Table of Contents

Behind the Veil at the Russian Court By Count I
PUBLISHER'S NOTE
CONTENTS
LIST OF PHOTOGRAVURES
BOOK I. 1855-1894 BEHIND THE VEIL AT THE RUSSIAN COURT
  CHAPTER I NICHOLAS I. DIES
  CHAPTER II ALEXANDER II. ON THE THRONE
  CHAPTER III ANECDOTES OF THE IMPERIAL FAMILY
  CHAPTER IV THE INFLUENCE OF THE GRAND DUCHESS HELENE PAVLOVNA
  CHAPTER V THE REFORMS OF ALEXANDER II. AND HIS MINISTERS
  CHAPTER VI THE ADLERBERGS AND THE SCHOUVALOFFS
  CHAPTER VII ST. PETERSBURG BEFORE THE WAR OF 1877-8
  CHAPTER VIII THE EASTERN WAR AND AFTERWARDS
  CHAPTER IX THE BERLIN CONGRESS AND ITS CONSEQUENCES
  CHAPTER X ALEXANDER'S LOVE AFFAIRS
  CHAPTER XI ASSASSINATION OF ALEXANDER II.
  CHAPTER XII ALEXANDER III. AND HIS CONSORT
  CHAPTER XIII THE IMPERIAL FAMILY IN 1881
  CHAPTER XIV THE FRIENDS AND MINISTERS OF ALEXANDER III.
  CHAPTER XV ALEXANDER III IS CROWNED
  CHAPTER XVI ST. PETERSBURG SOCIETY FROM 1883 TO 1894
  CHAPTER XVII THE FOREIGN POLICY OF ALEXANDER III.
  CHAPTER XVIII ALEXANDER'S MINISTERS
  CHAPTER XIX THE POLICE UNDER ALEXANDER III.
  CHAPTER XX THE TRUTH ABOUT BORKY
  CHAPTER XXI LAST DAYS AT LIVADIA
BOOK II. 1894-1913
  CHAPTER I FUNERAL AND WEDDING BELLS

CHAPTER II A CHARACTER SKETCH OF NICHOLAS II.

CHAPTER III THE EMPRESS ALIX

CHAPTER IV THE IMPERIAL FAMILY TO-DAY

CHAPTER V THE ZEMSTVO OF TVER INCIDENT AND WHAT CAME OF IT

CHAPTER VI THE ENTOURAGE OF THE EMPEROR AND EMPRESS

CHAPTER VII THE CORONATION OF NICHOLAS II.

CHAPTER VIII THE SPRINGTIDE OF DISCONTENT

CHAPTER IX THE WAR WITH JAPAN

CHAPTER X MUKDEN AND TSUSHIMA

CHAPTER XI THE BIRTH OF THE TSAREVITCH

CHAPTER XII THE DEATH OF MADEMOISELLE VIETROFF

CHAPTER XIII THE BEGINNING OF THE REVOLUTION

CHAPTER XIV PEACE WITH JAPAN; WAR AT HOME

CHAPTER XV THE FIRST TWO DUMAS

CHAPTER XVI THE CAREER OF M. STOLYPIN

CHAPTER XVII A CHARACTER SKETCH OF M. KOKOVTSOV

CHAPTER XVIII THE FOREIGN OFFICE UNDER NICHOLAS II.

CHAPTER XIX ST. PETERSBURG SOCIETY AT THE PRESENT DAY

CHAPTER XX THE EMPRESS ALEXANDRA FEODOROVNA AND HER CHILDREN

CHAPTER XXI THE 300TH ANNIVERSARY OF A DYNASTY

Contents.
List of Photogravures
(etext transcriber's note)

THE CHILDREN OF THE TSAR

Grand Duchess Olga   Grand Duchess Tatiana
Grand Duchess Marie Grand Duchess Anastasia

The Tsarevitch Alexis

Photos: Boissonnas & Eggler, St. Petersburg

Behind the Veil at the Russian Court
By Count Paul Vassili

With
Twenty-Three Illustrations in Photogravure

Cassell and Company, Limited
London, New York, Toronto and Melbourne
1913

PUBLISHER'S NOTE

SOME thirty years ago considerable interest was aroused by the publication, in the *Nouvelle Revue*, of Letters dealing with the Society of the different European capitals. These letters were by Count Paul Vassili.

They were clever, amusing, and, it must be owned, rather ill-natured letters. People wondered at the extraordinary amount of truth which they contained, at the secrets they revealed. The real name of their author to this day has never been disclosed; yet Count Vassili existed. He held an important post at the Russian Court, he had travelled widely, and everywhere had been welcomed as befitted his rank in the world. Cynical, intelligent, and wonderfully observant of everything that went on around him, his greatest interest in life was to commit to the leaves of a diary all that he saw or heard.

That diary, which stretches from the time of the Crimean War to the present year, it was his intention to publish before he died. Alas, death came too soon. The Count passed away a few months ago.

Nevertheless, the volumes which contained this diary became accessible, and their contents are now given to the public with the conviction that they will be read with the same interest that always attended the writings of Count Vassili.

At the same time, we would warn the reader that the present volume is not historical, but merely anecdotal. Yet sometimes anecdotes are also history. They very often explain events wide in their influence over the affairs of the world in general and Royal Houses in particular, which at first sight seem extraordinary, whilst, in reality, they are but the development of some small circumstance.

So far as we know there exists no chronicle of the Russian Court, and true anecdotes concerning it are extremely rare. Much has been written on the subject by outsiders upon hearsay; but here we have a book penned by a man who spent his life in the *milieu* which he describes, who knew intimately the people he writes about, who was present at most of the scenes which he describes. That alone would ensure an interest to this volume. We therefore hope that it will amuse its readers, and perhaps contribute in a small degree to reveal the truth concerning Russian Society and the Imperial Family.

More we cannot say, except that we leave to Count Vassili the entire responsibility of the judgments expressed and the facts divulged.

CONTENTS

PAGE

PUBLISHER'S NOTE — V

BOOK I. 1855-1894

CHAPTER

1. NICHOLAS I. DIES	3
2. ALEXANDER II. ON THE THRONE	16
3. ANECDOTES OF THE IMPERIAL FAMILY	25
4. INFLUENCE OF THE GRAND DUCHESS HÉLÈNE PAVLOVNA	38
5. THE REFORMS OF ALEXANDER II. AND HIS MINISTERS	48
6. THE ADLERBERGS AND THE SCHOUVALOFFS	60
7. ST. PETERSBURG BEFORE THE WAR OF 1877-8	71
8. THE EASTERN WAR AND AFTERWARDS	79
9. THE BERLIN CONGRESS AND ITS CONSEQUENCES	89
10. ALEXANDER'S LOVE AFFAIRS	99
11. ASSASSINATION OF ALEXANDER II.	108
12. ALEXANDER III. AND HIS CONSORT	116

13. THE IMPERIAL FAMILY IN 1881   122

14. THE FRIENDS AND MINISTERS OF ALEXANDER III.   130

15. ALEXANDER III. IS CROWNED   143

16. ST. PETERSBURG SOCIETY, FROM 1883 TO 1894   152

17. THE FOREIGN POLICY OF ALEXANDER III.   163

18. ALEXANDER'S MINISTERS   171

19. THE POLICE UNDER ALEXANDER III.   179

20. THE TRUTH ABOUT BORKY   185

21. LAST DAYS AT LIVADIA   192

BOOK II. 1894-1913

1. FUNERAL AND WEDDING BELLS   203

2. A CHARACTER SKETCH OF NICHOLAS II.   212

3. THE EMPRESS ALIX   224

4. THE IMPERIAL FAMILY TO-DAY   238

5. ZEMSTVO OF TVER INCIDENT AND WHAT CAME OF IT   250

6. THE ENTOURAGE OF THE EMPEROR AND EMPRESS   261

7. THE CORONATION OF NICHOLAS II.   270

8. THE SPRINGTIDE OF DISCONTENT   278

9. THE WAR WITH JAPAN   288

10. MUKDEN AND TSUSHIMA   296

11. THE BIRTH OF THE TSAREVITCH   308

12. THE DEATH OF MADEMOISELLE VIETROFF   320

13. THE BEGINNING OF THE REVOLUTION   324

14. PEACE WITH JAPAN; WAR AT HOME   334

15. THE FIRST TWO DUMAS   343

16. THE CAREER OF M. STOLYPIN   353

17. A CHARACTER SKETCH OF M. KOKOVTSOV   364

18. THE FOREIGN OFFICE UNDER NICHOLAS II.   375

19. ST. PETERSBURG SOCIETY AT THE PRESENT DAY   383

20. THE EMPRESS ALEXANDRA FEODOROVNA AND HER CHILDREN   392

21. THE 300TH ANNIVERSARY OF A DYNASTY   399

LIST OF PHOTOGRAVURES

THE IMPERIAL FAMILY OF RUSSIA, 1913   *Frontispiece*

Facing page

EMPEROR NICHOLAS I.   16

EMPEROR ALEXANDER II.   16

GRAND DUKE CONSTANTINE NICOLAIEVITCH   34

GRAND DUKE MICHAEL NICOLAIEVITCH   34

GRAND DUKE VLADIMIR ALEXANDROVITCH   34

GRAND DUKE ALEXIS ALEXANDROVITCH   34

EMPEROR ALEXANDER III.   116

EMPRESS MARIE FEODOROVNA   116

NICHOLAS II., TSAR OF RUSSIA   212

ALEXANDRA FEODOROVNA, TSARINA OF RUSSIA   225

THE WINTER PALACE, ST. PETERSBURG   342

PRINCE GORTSCHAKOV   364

COUNT IGNATIEFF   364

M. DE GIERS   364

M. KOKOVTSOV   364

M. STOLPYIN   364

GRAND DUCHESS OLGA   392

GRAND DUCHESS TATIANA   392

GRAND DUCHESS MARIE   392

GRAND DUCHESS ANASTASIA   392

THE TSAREVITCH ALEXIS   392

BOOK I. 1855-1894 BEHIND THE VEIL AT THE RUSSIAN COURT
CHAPTER I

NICHOLAS I. DIES

IN the vast halls of the Winter Palace, on the 18th of February—the 2nd of March according to the Gregorian Calendar—of the year 1855, a great crowd was waiting amidst a profound silence and intense grief for news it expected as much as it dreaded.

In the large square in front of the big building which had seen enacted within its walls so many momentous events in the history of Russia and the life of its Tsars, another crowd was gathered. The whole of the long night it had stood there in the snow and cold, with its eyes fixed upon a corner window—that of the room where all knew their Sovereign lay dying. Women were seen weeping, for, in spite of what was said abroad, Nicholas was beloved by his people, and they felt that his demise, occurring as it did at a critical moment in the destinies of his Empire, was an event fraught with mighty consequences.

Inside the Palace all the dignitaries of the Court and the Military Authorities, as well as those of the Civil Service, also were keeping watch: a sad vigil, which already had lasted two days—days full of anxiety both for the present and for the future. From time to time a door was opened to let in a new arrival, or to give passage to a messenger from the sick-room. At once the messenger would be surrounded by eager questioners, but all that he could say was that, so far, there had been no change, though the doctors had not given up all hope.

Inside the dying monarch's bedroom his family and a few trusted friends were gathered round the small camp bed upon which he was lying, fighting for breath. The Empress was sitting beside her Consort, holding his hand in hers. At the foot of the bed the Heir to the Throne was standing, his eyes fixed upon his father, and with tears slowly rolling down his cheeks. They all waited—waited for the last words of the mighty Sovereign for whom the gates of eternity were already opened. They all hoped for a sign, a farewell, a recommendation as to what was to be done when he would be no more; and in this sad watch they forgot time and aught else, even the news from the distant Crimea, where Russian soldiers were defending their country's flag against an angry foe.

But the dying man had not forgotten. Slowly he raised himself upon his hard pillow and beckoned to him one of his trusted friends; with gasping breath he asked him: "Any news from Sebastopol?" and when answered that none had come, "A messenger must have arrived this morning; go and ask what news he has brought, and tell me—tell me everything."

The friend went out; when he returned, his face was white, because he knew that the message which he brought was one of woe. But one thing he could tell, and that was that Sebastopol still held out, and that it could resist longer than the enemy expected. That he told. Nicholas listened in silence, and then in a clear voice, such as had not been heard since the beginning of his short illness, he said:

"I send them my thanks, my blessing, my gratitude; tell them so."

The Heir to the Throne came closer to his father, and knelt beside him.

"Hear me, my son," spoke the dying man. "You are going to be a great Emperor to-morrow. Love your people, do for them that which I was not able to do; conclude peace if you can, but an honourable peace. Do not trust to Austria, and do not forget its ingratitude for the help which I gave it in 1848. Austria is our enemy, I see it too late.... Love your mother, reverence her always, and do not allow your dreams to take the upper hand. A Sovereign has no right to dream. He can only work, and endure. I know you want to give the serfs their liberty; I have wished it too, and you will find among my papers documents concerning this subject; but, my son, take care: a nation easily abuses liberty if granted to it too soon. Do not estrange yourself from the nobility: it is the strength of Russia, together with our Holy Church; and remember that if you show yourself too great a Liberal, you will only create difficulties for yourself, and you will not die in your bed as I do; you will fall under an assassin's knife."

Profound silence reigned in the room after these solemn words had been spoken; the Empress was quietly crying, all the Imperial Family stood gathered round her. Nicholas I.

scanned all these sorrowful faces, and sighed as if not seeing among them one whom he expected to be there, and from his parched lips came out one word, a single name: "Barbara." Then the Empress got up, and going out of the room, returned soon in company with a woman whom she was holding by the hand. She led her to her husband's bedside, saying softly: "Bid good-bye to him."

"*Merci, madame*," was the broken reply, as, bending down, Mademoiselle Nélidoff kissed the Emperor's hand, sobbing heartbrokenly as she did so; and he repeated the words after her, "*Merci*, Charlotte," thus calling the wife of his youth by the name she bore in that past but not forgotten time when he first knew her, before the Crown of All the Russias had been put upon her head.

And that was all. The dying man only spoke to utter words of thanks to the faithful servants who surrounded him, and then his voice was heard no more, save to pray to the God to Whom he was about to give up his soul.

A priest was called, who gave him a last blessing, and then calmly, fearlessly, clinging to his wife's hand and to a crucifix which he pressed upon his breast, Nicholas I. breathed his last.

The doors of the bedroom were thrown open, and Alexander II. appeared upon the threshold as he passed from the chamber of death into the Throne Room, where his courtiers were gathered. To them he said with a broken voice:

"*Au nom de mon père je vous remercie pour vos services, messieurs.*" And later on, when the emotion of the first moment had passed, it was noticed and commented upon that the first words of the new Sovereign to his people had been uttered in French, as if to lay claim to the tendencies of which he had been suspected during his father's reign.

At the same moment the large window opening on to the balcony overlooking the square in front of the Winter Palace was unclosed. An aide-de-camp general appeared, and addressing the crowd standing outside: "Our Most Gracious Sovereign the Emperor Nicholas Paulovitch is dead," he said in a loud voice; "let us pray for his soul!"

The crowd fell upon their knees, and the chant of the solemn service rose and fell in harmonious cadence amidst the noises of the street, which were hushed as soon as the sad strains were heard.

So began a new reign.

The one that had thus come to a tragic close had been one of the most eventful in Russian history. Nicholas I. was unmistakably a great Sovereign, the last one of that autocratic type that had given to the world Ivan the Terrible, Peter the Great, and, in a certain sense, Catherine II.

He had ascended the Throne surrounded by solemn circumstances, amidst almost overwhelming difficulties, with his Empire in the throes of a rebellion that had for its leaders some of the greatest nobles in Russia. The time was not yet forgotten when these nobles had dethroned their emperors, and some of the assassins of Paul were still alive to encourage by their example those inclined to follow in their footsteps.

Many, even amongst the people, did not believe that Alexander I. had died in Taganrog; many others did not recognise the abdication and surrender of his right to the Crown of the Grand Duke Constantine in favour of his brother. They looked upon Nicholas as a usurper. When the standard of rebellion was raised during that eventful month of December, 1825, it was the conspirators who were supposed to be fighting for the right cause and the supporters of Nicholas for the wrong one. As for the people, they understood so little what was going on that they believed the famous Constitution, about which so many were speaking, was the work of the Emperor Constantine, as he was supposed to be.

When the public anxiety and emotion in St. Petersburg was at its height, when half of the troops had already gone over to the mutineers, Nicholas I. showed of what stuff he was made. Entrusting his wife and children to a few trusted followers, he appeared alone and unarmed on the square in front of the Winter Palace, and in a thunderous voice commanded the crowd to fall upon their knees and obey his orders. And such is the strength of a really strong personality, in alliance with a fearless disposition, that he was instantly obeyed, and soon an immense "Hurrah!" greeted him from those same people who, a few short moments before, had been ready to tear him to pieces.

In this manner was the rebellion crushed at once.

Its leaders were ruthlessly punished. A Prince Troubetzkoy, a member of the illustrious family of Volkhonsky, a Muravieff apostle, the noblest blood in Russia, saw themselves condemned and treated like vulgar criminals. Siberia witnessed a long procession of chained convicts, reminding it of the times when Menschikoff, Biren, and many others expiated the misfortune of having fallen under Imperial disgrace. Women gave a touching example of devotion to their husbands and to their duty. The Princess Troubetzkoy, the Princess Volkhonsky, as well as the wives of other conspirators, claimed as a favour the right to share their husbands' exile and prison. There, in the wilds of the Siberian woods, they gave birth to children, who, later on, were to be restored to the fortunes of their fathers and to their rank. And, strange to say, no word of rebellion was said, no murmur was heard; they all suffered bravely, thus showing that they were worthy of the great names which they bore.

But this conspiracy of the 14th of December, as it is still called, embittered the character of the Emperor Nicholas. It affected, also, the gentle Empress, who contracted, from sheer fright for her dear ones, a nervous affliction, which caused perpetual trembling of her head, of which she never was cured.

The dreams which every new Sovereign indulges in when he ascends his Throne were rudely dispelled from the very first, and since that sad day the spectre of revolution never left the Emperor's side. It influenced all his actions, and it imparted to him a hardness absolutely foreign to his original nature. He firmly believed himself to have been designed by Providence to crush revolution, and he devoted all his energies to that task.

Later events transpired which encouraged him still more in that decision and confirmed his belief. He found himself confronted, immediately after a long and difficult war with Turkey, by the Polish rebellion. That was a bitter blow to his pride and heart. He had loved the Polish army, had firmly thought he could do away with the prejudices that existed against him and his nation in Poland; he had had himself crowned in Warsaw, and had showered graces and gifts upon his Polish subjects. All that was forgotten; he found himself surrounded by traitors, even among those whom he thought he could trust, if only on account of the old French proverb: "*Noblesse oblige.*" And they had turned against him—those whom he had loved. Prince Sanguszko, who had been his personal aide-de-camp; Prince Adam Tsartoryski, who had been the intimate friend and confidant of Alexander I.—they all went over to the mutineers. Personal ambition had a great deal to do with this action. It is said, even, that Prince Tsartoryski addressed himself to Nicholas I., asking him to recognise him as Viceroy of Poland, in return for which he would undertake to put an end to the rebellion. The message did not reach the Emperor, as the person who was asked to transmit it categorically refused to do so. One can well fancy in what spirit it would have been received had it come to the Emperor's ears. But all the nobleness in the character of Nicholas I. revolted at this base ingratitude, and, as a result of these blows dealt him by fate, he became a hard and embittered man, relentless sometimes, stern always. They say he rarely smiled, and yet his was a gentle nature, full of kindness and generosity such as is rarely met with in a Sovereign, and profoundly unselfish.

All those who knew him well, his family, his entourage, his children, his servants, they all would have given up their lives for him with joy. No one ever appealed to him for relief in vain. He loved to do good, to help others. The only things which he could not forgive, because he despised them, were ingratitude, or want of self-respect. He had principles, and what is more, he lived up to them. He never would consent to any compromise, and this perhaps was the primary cause of the unfortunate Crimean War.

He had hurt the vanity of Napoleon III. by refusing him the title of *Monsieur mon frère*, and so declining to admit him as an equal to the circle of European Sovereigns.

He sent his troops to help the Austrian Government to subdue the revolt of the Magyars because he believed it was his duty to do so, without any illusion as to the reward which he would get for this act of chivalry.

Talking of this reminds me of an episode connected with that event. When Nicholas had decided to send his troops to Hungary, he announced his resolution in the town of Moscow, at the Kremlin Palace, to the nobility and the notables of the ancient capital. His words were received with immense enthusiasm, and a loud "Hurrah!" was the reply to them. The Emperor looked round him, and suddenly noticed that one of his personal friends, the same man who seven years later was to bring him for the last time before he died news of Sebastopol, that that man alone kept silent and in the background. When all was over and the Sovereign had retired to his own rooms, he had him called and asked him: "Why did you not shout

'Hurrah!' with the rest?" "Because I was thinking of the day when Austria would astonish your Majesty with its ingratitude," was the unexpected reply. Nicholas sighed. "You may be right," he said, after a pause, "but I haven't sent my troops to help Austria, I have sent them to help a brother Sovereign."

This anecdote gives the key to the character of this extraordinary monarch, the Sir Galahad of crowned heads, who up to the last moment would not believe that England and France would fight against him for the interests of Turkey, and who never wavered in his trust in Queen Victoria, whom he immensely admired since the visit which he had paid to her at Windsor when she was quite a young wife, and whose portrait adorned his writing-table to the last days of his life. Intensely as he hated English politicians and politics, he made a distinction between the Queen and her Ministers, and whilst distrusting the latter, had the utmost respect for the former, though at the same time not being able to understand the mechanism of constitutional government, nor how impossible it was for an English Sovereign to go against her Parliament or the opinion of her responsible advisers. He attributed to timidity on the part of Queen Victoria the failure of his attempt to come to a direct understanding with her, as he had tried to establish by means of a correspondence, which had not relieved the tension existing between the Court of St. James and that of St. Petersburg in regard to the Eastern Question; and anyone who would have told him that his personality was not sympathetic to the Queen would have profoundly surprised him. In his opinion all Sovereigns ought to like one another, and prejudice in regard to each other was a thing he would not admit, any more than he would admit the right of intruders, such as, in his opinion, were Napoleon III. and Louis Philippe, to hold their own against monarchs "by the grace of God."

Nicholas I. has been accused of being narrow-minded. This was not the case at all, but he was extremely firm in his opinions, and not empty of prejudices. His hatred of revolution was keen, because he held that one never knew where it would lead to, nor how it would end. His mother, the Empress Marie Feodorovna, had brought him up to feel a horror and execration of the French Revolution, and that mother he worshipped. She had been a visitor at the Court of France during the reign of Louis XVI., and had formed an enthusiastic friendship for the unfortunate Marie

Antoinette, who had welcomed so heartily the Comte and Comtesse du Nord during their journey to France. The fate of the hapless Queen was a frequent subject of conversation among the Imperial Family in St. Petersburg, and it is no wonder that it excited hatred against all the instruments of it. Moreover, the French emigrants had been very well received by the Empress Catherine, and they had rapidly spread their prejudices against the new ideas among the Russian aristocracy, and at that time it was the aristocracy alone who ruled public opinion. It upheld all Nicholas's prejudices, even outdid them, and certainly no one was bold enough to tell him that they were, perhaps, stretched too far, and that the world must advance on the road of progress and liberty.

But the Emperor, in spite of this shortcoming of his otherwise powerful mind, was fully aware that his country ought to follow to a certain point the development of science, literature and politics of the rest of Europe. What he wanted was to regulate that development, and there was his error. The human mind cannot be treated like a soldier at drill. It must be left a certain latitude of criticism and liberty, if only to neutralise its efforts at independence. This the Emperor did not admit. He considered literary men in the light of pests, and was sensible to the appreciations of the press when these were directed against his Government, whilst totally indifferent when they touched his own person. Curious mixture of haughtiness and sensitiveness, which no one who did not know him well could understand.

In his private life Nicholas I. was, above all things, a gentleman. His wife he loved tenderly, and always and upon every occasion treated her with the utmost respect. He was not a ladies' man like his son. Indeed the only *liaison* which he had, and which was known, and not merely suspected in Society, was his love for Mademoiselle Nélidoff, a maid of honour of the Empress, who had succeeded in captivating him by the cleverness of her mind, and who loved him on her side as few men have ever been loved by women.

Mademoiselle Nélidoff was a remarkable person. Few have been gifted with such tact, such intelligence, such penetration, and such a spirit of self-sacrifice as she showed during the whole of her long life. Her intimacy with the Emperor lasted many years, and never once did she allow herself to fail in the least mark of respect towards the

Empress, or to assert herself in any way. She was always humble in her demeanour towards the latter, always submissive, never aggressive in the least. Nicholas used to come to her rooms every afternoon to talk over the events of the day; but the most bitter enemy of Mademoiselle Nélidoff could not say that she ever mixed herself up in politics, or tried to play a rôle in Society, as many so circumstanced would have done. She maintained the dignity of her womanhood so well that the world, whilst it knew, yet could not affirm that she had won the affections of her Sovereign, who, in his turn, never showed to her in public any particular attention. The only time that he ever did so was at the very beginning of their *liaison*, during a review in the park of Tsarskoye Selo. The Empress, as usual in such cases, drove in front of the troops, in an open carriage with her lady-in-waiting, who happened on that day to be Mademoiselle Nélidoff. The Emperor, who was on horseback, accompanied the carriage, and with an affectation totally foreign to his usual strict observance of the conventions of life, remained the whole time beside the carriage, and bending from his saddle, talked with the young maid of honour, who in her turn became white and red, and appeared to be very unhappy. The Empress, too, was quite upset, and an eye-witness of this occurrence related afterwards that she was with difficulty restraining her tears. But apart from this single occasion, never once did Nicholas show in public that he was interested in the charm of character and conversation of Mademoiselle Nélidoff.

The latter contrived to keep the good graces of her Imperial mistress, and ended by winning her heart by her tact and submissiveness. And when the Emperor was dying, it was the Empress Alexandra Feodorovna herself who had the generosity to bring to her husband's bedside, for a last farewell, the woman who had loved him so well.

Mademoiselle Nélidoff never appeared in Society after the Emperor's death. She continued living at the Winter Palace, and went on fulfilling her duties to the Dowager Empress until at length the latter died. Then gradually the name of the woman who had won the heart of Nicholas I. was forgotten. She retired entirely from the world, and, save a very few chosen friends, never received anyone, or ever spoke about the past. The silence of the grave closed upon her long before she was dead. Her constant visitors were her brother-in-law, the husband of her deceased sister, and his two sons, whom she dearly loved, but even with them she remained silent as to the great drama of her life. No word ever passed her lips concerning those past years of her youth, no confidence was exchanged with anyone as to what she had felt whilst her romance had lasted. She died at a very advanced age a year or two before the closing of last century, after having burned all the papers or letters which she possessed. The newspaper notices that she had passed away was the first intimation received by many of those to whom her name was familiar from childhood, of the fact that she had not long before passed from the land of the living to that of eternal peace and rest.

CHAPTER II

ALEXANDER II. ON THE THRONE

AT the time he ascended the Throne Alexander II. was very popular. People had begun to get tired of the despotic rule of his father, and the Crimean War with its loss of life and prestige and the disasters which it had brought upon the nation had, as is usual in such cases, aroused discontent against the existing order of things. Many Russians who had lived abroad, and witnessed the perturbations occasioned in the whole of Europe by the Revolution of 1848, held the opinion that in Russia, too, something ought to be done to meet the aspirations of the intelligent classes of Society towards an improvement in the Government. The great qualities of the Emperor Nicholas were not questioned, but it was felt that a monarch could not be everywhere, nor see for himself all the needs of the nation, and that with a Sovereign less conscientious than he was a system of absolutism such as he had maintained was not possible. The Heir to the Throne, on the contrary, was credited with the desire to govern more or less according to constitutional principles, to try and introduce into Russia some of the reforms that had gradually permeated the rest of Europe. It was known that his great ambition was to emancipate the serfs, that he was humane, kind, and not the partisan of a tyrannical inquisition as to the opinions of his future subjects. As is usual in Royal Houses, the Emperor and his son had been at variance on many points, and all those who were

EMPEROR NICHOLAS I.   EMPEROR ALEXANDER II.

tired of Nicholas looked towards his successor to reform the many abuses that were known to exist. The Crimean War had been opposed by him, and this alone would have made him popular; and yet, when the event dreaded by a few and desired by many had taken place, when the remains of Nicholas had been laid to rest with those of his ancestors in the fortress of St. Peter and St. Paul, it was felt that somehow a great light had gone out, and that it remained a question whether the critical condition of the country could be bettered by the efforts of his successor. Alexander II. also had enemies; these for the most part were men in power whom it was difficult to remove at such a moment of national peril, and between them and his own personal friends, who wanted to replace them at once, the new Sovereign found himself in a most difficult and embarrassing position, from whence he had not sufficient strength of will to extricate himself.

The young Emperor had a great defect, which, to a certain extent, is inherited by his grandson, the present Tsar, and that is a lack of firmness and endurance in his character. He was easily influenced, easily led, and apt to be easily discouraged by the slightest difficulty.

Exceedingly sensitive, he never forgave an injury or pardoned a criticism. At heart he was really more autocratic than his father, but, having been brought up with immense care and by people imbued with Liberalism as it was understood at that time in Russia, he exhibited a curious mixture of despotic and revolutionary ideas. Some may think it anomalous to apply the term "revolutionary" to a Tsar of Russia, but was not the emancipation of the serfs a revolution? Not in its fact, but in the way in which it was conducted. Nicholas had dreamed about it, but he had realised that a reform of such magnitude could not be rushed; he saw in it dangers of further conspiracies against the Throne, such as that of December 14, but of greater possibilities, because they would not be confined to the upper classes, but would be the revolt of unknown forces of the nation against an authority which for ages had refused to acknowledge their existence.

Alexander II. was devoid of the power of realising the consequences of events, and only gave his attention to the difficulties of the moment. There was in him a strange blending of superstition and recklessness which he never lost during his whole life. He was humane, and at the same time could become intensely cruel; he was vindictive—the greatest defect that a Sovereign can have—and his vindictiveness persisted throughout his life. He was intelligent, cultured, but not clever; he had none of the qualities indispensable to a great statesman, and depended for his opinions to a large extent on those by whom he was surrounded, and of these the men who flattered him most had the greatest influence. He was exceedingly vain, and the many mistakes that marked the close of his reign arose in part from wounded vanity. He had principles; indeed, it would have been impossible for his father's son to be without them, but he did not live up to them, and at times he could act like the most unprincipled of men. Few understood him, and it is doubtful whether he understood himself, but he had full consciousness of his power, and of all that it gave him, whilst not overburthened with the sense of the responsibility that it entailed, which Nicholas I. had felt so acutely. With several of his father's failings, he had none of the grand traits of the latter's character; he was the type of an absolute Sovereign, but not that of an autocrat; he could neither punish nor forgive with dignity, and though he gave easily, yet his was not a generous nature.

In the year of grace 1855, however, few were acquainted with the character of Alexander II. That character, indeed, did not reveal itself in its true light until after the disappointments of his reign had done their work. At first the whole nation gave itself up to the task of helping the Emperor, and when he received the solemn oath of allegiance to his Crown from the principal dignitaries of the Empire, on the morrow of his father's death, he was greeted by them with very sincere enthusiasm. The ceremony took place in the private chapel of the Winter Palace, in the presence of the whole Imperial Family, including the Empress Mother, who with indomitable courage was present in order to support her son. She was dressed all in white, in accordance with the Russian convention, which forbids the wearing of mourning at the accession festivities of a Sovereign. The young Empress, too, appeared in a white dress, unadorned, however, with a single jewel, and it was noticed by everybody with what reverence she approached her mother-in-law and kissed the latter's hand, bending so low that her knees almost touched the ground.

The Emperor every now and then wiped his eyes with the back of his hand, and after the ceremony addressed a few words to the members of his military household, thanking them for their past services and asking them to show to him the same devotion that they had shown to his father. He then also solemnly transmitted to them the touching message of gratitude which Nicholas had caused to be inserted in his will, and which was addressed by him to all those who had held office under him. He added a few words of his own expressing the hope that peace, *honourable peace*, would soon be concluded. The speech was delivered in Russian, so as to be understood by all. It was very favourably received both at home and abroad, and the European Bourses rose in consequence. The general situation, however, was still felt to be full of danger and anxiety; everyone knew that the task before the new Sovereign was arduous in the extreme, and that it was impossible for him to begin anything in the way of interior reforms until peace had been concluded.

At length the Congress met in Paris, thus increasing the prestige of the Napoleonic dynasty which Nicholas had always refused to acknowledge, and though Alexander II. did not like him, it was Count Orloff, the trusted and intimate friend of his father, who was appointed by him as his representative at this assembly, upon which the fate of Russia depended.

Count—afterwards Prince—Orloff was one of the curious figures of the previous reign. He was a stern old man, even more autocratic perhaps than his master, but kind at heart, and always careful not to abuse the power which he wielded. He was the head of the famous "Third Section," as it was called, or the Department of the Secret Police, of the Empire, and had the right to seek his Sovereign's presence unannounced whenever he thought it necessary. At that time it was usual for Court society to carry all its family grievances to the foot of the Throne, and to ask the Emperor to pronounce a final verdict upon them. That verdict always depended on the report made by the head of the Third Section, and to Count Orloff's credit it must be said that he never profited by the family secrets with which his office had made him familiar. He was the type of an old Russian *grand seigneur* or *barine*, as the Russian peasantry say, with a dignity that never left him for a single moment, even in the most trying circumstances; a man who fearlessly expressed his opinion to his Emperor as well as to those with whom he came into contact in his official position. He was intensely feared, but at the same time immensely respected. The nation knew that its honour was safe in his hands, and he was perhaps the only man in Russia with sufficient authority to sign the Treaty of Paris; the humiliation of which would never have been forgiven to anyone else.

Before he left for France he was received in audience by the young Empress Marie Alexandrovna, and it was related then that she asked him to notice particularly the Empress Eugénie and her manners and dresses. The old man replied brusquely that he was not sent to the French Court to pay any attention to a crowned adventuress, and, added he, "*Vous devriez, madame, être la dernière à vous intéresser à ce monde là!*"

Of course, I do not vouch for the truth of the anecdote, but it was related everywhere at the time.

Count Orloff received the title of Prince on his return from Paris, and died not very long afterwards. He left an only son, who for a great number of years represented his Government on the banks of the Seine, under the Third Republic. His widow, *née* Gérebtsoff, an exceedingly clever woman, gifted with a very caustic wit, which made her rather disliked in St. Petersburg, retired to Florence, where she possessed a splendid palace, and passed her life there is quasi royal state. She was a favourite with the Emperor Nicholas, who appreciated her austerity of principles and her devotion to the Imperial House, but it was said that the Empress stood in awe of her, and the Grand Dukes and Grand Duchesses feared her exceedingly. Her verdicts in Society were dreaded, and either made or marred worldly reputations. She execrated the Princess Lieven, and used to declare that social spies—as she called people with the political proclivities of the famous Princess—were just as contemptible as those who did the dirty work of a spy for money. She could not forgive meanness, and she considered it the worst of meannesses to repeat what had been told one in confidence. Entirely trusted by her husband, she knew more Imperial and social secrets than anyone else in St. Petersburg, and never could she be accused of an indiscretion. Princess Orloff was a great character; and it is to be regretted that the type of woman she represented has almost ceased to exist.

The great event after peace had been concluded was the Coronation of the new Emperor. Every European State sent representatives to attend it, and it was the grandest ceremony witnessed for many years even in Russia. France was represented by the Duc de Morny, Napoleon's half-brother, and to this day are related anecdotes of the mercantile spirit that characterised that illegitimate descendant of a queen, and that made him use his position, and the accruing privileges, to conduct financial operations which turned out to be very profitable. For instance, he took with him, under the diplomatic privilege which exempted him from Customs dues, a whole cellar of the rarest wines, which he afterwards sold to his acquaintances at prices perhaps higher than they would have paid to a wine merchant. He also transported among his luggage his picture gallery, already famous at the time, and he sold or exchanged some of his art treasures under most favourable conditions. But he lavished on Russian Society splendid hospitality, and won all his lady friends' hearts by the amiability with which he brought them dresses and hats from Paris. His mission was most successful, because his tact was great, and his appreciation of men and things generally a true one, based as it was on shrewd observation as much as on personal intuition. Before he left Russia he married the young Princess Troubetzkoy, whom rumour said was a favourite of Alexander II. Her mother had served as a lady-in-waiting to the Empress Alexandra Feodorovna, and was the subject of much Court gossip when Prince Troubetzkoy gallantly stepped in, and made her his wife. The Duchesse de Morny was their only daughter.

Austria was represented at the Coronation of Alexander II. by Prince Esterhazy, whose wonderful diamonds, with which his Hungarian costume was trimmed, excited an immense sensation; England's representative was Lord Granville, whose ball was one of the most splendid given during the time of the festivities. Belgium had dispatched the Prince de Ligne, who, though the first personage of the kingdom, was not perhaps so warmly welcomed as would have been the case had his wife not been a Pole by birth, a Princess Lubomirska; Prussia had sent Prince Frederick William, who in later years was to become the first Crown Prince of United Germany. In truth, nothing was lacking to make this pageant a memorable one in the fullest sense of the term.

Fair women also graced it with their presence, and foremost among them were the two sisters of the Emperor, the Grand Duchesses Marie and Olga Nicolaievna, the latter married to the Crown Prince of Würtemberg, and his sister-in-law, the lovely Princess Alexandra of Saxe-Altenburg, married to the Grand Duke Constantine. Pictures can give but a faint idea of her extreme beauty, and her marvellous grace. For years she was a conspicuous figure at Court, where her husband also had a prominent position and great influence over his brother, who frequently took his opinion and advice. He was supposed to be the promoter of Liberal reforms, and consequently was disliked by the Old Russian party. In spite of certain apprehensions the Coronation festivities passed off quite brilliantly, and without the slightest hitch. They had in a certain sense helped to allay the state of tension that had existed between the Cabinets of Paris and St. Petersburg ever since the accession of Napoleon to the French Throne. The Duc de Morny had succeeded in ingratiating himself in the good graces of Alexander II., who was always keenly sensitive to those gifts of small talk and conversation that the half-brother of the ruler of France possessed to such perfection. He would have liked Morny permanently as Ambassador in St. Petersburg, and Prince Gortschakov—who at that time was already at the head of Foreign Affairs in Russia—would have felt pleased had this been the case.

The relations between the two statesmen remained always cordial, even when those of their respective countries suffered again an alteration owing to the unfortunate Polish mutiny in 1863. It was at that time that De Morny wrote to the Imperial Chancellor in the following terms:

"29 Novembre, 1863.

"MON CHER PRINCE,

"*Votre lettre m'a fait plaisir et peine; plaisir pour ce qui me concerne personnellement, peine pour ce qui a rapport aux relations entre nos deux pays. Enfin, j'espère toujours qu'elles s'amélioreront, et vous pourrez compter sur moi pour y travailler.*"

Unfortunately for himself, and perhaps for France, the Duc de Morny was not destined to see the improvement in French relations which eventually resulted in the Franco-Russian alliance.

CHAPTER III

ANECDOTES OF THE IMPERIAL FAMILY

WHEN Alexander II. ascended the Throne the Imperial family was composed of his three brothers, two sisters, his aunt the Grand Duchess Hélène Pavlovna (widow of the youngest brother of the Emperor Nicholas I.) and her daughter the Grand Duchess Catherine (married to Duke George of Mecklenburg, and living with her husband in St. Petersburg) and of Prince Peter of Oldenburg, the son of the Grand Duchess Catherine Pavlovna, the youngest daughter of the late Emperor Paul.

We shall refer to all these august personages in turn, but will begin by mentioning the two Empresses, the wife and the mother of the new Tsar.

The Empress Marie Alexandrovna was a fair, slight woman, very delicate in health, who during the first years of her marriage had led a singularly quiet existence in which her numerous babies played an important part. Her husband had fallen in love with her, much to the surprise of everybody. He had been sent to Germany with the idea of marrying him to a German princess of higher rank than the daughter of the Duke of Hesse, but the latter had appealed to him by her meek manner and kindness of disposition. She had led a most unhappy life at home, and therefore looked upon her marriage with the Grand Duke Alexander quite as much as a means of escape from that as a brilliant match, such as reasonably she could not have hoped for; and her feeling of intense gratitude towards him made her later on bear with an extraordinary patience his numerous infidelities.

Whilst her mother-in-law lived, Marie Alexandrovna never asserted herself in the least, but later on she developed a great interest in the numerous charitable institutions placed under her patronage, and especially in the education of young girls belonging to the poorer nobility. So long as her health permitted her to do so, she regularly visited the various institutions where they were brought up, and personally superintended the yearly examinations, knowing the schoolgirls by name and later on following them in their future careers. She was very reserved, very religious, very good, excessively conscientious, and devoted to everything Russian and orthodox. During the months preceding the Turkish War of 1877, she openly supported the Slavonic party, and was very much under the influence of a certain coterie, of which the most prominent members were her confessor, Father Bajanov, and one of her ladies-in-waiting, the Countess Antoinette Bloudoff, about whom we shall have something more to say later on. Very unhappy in her married life, she sought in religion a comfort for the deceptions which she felt very bitterly, but nevertheless was too proud to admit. Extremely cultured, she used to read a great deal, and was *au courant* with everything that went on either in the literary or the scientific world. Politics interested her greatly, though she would never express a political opinion in public.

Few princesses have controlled a Court to the degree of perfection that she did, and her manner, in that respect, never left anything to be desired; nevertheless, her receptions were always cold, and it was difficult to feel at one's ease in her presence. She was extremely respected, but she never unbent, though full of sympathy for the woes or joys of others. At first she had tried to be of use to her husband, but soon found out that he had very little time to give to her, and that her constant ill health bored him to the extreme. All her hopes and ambitions, therefore, had turned and were centred upon her eldest son, the Grand Duke Nicholas, to whose education she had attended with the greatest care, going so far as to read the same books that he did, and to practically follow with him his course of studies. She loved him passionately, and her affection was fully justified, for the young man was not only attractive in the extreme, but also gifted with the rarest qualities of heart and mind. There is no doubt that had his life been spared he would have made a remarkable Sovereign, but he died at the early age of twenty-two years, from the results of a fall from his horse, which caused a disease of the spine. He was about to be married to the Princess Dagmar of Denmark. The Empress never recovered from this blow, and from then her own health began steadily to decline. She grew silent and melancholy, and her sadness increased still more after her only daughter's marriage with the Duke of Edinburgh, and consequent departure to live in England. Then came further disappointments, political anxieties, all the terrors of Nihilism and its constant menace to the Emperor. Domestic sorrows, too, ensued—the association of Alexander II. with the Princess Dolgorouky; and at last, when the poor Empress died, it was more from a broken heart than from the illness from which she had suffered for a number of years.

Marie Alexandrovna was strict upon all matters of etiquette, and during her reign precedence was observed at Court in the most rigid manner. She was not very popular among Royal circles in Europe, partly on account of that devotion to ceremonial, which became almost an obsession with her. She had a very high opinion of her rank as Empress of Russia, and it is said that when she went to England on the occasion of the birth of the first child of the Duchess of Edinburgh, she was not satisfied with the reception she had there, and declared that she would never return to a country where they did not appreciate the honour that she had conferred upon it by her presence. Her great delight were her visits to Darmstadt, where she had built for herself, in the neighbourhood of the town, a castle called Heiligenberg, which she left in her will to her brother Prince Alexander of Hesse, who was her great favourite, notwithstanding his unequal marriage with Mademoiselle von Haucke. That marriage nearly caused the banishment of the Prince from the Russian Court, so incensed was the Emperor Nicholas, not so much at the marriage itself, but at the circumstances that had attended it. Mademoiselle Julie von Haucke was a maid of honour to the Empress; the Prince fell in love with her, and the romance was accidentally discovered one day during an official dinner, when the young girl suddenly fainted. The

Prince was ordered by the Tsar to marry her, and both were exiled from the Court, in spite of the tears of the Tsarevna.

Mademoiselle von Haucke was in her turn granted the title, first of Countess, and, later on, of Princess of Battenberg, and she remained always upon good terms with her Imperial sister-in-law.

The Empress Alexandra Feodorovna, the consort of Nicholas I., was most incensed at this escapade of the brother of her daughter-in-law, and the relations between the two ladies became very strained in consequence. In fact, they had never been very cordial, because the Empress, in spite of her great kindness and amiability, imposed upon the Tsarevna and rather crushed her. The young timid girl never felt at her ease before the elder lady, with her grand eighteenth-century manners. Even after she became Empress she was always nervous in presence of her mother-in-law, whom, nevertheless, she continually treated with the utmost respect.

Alexandra Feodorovna was extremely liked among St. Petersburg Society, into the interests of which she had entered almost from the first day of her arrival in Russia. She knew everybody, had learned by heart the different family alliances and the genealogy of all the people who were introduced to her. Without being regularly beautiful like her mother the famous Queen Louise of Prussia, she had an extraordinary charm of manner and wonderful grace in all her movements. It is said that when she entered a room it was with such quiet dignity that everybody felt awed, but at the same time delightfully impressed. She liked Society, and was always surrounded by her friends. Every evening a few people were invited to take tea with her and the Emperor, who in that way learned to know persons and to hear what was going on through other channels than his Ministers. Even after her widowhood, the Empress continued to receive guests in a quiet way, until her health, which had always been extremely delicate, forbade it. Then she used to get the members of her family to gather round her, and amuse her with their tales and stories as to what was going on in the world. Her favourite brother was Prince William of Prussia, afterwards the Emperor William I., and in him she used to confide whenever she found any difficulty in her path. The two remained close friends until the Empress's death, and the friendship was continued by Alexander II., who was always upon intimate terms with his Prussian uncles, and nearly always favoured the policy of a *rapprochement* with Germany.

As I have said already, the Emperor Alexander had three brothers. The elder of them, the Grand Duke Constantine Nicolaievitch was a very remarkable man. Singularly clever, he had been most carefully educated, and with zeal that is rare among members of Royal Houses, had profited by this education, and developed the gifts which nature had showered upon him. He had strong Liberal leanings, and was the adviser of his brother in the great reforms which followed upon the emancipation of the serfs. It can safely be affirmed that without him the emancipation would not have taken place so soon. It was he who brought to the Sovereign's notice the men who were able to help him to put his generous intentions into operation, and supported them in spite of the violent opposition which they encountered. It was he who called into existence the different commissions over which he presided, and induced the Emperor to appoint to a responsible post in the Ministry of the Interior Nicholas Milioutine, the brother of the future Field-Marshal Count Dmitry Milioutine. To the efforts of the former, seconded by the famous Samarine and by Prince Tcherkassky, were due the principal reforms which marked the reign of Alexander II.

At one time the Grand Duke was the most praised and the most hated man in the whole of the Empire. The Old Russian or Conservative party declared him to be a dangerous Radical, whilst the Liberals praised without limit the courage he showed in prompting his brother to lead Russia on the path of necessary reforms, and to continue the work of Peter the Great by bringing her into line with other European nations. At his house could be met all the intelligent men in Russia, no matter whether or not they had an official rank. He was the first to try to break through that circle of bureaucracy in which the country was confined, the first to attempt to do away with the *Tchin*, that plague of Russia. He had the instincts of a statesman, though through the tendency of his education he did not admit that a statesman could influence his nation against the wishes of its ruler, and held that it was that ruler alone who could decide as to what was good or bad for it. In his heart of hearts, he secretly envied his brother, and would fain have been in his place. He was, indeed, accused by his enemies of having ambitious designs against his lawful Sovereign; but that was an absurdity, for the Grand Duke was above everything else a Romanoff, who only cared for the welfare of his House, and had its respect for its head. What he certainly would have liked would have been to be granted more official authority than was the case.

At last, however, the governmental talents of the Grand Duke were put to a test. He was sent as Viceroy to Warsaw, when revolutionary trouble was brewing. It was hoped that by the introduction of Liberal reforms, and a kind of autonomy, under the guidance of a member of the Imperial House, the threatened storm would be averted. Constantine went to Warsaw, and with his beautiful wife he held a Court there; they both tried to make themselves popular with all classes, going so far as to call a son that was born to them by the Polish name of Viatcheslav. Further, to give more significance to the mission of peace he had undertaken, he called to the head of his Ministry one of the rare Poles who really understood the needs of their country, the Marquis Vielopolski.

It was all in vain; the insurrection broke out, Vielopolski was compelled, amid execrations and curses, to fly from Warsaw, the Grand Duke himself was fired upon, and had to acknowledge that his essay of a constitutional government on the banks of the Vistula had failed. He went back to St. Petersburg, to find his influence with his brother singularly diminished, and himself looked upon as a revolutionary to whose policy was due all the horrors and difficulties which followed upon the unfortunate rebellion of 1863. His political career was ended.

He then concentrated all his efforts upon the Navy. He was High Admiral and Commander-in-Chief of all the naval forces, but there again misfortune pursued him. His was a great mind, capable of great conceptions, but quite unable to grapple with details. His administration was not a success, and he carried his neglect so far that rumours went about that a great proportion of the secret funds granted to the Navy had found their way into his pockets.

The war with Turkey in 1877 revealed the unsatisfactory condition of the Navy, but Alexander II. was still too fond of his brother to deprive him of his post, and it was only after the Emperor's assassination that the Grand Duke Constantine, whose relations with his nephew the new Tsar were most unsatisfactory, himself resigned his various offices. The Grand Duke was fond of spending money, and was in his later years essentially *un homme de plaisir.* After having been passionately in love with his wife, the Princess Alexandra of Saxe-Altenburg—who certainly was one of the most beautiful women of her day—he ended by completely neglecting her; they scarcely saw each other until the last illness, which prostrated the Grand Duke, when his consort, forgetting old grievances, went to nurse him in the distant Crimea, where he had retired.

His eldest son, the Grand Duke Nicholas Constantinovitch, was the hero of a scandal which resulted in his exile to Taschkent, where he remains to the present moment, having married there the daughter of a police officer.

As for the other children of the Grand Duke Constantine Nicolaievitch, one daughter is the Dowager Queen of Greece, who is so beloved everywhere, and whose popularity in her adopted country is as great as it is in her own; the other, the Grand Duchess Wéra, died a short time ago, the widow of Duke Eugène of Würtemberg. The second son, Constantine Constantinovitch, is the cleverest man in the Imperial Family; he has written several volumes of verses, and is President of the Imperial Academy of Sciences. His youngest brother, the Grand Duke Dmitri, is a keen sportsman, and one of those happy creatures that have no history.

The second brother of Alexander II., the Grand Duke Nicholas Nicolaievitch, was a very handsome man, whose features closely resembled those of the Emperor Nicholas. But with this resemblance the likeness ended. He was not stupid in the strict sense of the word, but ignorant, self-opinionated, stubborn, and very vindictive, a trait he shared in common with his elder brother. There is a curious anecdote about him, for the authenticity of which I can vouch. He was once president of a commission, one of the members of which was a great personal friend of the Sovereign, a man who always had his *franc parler,* and whose opinion had often been taken into consideration by the stern Nicholas I. This man disliked the Grand Duke, and having suddenly noticed that the latter counted under the table upon his fingers whilst discussing certain credits for the Army, interrupted brusquely with the remark:

"Monseigneur, quand on sait settlement compter sur ses doigts, on se tait."

The scandal can be imagined.

In spite of this deficiency in his arithmetical attainments, the Grand Duke was entrusted with various military commands, and was Commander-in-Chief of the Army during the war with Turkey. It is well known how utterly incompetent he showed himself in that capacity and the disasters which were due to his obstinacy and want of foresight. Public opinion was very bitter against him for his incapacity. He died only a few months before his brother, the Grand Duke Constantine, and his splendid palace was acquired by the Crown for the purposes of a college for young girls, which is known as the Xenia Institute, and which was founded by the late Emperor at the time of his eldest daughter's marriage.

The Grand Duke Nicholas left two sons, both of whom are married to daughters of the King of Montenegro.

The youngest brother of Alexander II., the Grand Duke Michael Nicolaievitch, died only quite recently, and was always very highly thought of and deeply respected by all the Imperial Family. Even his stern nephew the Emperor Alexander III. reverenced him, and frequently turned to him for advice. He had occupied for many years the responsible position of Viceroy of the Caucasian provinces, and had filled it to general satisfaction. His wife, the Grand Duchess Olga Feodorovna, by birth a Princess of Bade, was one of the most cultured princesses in Europe, and a woman of brilliant intellect, kind heart, and charming manners. She was the type of the *grande dame* of past days, full of gentleness and dignity, and altogether an exception to the general mould after which princesses are fashioned. Her conversation was exceptional, and her powers of assimilation quite remarkable. When she liked she could win all hearts, even those of her enemies.

On her return from the long absence in the Caucasus her house became the rendezvous of all the intellectual and artistic elements of St. Petersburg Society, and she was rather feared by the other ladies of the Imperial

BROTHERS OF ALEXANDER II.

Grand Duke Constantine Nicolaievitch   Grand Duke Michael Nicolaievitch

BROTHERS OF ALEXANDER III.

Grand Duke Vladimir Alexandrovitch   Grand Duke Alexis Alexandrovitch

Family for her authoritative manners and domineering spirit.

The Grand Duke distinguished himself during the Turkish War, where he won the Grand Cross of St. George and the baton of Field-Marshal. He was a tall man, with the characteristic features of the Romanoffs, a long beard, and altogether the look of a thorough *grand seigneur*. He kept in favour during three reigns, and was extremely regretted when he died, especially by the Dowager Empress. His wife had predeceased him by a number of years; she died on her way to the Crimea from the shock which she sustained when she heard of her second son's marriage with the Countess Torby.

The grand ducal couple had a large family—six sons and one daughter, who is now Dowager Duchess of Mecklenburg-Schwerin.

Of the three daughters born to the Emperor Nicholas I. and the Empress Alexandra Feodorovna, the second, Alexandra, died a few months after marriage; she was extremely beautiful, and it is said that her mother never recovered from the blow caused by her death. The youngest—the Grand Duchess Olga, with whom an Austrian Archduke had been in love, and whose proposed marriage had failed on account of religious questions—became Queen of Würtemberg, and had neither a happy nor a pleasant life. She also was extremely beautiful, and possessed of her mother's grand manner, a Sovereign every inch of her, with that born dignity which it is next to impossible to acquire. Her husband was her inferior in everything, and no children were born to her in whom she could have forgotten her other disappointments. She died after a lingering illness, very much regretted by those who knew her well, but almost a stranger to the country over which she had reigned.

Not less lovely, but with a very different disposition, was her eldest sister, the Grand Duchess Marie Nicolaievna, who married the son of Prince Eugène de Beauharnais and Princess Amelia of Bavaria. Clever, with a shade of intrigue, wonderfully gifted, but of a passionate, warm disposition, she made a very inferior marriage, from sheer disappointment at having missed a brilliant alliance which her coquetry had caused to be abandoned. Extremely fascinating, a fact of which she was perfectly aware, she was a general favourite in society, and so much beloved that by a kind of tacit agreement everybody united their efforts to hide from her stern father her numerous frailties. When at length the Duke of Leuchtenberg wanted to make a scandal and separated from his wife, the Emperor interfered, and granted to his daughter's children the title of Prince (or Princess) Romanovsky. She afterwards married Count Gregoire Strogonoff, but lacked the courage to tell the fact to the Emperor, and Nicholas I. died in ignorance of it. There is no doubt he would never have forgiven her, though the Strogonoffs rank among the great nobles of Russia. The union, indeed, was only acknowledged by Alexander II. after a long struggle. The Grand Duchess bought a villa in Florence, and spent there a great part of the year, surrounded by artists and indulging in her taste for painting and sculpture. She had been elected President of the Academy of Arts in St. Petersburg, and her efforts were certainly directed towards the development of artistic activity in her native country. She died in Russia, whither she had wished to be brought back when it became evident that she was attacked by an incurable disease. By her first husband she left two daughters and four sons, one of whom was killed during the Turkish campaign. By her second marriage she had one daughter, called Hélène, who was the favourite of the present Dowager Empress; she was twice married, first to a Colonel Scheremetieff, and secondly to an officer named Miklachevsky, and died not long ago. She bore an extreme likeness to her grandfather, the Emperor Nicholas I., and, though a very great lady in manner, was not a favourite in St. Petersburg Society, which found her haughty and stiff.

The magnificent palace of the Grand Duchess Marie Nicolaievna, which had been given to her as a wedding present by her father when she was united to the Duke of Leuchtenberg, was sold to the Crown by her children after her death. It is at present the seat of the Council of the Empire, and except the walls nothing is left to remind one of the lovely woman who was once the mistress of it, nor of the festivities of which it was the scene for so many long years.

CHAPTER IV

THE INFLUENCE OF THE GRAND DUCHESS HÉLÈNE PAVLOVNA

AMONG the remarkable women whom it has been my fortune to meet, the Grand Duchess Hélène Pavlovna certainly holds the first place. For a long series of years she was the most important member of the Russian Imperial family, and her influence was exercised far and wide, and even outbalanced that of the reigning Empress. She was not only a leader of society, but a serious factor in both foreign and home politics. It was she who gave to her nephew, the Emperor Alexander II., the first idea of the emancipation of the serfs, and more than that, it was she who gave him the first hint as to how this reform could be accomplished. Assisted by the advice of several remarkable men, such as Nicholas Milioutine, Prince Tcherkassky, and others, she gave their liberty to the peasants of her property of Karlovka in the Government of Poltava. This event sounded the first knell of the old regime, and it is to the everlasting honour of the Grand Duchess that it came to be heard through her generous initiative.

She was no ordinary person then, this Princess, who, after a childhood spent at the small Court of Stuttgart, was suddenly introduced to all the splendours of that of St. Petersburg. Left a widow at a comparatively early age, she could not, so long as her brother-in-law the Emperor Nicholas reigned, aspire to a political rôle. Yet her serious mind was tired of the vain and empty life she was condemned to lead, so she contrived to make her palace the centre of artistic and literary Russia. Every author, painter or sculptor was welcomed there, and every politician too. It was murmured, and even related, that the report of the liberty which was indulged in the conversations held at these gatherings reached the Emperor himself, who once remonstrated with his sister-in-law on the subject and received from her the proud reply: "*Il vaut mieux pour vous, Sire, qu'on cause chez moi tout haut, plutôt que de conspirer chez les autres tout bas.*"

Nevertheless, she was obliged to restrain herself in the expression of her opinions after these remarks were made to her, and it was not until her nephew ascended the throne that she began to play an open part in politics, and to acquire real influence in that direction. Her palace soon became a centre of Liberalism, as it was understood at the time, and it is certain that her evening parties, to which everyone of importance in Russia, with or without Court rank, was invited, were of great use to Alexander II., who found it convenient to meet at his aunt's house people whom it would have been next to impossible for him to see anywhere else.

The Grand Duchess Hélène, among her great qualities, possessed the rare one of being able to discover and appreciate people of real merit. "*Elle se connait en hommes,*" was the judgment passed upon her by Bismarck, who also knew how to judge the merits of individuals. Her clear brain was unaffected by prejudice, although she appreciated the important part it plays in the judgments of the world. She was altogether superior to these judgments, even when they were passed upon herself. Thus she never wavered in her friendship for Nicholas Milioutine, who, in spite of the cruel insinuations that were made in St. Petersburg Society regarding that friendship—insinuations that the high moral character of the Princess ought to have preserved her from.

Strange to say, the person who most warmly defended the Grand Duchess against these calumnies was the Empress Marie Alexandrovna herself. She did not like her aunt, nor sympathise with her opinions, but she had a strong sense of justice, and, moreover, felt that, as the first lady in the Empire, it was her duty to protect the second one from unmerited disgrace. She therefore consented to meet Milioutine one evening, and after he had been presented to her she received him with kindness, and even discussed with him a few points concerning the emancipation of the serfs that was then the topic of the day, and the mere suggestion of which had brought such a storm about the heads of those who were in favour of it. It was upon that occasion that the Empress expressed the judgment which was considered so true at the time, and sounds so strange to-day: "*Il m'a toujours semble que ces grands mots de conservateurs, de rouges, de revolutionnaires n'avaient pas de partis.*" Poor Empress! Subsequent events were to afford a terrible contradiction!

So long as the Liberal reforms were on the *tapis*, the salon of Hélène Pavlovna retained its importance. People used to try their utmost to be received by her, because they knew that it offered them the possibility of meeting and even speaking with the Sovereign. All the Ministers of Alexander II., General (afterwards Count) Milioutine, M. Abaza, M. Valouieff, the famous Samarine, were habitués of her evening parties. It was at her instigation that the question of compulsory military service was first mentioned to the Emperor. It was during a dinner which she gave to Prince Tcherkassky, before the latter's departure for Poland, that the reform of the Legislative Code was first discussed, and the introduction of the *juges de paix*, in imitation of those of France, was decided.

Whenever a step was made in the road of progress and Liberalism, it was the Grand Duchess Hélène who was the first to notice it, and to show her appreciation of it. Ofttimes she carried her enthusiasm too far, and harmed instead of doing good to the causes which she had taken to heart.

Gossip began to accuse her of intrigues, which, if the truth be said, were not absolutely foreign to her nature. She liked to make herself important, to be thought the principal personage in Russia, to be considered as the person who had the greatest influence over her nephew Alexander II. It was a very innocent little weakness, but it made her sometimes ridiculous, and certainly her opinions would have had greater weight had she not talked so much, and especially restrained her friends from talking so much, about her influence and her importance. She aspired to the position of a Richelieu, and did not realise that it was rather as that of his councillor, the famous Père Joseph, she could have attained more easily her goal, which was that of governing and reforming Holy Russia.

With all this, however, she exercised a great influence on St. Petersburg Society; she was a really great lady, a princess of the old style, pure and proud, who looked upon the world from an ivory chair, who never allowed herself any meanness, any petty vengeance, or forgetfulness of the position she filled in the world. She was an incomparable hostess, though her evening parties were thought dull by those whose powers of conversation were limited, or who cared only for small talk. No one knew better than she how to receive her guests or to put them at their ease, and though slander or gossip were excluded from her conversation, yet she sometimes unbent, and would relate with much spirit anecdotes concerning her arrival in Russia, and the first years of her married life. This reminds me of one occasion when she told us the following amusing story of the Emperor Nicholas's sternness in all questions of military service. It was so funnily related that I entered it in my diary as soon as I got home, and I will repeat it now, as I heard it from her lips on that day. The conversation had centred by accident on the Emperor, and someone said that he had been capable of very cruel things. The Grand Duchess instantly protested with energy.

"The Emperor was not cruel," she said; "he punished when it was necessary, but I never remember his punishing anyone unjustly, or having done any really cruel act. He was, with all his severity, the kindest of men. The only time that I have heard of his having been cruel was on one occasion"—and she smiled at the remembrance of what she was going to relate—"and that was as follows: The Emperor very often used to drive out quite alone through the streets of St. Petersburg to see what was going on. At that time there was a guard-house close to the Alexander Nevski Convent. Now it was the custom when the Emperor—and for the matter of that any member of the Imperial Family—happened to pass there, for the guard to come out and present arms, and if the officer in command had been obliged for some reason or other to remain indoors, the senior non-commissioned officer came out in his place. Now on that particular occasion the officer on guard happened to be a certain Captain K——, who, thinking that no one would ever hear about it, had simply undressed and gone to bed, leaving his subordinate to see to things during the night. The Emperor had slept badly, and went out at the early hour of six o'clock. When he passed the guard-house and saw that the officer did not come out, he had his carriage stopped, and inquired where the officer was. Upon receiving the reply that he was indoors, the Emperor went in. The first sight that met his eyes was Captain K——, sleeping upon the camp bed which was reserved for the officer in case of need, and completely undressed. The Sovereign shook him by the arm. One can fancy the feelings of the unfortunate man when he saw who it was that was awakening him. 'Get up,' said the Emperor, 'and follow me. No; don't dress yourself—come *as you are*.' And he dragged him *as he was*, without even the most indispensable garment on, and ordered him to sit beside him in his carriage. Thus, completely undressed, he brought him back to the Winter Palace, whence he ordered him to be sent, still undressed, to the Caucasus, where he was degraded to the rank of a common soldier. That was the only cruel deed I knew the late Emperor to do," added the Grand Duchess, "and then he very soon pardoned Captain K—— and restored him to his favour. It is certain that the captain would in time have made a career, in spite of this unfortunate incident, had he not been killed during the Hungarian campaign."

I repeat this story to afford some idea of the conversation at these celebrated evening parties at the Palais Michel, as the home of the Grand Duchess Hélène was called, and to show that, with all her reputation of a blue-stocking, she was not above repeating a funny anecdote to amuse her guests. It is therefore a mistake to say that her conversation was pedantic, and that outside of politics nothing ever amused her. She could laugh, in spite of her stiffness, which was more apparent than real, and her ceremonious manners proceeded rather from her education than from the haughtiness with which she was credited.

After the Polish mutiny of 1863, the importance of the Grand Duchess Hélène decreased. A certain reaction had already set in, after the enthusiasm which had accompanied the manifesto of February 19th, 1861, granting liberty to the serfs, and the old Conservative party had succeeded in proving to the Emperor that he had underestimated the difficulties of the reform, especially in its connection with the agrarian question. At the same time the disappointment which attended the essay in constitutional government in Poland by the Grand Duke Constantine was causing acute irritation. It had been whispered at these weekly gatherings at the Palais Michel that if the Emperor's brother succeeded in Warsaw something of the same kind might be tried in St. Petersburg, and a responsible Cabinet instituted on the lines of those of Western Europe. The attempt having failed, its discredit fell on the promoters of it, primarily on the Grand Duke and his aunt, whose advice he had been credited with following. Several councillors of the Emperor, like old Count Panine, represented to him that too much latitude had been allowed the Grand Duchess Hélène, and that she ought to be reminded that in Russia it was not allowed to discuss the actions of the Sovereign, and still less to disapprove of them. After this a certain coolness existed between aunt and nephew, and the journeys abroad of the Grand Duchess became longer and more frequent; but when she was in St. Petersburg she did not change her habits, and continued to receive her friends, to give her parties, and to express her opinions. Gradually, however, the tone of her salon changed, and artistic matters were more to the front than had been the case before. She also gave her attention to charitable and scientific institutions, and the hospital of experimental medicine which bears her name testifies to the present day of the interest with which she followed the progress of medical science. She died at a relatively advanced age, in the beginning of the year 1873.

Her daughter, the Grand Duchess Catherine, tried to follow in the footsteps of her mother, but though kind-hearted, she had not the brilliancy of the Grand Duchess Hélène, and so did not succeed in replacing her. Her dinners and parties, even when the same people attended them, lacked the animation, and especially the ease, which had distinguished the former gatherings at the Palais Michel.

The Grand Duchess Hélène had as friend and helper her lady-in-waiting, the Baroness Editha Rhaden. Just as remarkable a person in her way as her august mistress, she was the life of the Palais Michel. Extremely clever, and still more learned, she made it her business to read everything that was worth reading, to know everybody worth knowing, and to study every question worth studying. She was also the channel through which news of the outside world and the opinions of the various political circles of the capital used to reach the Grand Duchess. She attended to her correspondence, and often replied to the letters which the latter received or transmitted her orders to those who looked to the aunt of the Sovereign for direction in matters of State. A curious note sent to Nicholas Milioutine testifies how thoroughly the Baroness Rhaden was identified with the aspirations of the party which had put its hopes under the patronage of the Grand Duchess Hélène. It was written in the month of October, 1860, just at the time when the commission which was elaborating the project of the emancipation of the serfs was bringing its work to a close, and when unexpected difficulties had suddenly cropped up. I give it here in its original French, together with a translation:—

"*Je suis chargée de vous annoncer une bonne nouvelle, secrète encore, c'est que le grand duc Constantin est nommé president du grand comité, et qu'à son retour l'Empereur présidera lui-même. Avais-je raison ce matin de croire à une Providence spéciale pour la Russie, et pour nous tous?*"

(I have been asked to give you some good news, which is as yet secret, and that is that the Grand Duke Constantine has been appointed President of the Grand Committee, and that after his return here the Emperor will himself preside. Was I not right this morning in thinking that there existed a special Providence for Russia, and for us all?)

Editha Rhaden was a charming person, rather given, perhaps, to exuberant enthusiasm, which prevented her from appreciating the real worth of things as well as of people, but with real intelligence, sound principles, and brilliant conversational powers. She was perhaps slightly *poseuse* and rather given to exaggerate both her own and her Imperial mistress's importance. A great stickler for etiquette, she contrived to give a ceremonious appearance to the smallest gathering, and she was famed for the magnificence of her curtseys whenever a crowned head came into a room. She lived only within the atmosphere of a Court, and when absent from it seemed lost and utterly out of her element; but she was thoroughly genuine, incapable of a mean act, and very much liked even by those who smiled at her innocent foibles. After the death of the Grand Duchess Hélène, whom she did not survive very long, she continued to receive those who had been habitués of the Palais Michel, and held a small Court of her own, whose importance she overvalued. When she died she was generally regretted, for she had tried to do all the good she possibly could, and no one could reproach her with a bad action or a bad use of the influence which at one time she unquestionably possessed.

Another important member of the Imperial Family was Prince Peter of Oldenburg, the cousin of the Emperor. His entire existence was given up to deeds of charity, or to questions of education. He was the founder of a school which has given to Russia some of its most distinguished citizens, and which to this day is considered to be one of the best in the Empire. The Mary Magdalen Hospital was also due to his initiative. He was almost venerated by all classes of society, and when he died even the cab-drivers of St. Petersburg were heard to mourn him as one of their best friends. His son, Prince Alexander, married the Princess Eugénie of Leuchtenberg, the daughter of the Grand Duchess Marie Nicolaievna by her first husband, the son of Eugène de Beauharnais, of Napoleonic fame. He is also a very distinguished man.

CHAPTER V

THE REFORMS OF ALEXANDER II. AND HIS MINISTERS

When Alexander II. ascended the Throne, it was known—and, what is more, it was felt—that by the force of circumstances alone his reign was bound to be one of serious reforms. It was known also both at home and abroad that these reforms would be strenuously opposed by all his father's friends, Ministers, and advisers. People wondered whether the young Sovereign would prove to have sufficient energy to change an order of things which it was to the interests of many old servants of the Imperial regime to retain as they were. Public opinion, however, was soon enlightened as to the intentions of the Emperor, because when he received deputations of the nobility, on the occasion of his Coronation, he publicly declared to them his intention to grant liberation to the serfs. His announcement caused a great sensation, but as time went on and the great reform, though discussed everywhere, was delayed, it was thought that the Government and Alexander himself feared the consequences of such a revolutionary measure. The problems which it raised were of the most serious character and threatened to shake the very foundations of the empire. The matter was especially complicated in its agrarian aspect, for the very right of property, as it had hitherto been understood in Russia, was jeopardised. One cannot wonder, therefore, that even a Liberal monarch hesitated before making the fateful stroke of his pen that would irrevocably settle the matter.

As is usual in Russia, a committee was appointed to study the question, and, thanks to the efforts of Prince Gortschakov, who was one of his strongest supporters, Nicholas Milioutine was appointed, under General Lanskoi, to bring into order the different propositions submitted to the committee; he was to endeavour to evolve a scheme that would be acceptable both to the enthusiastic supporters and the indignant opponents of the reform, the principle of which, nevertheless, the latter felt could not be avoided any longer.

It is not within the limits of this book to deal with the individuality of Milioutine, nor of the influence exercised by him during the eventful years which followed the accession of Alexander II. to the Throne. He was a most remarkable man, both as regards intellect and character, but he was one of the most disliked personages in Russia. By a strange stroke of destiny, after having borne the reputation of being an extreme Radical, and being under suspicion of the Emperor himself, who for a long time refused to employ him, Milioutine, thanks to the protection of the Grand Duchess Hélène and of Prince Gortschakov, found himself called to collaborate with the Sovereign in the most important act of his reign. Later on, as soon as the reform over which they had both worked had become an accomplished fact, Milioutine fell once more under his Sovereign's displeasure and was rudely dismissed before he had been able to show what he could do towards regulating the machine which he had set in motion.

The dismissal of Milioutine was typical of Alexander II. and of the indecision which was one of the defects in his character. He never had the patience nor the necessary endurance to wait for the natural development of events and for the consequences of his actions; he considered that they were bound to be successful, simply because he wished them to be so. His was a nature that expected praise and gratitude not only from individuals but from nations. He had nursed big dreams of glory, and would have been perfectly happy had the enthusiasm with which he was greeted by his subjects on that eventful day of February 19th, 1861, lasted for ever. That it did not do so made him angry, all forgetful of the fact that the brightest day is sometimes followed by the blackest night.

Alexander, indeed, had a great deal of childishness in his character. As a child breaks his playthings, so he would treat people who had ceased to please him; and this fatal trait of character, which so often made him withdraw to-day what he had given yesterday, was one of the many causes that shattered the popularity which at one time seemed so deep and lasting.

No one who was in St. Petersburg at the time of the emancipation of the serfs will ever forget the morning of that great day in February, 1861. The excitement in the capital was intense. Up to the last moment people had doubted whether the Sovereign would have the courage to put his name to the measure. Even the most Liberal among the upper classes, those who for a long time had wished for the day when slavery would be abolished, were fearful of the manner of its accomplishment. It must not be supposed that the old Russian nobility were entirely against the emancipation. What they objected to was the lines upon which the Emperor wanted it to be brought about, and the forced expropriation of what belonged to the landlords in order to give it to the peasants. Those who knew these peasants well felt how very dangerous it was to imbue these ignorant people with the idea that the Sovereign could take from his nobles lands to give to the peasants. Events have proved that these adversaries of the great reform were right; it was this fatal mistake that spoiled the great work which, conducted differently, would have immortalised Alexander II. not only as a humane, but also as a wise Sovereign.

All this was discussed on the eve of that February 19th, and everybody knew that frantic efforts were being made on both sides to delay or to hasten the important decision. It was said that some of the promoters of the projected reform, in order to break down the last hesitations of the Sovereign, had tried to frighten him with the threat of an insurrection of the masses if it was not promulgated. A curious note from the Grand Duchess Hélène to Milioutine shows us the apprehensions felt in high quarters as to what might follow a deception of the hopes raised among the peasant class.

"I think it right to warn you that my servants have told me that if there was nothing for the 19th, the *tchern* (populace) would come before the Palace and ask for a solution. I think one ought to pay some attention to that piece of gossip, because at the present moment a demonstration would be fatal for our hopes."

As a matter of fact, no demonstration was ever planned, or could have taken place in view of the precautions taken by the police; but this apprehension of the Grand Duchess was typical of the nervous excitement among the upper classes at the time.

The Emperor, however, had made up his mind, though it seems that at the very last moment some kind of fear had taken hold of him. On February 18th, the anniversary of his father's death, he had driven to the fortress and for a long time prayed at his father's tomb. Did he remember then the words spoken by the dying Nicholas when, with that sense of prophecy given to people at their last hour, he had told his son that if he brought about all the Liberal measures of which he was dreaming he would not die in his bed? On his return to the Winter Palace, however, Alexander II. seemed unusually grave and silent.

Whether he slept or not no one knows, and the next morning was brought to him the famous manifesto composed by the Metropolitan of Moscow, the venerable Philaret, which began with the words, "Make the sign of the Cross, thou Russian people." When Count Lanskoi, then Minister of the Interior, handed the momentous document to the Emperor, he took it from him with hands that trembled in spite of his efforts to remain calm, and asked to be left alone for a few moments.

What passed in his mind during those minutes? Did he see, as in a dream, the past and his father's wishes and his father's hopes, and the future with its hideous end, the day when, maimed and bleeding, he would be brought back to that same room to die, struck by one of those whom his hand was going to free? He never told anyone the struggles of his soul on that day, and when he recalled Lanskoi there was no sign of emotion on his face. He signed the manifesto with a firm hand, and it was at once made public.

A few hours later Alexander II. left the Winter Palace in a victoria, alone and without escort. The square in front of the old building was crowded with people, and when the Sovereign appeared, such a cry of greeting arose as Russia had never heard until that day. The enthusiasm cannot be described, people surrounded the Imperial carriage and pressed round their liberator, women sobbed and children wept, and even among the onlookers emotion was intense. Many had come there attracted by mere curiosity to witness the scene, many who deplored the occasion that had given rise to it, and even they were seized with the general emotion. One lady alone kept cool. It was the old Countess Koutaissow, whose sister had been the mistress of Paul I., who was the representative of the old Conservative element in St. Petersburg society, and bitterly opposed to the reforms of the new reign. When asked whether she had not felt affected by the general enthusiasm she replied, quietly: "No; I only rejoiced that I am too old to see the masses that have just been emancipated rise against their Sovereign and his successors, and I mourned the fate of my children who will see the consequences of to-day's folly."

None of the reforms which marked the reign of Alexander II. was completed, but it is certain that, notwithstanding their faults, they signalled the dawn of a new era in which it was no longer possible to step back; but they brought neither peace to the country nor glory to the Sovereign, who had believed, in his ignorance of men and things, that they would ensure him a place among the rulers of his country next to that of the Great Peter. But Peter had a will of his own, and Alexander II. had merely fancies.

It cannot be denied, however, that at the beginning of his reign he was surrounded by clever men and by gentlemen, which is more than can be said of his two successors. *La noblesse*, to use the old French word, had still something to say, and it is doubtful whether Alexander would have accomplished what he did had he not been helped by a section of that much maligned class of society.

Foremost among his Ministers was the brother of Milioutine, to whose efforts the emancipation of the serfs owed so much, General Dmitry Alexieievitch Milioutine, who for more than twenty years held the portfolio of War Minister. To his efforts was due the reorganisation of the Army, as well as the introduction of compulsory military service, another of the measures that raised a storm of indignation throughout the whole country. Milioutine was perhaps the most remarkable personality in the group of men who thought to immortalise themselves together with the Sovereign whom they served. He was a small, quiet individual, with sad, grey eyes, and with an iron will beneath his frail appearance. He was the only one among Alexander II.'s advisers that came to power with a definite plan, from which, in all justice it must be said, he was never known to swerve aside. He had at heart the welfare not only of his country but also of the soldier whose fate lay in his hands. He tried to ameliorate that fate, and to him must be ascribed the abolition of corporal punishment in the Army and a whole list of measures which had for their purpose the training and education of the soldier. Military schools were one of his principal cares; he wanted to establish a regular system of training not only for officers, but for the non-commissioned officers, who in his opinion were the pillars of a proper organisation of the Army. He was an indefatigable worker, who entered into every detail, and who never neglected the most insignificant points. Had he been ably seconded, there is no doubt that the beginnings of the war of 1877 would not have been so disastrous as they were, but the Grand Duke Nicholas was his enemy, and did all that he could to counteract the measures adopted by the Minister, who often had to do, in obedience to the Emperor's personal orders, what he secretly disapproved.

Milioutine was not liked. All the old generals who had fought during the previous reign reproached him for what they called his "revolutionary ideas," and the younger generation, who through his reforms found itself burthened with new and unpleasant duties, was vigorously opposed to him. The old warrior, however, paid no attention to the outcry raised, and allowed the personal attacks of which he was made the subject to pass unnoticed. He never tried to revenge himself on his foes; never made use of the power which he wielded to harm anyone, and always listened to criticism, being of opinion that one can always learn something from it. He was hated by the Heir to the Throne, and when Alexander III. succeeded his father in the tragic circumstances which everybody knows, it was felt that Milioutine's days as Minister were numbered. He knew it himself, and had the situation been less grave he would at once have offered his resignation. A few short months, however, saw it become an accomplished fact, when the Liberal Cabinet, headed by Count Loris Melikoff, of which he was a member, had to retire before the autocratic programme which M. Pobedonostseff had induced the young Emperor to adopt.

Milioutine never returned to St. Petersburg after that day. He retired to the Crimea, where he possessed a villa, and never more turned his attention towards public affairs, preserving a dignified silence both as to his wrongs and to his political activity in the past. The present Sovereign made him a Count, and later on conferred upon him the dignity of Field-Marshal. When the Count was in the Crimea, Nicholas II. never forgot to visit the old veteran, living so quietly amongst his roses and the many flowers of his garden. There he died at the beginning of 1912, two days after his wife, at the advanced age of ninety-four, having kept unimpaired to the last his brilliant qualities and his remarkable intelligence. Few statesmen have had the dignity of Count Milioutine; few have known better how to behave when in power, and to live when out of it.

Of a different type from the General was Count Panine, who at the time of the emancipation of the serfs held the portfolio of Justice. He was a *grand seigneur* in the fullest sense of the term, *un homme d'autrefois* immutable in his principles, and who, when he saw he could no longer please his Sovereign, retired rather, as he himself said, "than bow his grey head before the idol of progress." Panine was the embodiment of that type of Russian functionary that will not admit a change of regime, and that look upon every reform as a danger. He was thoroughly retrogressive in all his opinions, and Liberalism or Liberty meant for him merely Revolution. He firmly believed that every concession made to the spirit of modern times was a danger to the Throne, and he was perhaps the only man who had the courage to tell Alexander II. so, and to retire from power rather than lend his hand to what he considered to be the degradation of that system of autocracy which he had defended during the whole of his long life.

By a strange freak of destiny, and one of those contrasts one only meets with in Russia, his only son was one of the first to adopt the new ideas of Liberalism. Together with some of his University comrades, he was arrested in 1861 under an accusation of Nihilism. Released on account of his father's services, Vladimir Panine married a charming woman, Mademoiselle Maltseff, and imbued her with his own revolutionary opinions. When he died quite young, leaving an only daughter, who found herself the sole heiress of the enormous fortune of the old Count Panine, the widow of the latter implored the Emperor to take the child away from her mother and to have her confided to her own care. In spite of the tears of the young Countess Panine, her daughter was taken forcibly away from her and placed in the institute for girls at Smolna, whence she was allowed to go out only to visit her grandmother. The relatives of the heiress tried to instil into her entirely different ideas from those of her father and mother. When out of sheer isolation the Countess Vladimir Panine married a young doctor named Petrounkevitch, whose Liberal opinions were in accordance with her own, everything possible was done to compromise both, and to effect thus the complete separation of little Sophie Panine from her mother. The latter, with her second husband, was forbidden to visit the capital, and they settled in Odessa. Meanwhile the heiress grew up, and, as so often happens in such cases, retained in the depths of her heart a perfect adoration for her mother and a thorough dislike for her father's sisters, who were among those who had tried most to isolate her from everything that was not in accordance with the principles in which they wanted her to be brought up. At length the child who had been the object of all this strife was married at seventeen to a very rich man, not, perhaps, her equal by birth, but whose financial position put him above the suspicion of having wanted her for her money. After a few years the couple were divorced, and the Countess Sophie Panine, by special permission of the Emperor, was allowed to resume her maiden name. She still lives in St. Petersburg, entirely devoted to good works; the revenues of her immense fortune are consecrated to the relief of poor students and to the building of cheap kitchens and night refuges. During the troubled times of

1905 it was rumoured that the Countess Sophie Panine was seriously compromised; and it was even said that she had been arrested. This proved to be incorrect, but it is evident that, in spite of the efforts made to imbue her with strict Conservative principles, the granddaughter of the most autocratic Minister of Alexander II. is in open sympathy with the very ideas against which he fought during the whole of his long life.

Prince Lieven and M. Valouieff were also remarkable personalities of the time of which I am writing. The former fell into terrible disgrace under Alexander III., and was ordered to leave St. Petersburg. This event caused a great scandal at the time, for the Prince and Princess were both prominent in society. For the Princess the blow was a terrible one, and she did not scruple openly to attack the new Sovereign until it was made evident to her that she had better refrain.

M.—afterwards Count—Valouieff and M. Abaza had a better fate. The first of these gentlemen, who for a long time had held the portfolio of Home Affairs, exchanged it for that of the Imperial Domains, and though he lost his influence he retained his position. He had the common sense not to try to go against the tide, and to give up of his own accord the power which otherwise would have been snatched from him. He was a pleasant, quiet man, and generally liked.

M. Abaza for some time was a very considerable personage in St. Petersburg society. He was one of the intimate friends of the Grand Duchess Hélène and of Baroness Editha Rhaden, and it was their influence that brought him before the notice of Alexander II. He was supposed to be a great authority on all financial matters, and twice had the portfolio of that department entrusted to his care. He was one of those who had submitted to the influence of the Princess Dolgorouky; and when she became the Sovereign's morganatic wife and received the title of Princess Yourievsky, Abaza tried to induce her to persuade the Emperor of the necessity of granting a Constitution to the nation. Ryssakoff's bomb put an end to those dreams in the most shocking and unexpected manner. With the death of Alexander II. the duties of his Ministers came to an end. His successor never forgave M. Abaza, not only his Liberal principles, but also his friendship with the Princess Yourievsky; and though he continued to be a member of the Council of State, and presided over many commissions, though he was granted orders and dignities, and even often consulted in grave matters of State, yet the political career of M. Abaza was practically ended on that eventful March 1st, 1881. When he died, many years later, leaving an enormous fortune, the event was noticed by only the usual obituary in the newspapers, and a remark made by Alexander III., who, having been told that the Princess Ouroussoff, daughter and heiress of the deceased statesman, inherited seven millions, said, "Only that! I thought he had stolen much more!"

CHAPTER VI

THE ADLERBERGS AND THE SCHOUVALOFFS

THE two most prominent families during the reign of Alexander II. were those of Count Adlerberg and Count Schouvaloff. The former, of German origin, did not boast of many ancestors, but had for two generations enjoyed the confidence of their Sovereigns. Old Count Vladimir Adlerberg, who received the title from Nicholas I., was not only Minister of the Imperial Household, but a personal friend of that monarch. His son Alexander was educated with the Emperor's sons, and in his turn was entrusted with the same post as his father had occupied, after the latter's death. No one could have filled that delicate position with more tact, more intelligence, and more kindness than he did. Admirably educated, he possessed a perfect knowledge of the French and German languages, and it was he who generally had the task of composing the letters which Alexander II. had occasion to address to other Sovereigns on important political matters. It was said that Count Alexander Adlerberg knew more secrets, both State and private, than any other man in Russia, and his discretion was beyond all praise. No lips were ever more securely sealed than his, and no man ever had his talent to forget what he had heard or seen. For the whole quarter of a century that the reign of Alexander II. lasted, that friend of his youth never left him; and although during the last months of the Emperor's life their relations became strained through the influence of the Princess Yourievsky, yet the Emperor would not dispense with the Count's services, so well did he appreciate the fact that nowhere would he find such a devoted and true friend. How devoted, the world perhaps did not guess. It could not have imagined that an occasion would arise when Count Adlerberg, who was supposed to have acquired his great position owing to flattery, would through his affection for his Sovereign risk his position in telling him the truth in a matter most near to his heart. Yet so it befell. When, after the death of the Empress Marie Alexandrovna, Alexander decided to unite himself in marriage to his mistress the Princess Dolgorouky, he asked Count Adlerberg to be present at the ceremony. The old statesman refused, and earnestly begged Alexander II. to abandon the idea. The Emperor was greatly incensed, and for a time it was thought that the Minister's position was shaken. He was urged by the entourage of the Tsar to give way, and as he could prevent nothing, at least to acquiesce to what was about to become an accomplished fact; but he remained firm in his resolution, declaring that his duty as Minister of the Imperial Household made it imperative for him to maintain the dignity of the Crown, and that he believed this was going to be compromised by the step which the Emperor was about to take.

Alexander II. was very vindictive, as all know, yet whatever he might have thought, he did not, save by a certain new reserve of manner, express his displeasure at Adlerberg's conduct. Perhaps even the reasons which the latter had given to him against the marriage had some weight, for when his valet asked him what uniform he wanted to wear for the ceremony, he told him to put out plain evening clothes, which he never wore save when he was abroad, adding that as his marriage was a private affair, he wanted to give it a private appearance. This incident was very differently commented upon at the time, and some saw in it a desire to reassure Count Adlerberg as to the intentions of the Sovereign and his determination not to put the Crown of the Romanoffs on the head of the woman for whom he had so deeply offended his first wife and all her children. But the shrewd Minister well knew that such a resolution, if really taken, would not be kept, and, as a matter of fact, it was only the intervention of death that prevented the justification of his opinion.

Count Adlerberg had married a lady of considerable culture, and one who never used her great position except to do good. She was by birth a Mademoiselle Poltawtsoff, the sister of Madame Skobeleff, the mother of the famous general. Countess Adlerberg at one time kept open house, and her parties were quite a feature of the St. Petersburg winter season. She was a great lover of music, and generally all the famous singers that visited the northern capital were to be heard at her Tuesday receptions. These were brilliant and animated, attended by all the wealth, beauty and fashion of the city. Invitations to them were eagerly sought, and as eagerly accepted. The hostess had for everybody a pleasant smile and word, and no one could have believed that the day would come when the very people who crowded her lofty rooms would desert them and would forget the many kindnesses which they had accepted at those receptions.

So it was, however, for Count Adlerberg's preferment lasted only as long as Alexander II. lived. His successor had always hated the Minister of the Imperial Household with a bitter hatred. Well informed people ascribed it to an incident in the life of the Grand Duke, in which the young Princess Mestchersky had played a part. This lady—who was maid of honour to the Empress—had inspired a violent passion in the Grand Duke, who at the time had no prospect of ever ascending the Throne, and he proposed to marry her. The death of his brother, however, with the change in his position that it entailed, put an end to all these plans. Count Adlerberg was the first one to represent to the Emperor the necessity for his eventual successor to make a match in conformity with his rank, and strongly urged the accomplishment of the last desire of the dead Tsarevitch, to see his brother united to the Princess

Dagmar of Denmark, whom he had been about to marry himself when his illness intervened and made havoc of all his plans. The Count did more. He induced a very rich man, well known in society, M. Paul Demidoff, to marry the Princess Mestchersky, to whom he also explained the necessity for sacrificing herself for the welfare of Russia and of the Imperial Family. The young lady understood, and in spite of the entreaties of the Grand Duke Alexander, allowed herself to be united to Demidoff. She died in child-birth the next year, and the Heir to the Throne consented at length to be married to the Princess Dagmar, whom later on he was to love so tenderly; but he never forgave Count Adlerberg his intervention at the time, and his first care when he became Emperor was to dismiss the old servant of his father and grandfather. Moreover, he did this with the utmost brutality.

It was quite unnecessary to send a messenger ordering the Count to return at once all the documents of State which he had in his possession; or, worse insult still, to appoint a Commission to inquire into the financial state of the Privy Purse of the late Emperor, which the Count had administered. Those who advised Alexander III. to this course were only covered with confusion, for affairs were found to be in perfect order; indeed, the late Minister of the Imperial Household had effected economies amounting to 380 millions of roubles. But the news that such an inquiry was about to take place was sufficient excuse for all those who had spent their lives in the Adlerbergs' house to turn their backs upon them and never again to visit them. The Count, who knew human nature better than most men, was not affected by this change, and no one could have borne himself with greater dignity.

He lived six years or so after leaving the political arena, yet he was never heard to utter one single word of complaint as to the treatment which he had received. When he died his body was barely cold when a legal functionary from the Emperor arrived to seal up all the papers of the former Minister, and his widow was hardly given the necessary time to remove herself from the house where she had lived since her marriage. Under a clause in the will of Alexander II., the Count had been given the right to use the house during his lifetime, and people were of opinion that this right might have been continued to his widow. It is certain that Alexander III. was neither just nor generous in his treatment of one of the foremost among the statesmen of his father's reign, and of one whose devotion to his Imperial master had never been questioned.

The Countess Adlerberg resented the treatment bitterly, and allowed herself to make remarks about the ingratitude of Sovereigns in general, and of Alexander III. in particular. She tried to gather around her all the elements of opposition to the new regime, but this did not succeed. She was aunt to General Skobeleff and to the Duchess of Leuchtenberg, who was a great favourite with the new Empress, and she thought that these alliances would give her back some of the importance she had lost. When the "White General" was recalled to St. Petersburg after his Paris speech, the Countess went to meet him at the station with an immense bouquet of flowers, and thereby made herself ridiculous, and added to the resentment which was cherished against her in Court circles. It was her last public manifestation. Very soon after that her nephew died suddenly in Moscow, and after Skobeleff's disappearance the name of the Countess Adlerberg disappeared also from the public ken. She was one of the *Dames à Portrait* of the Empress, and took her place at Court when it was necessary, but she soon left off doing even that, and at last settled in Tsarskoye Selo, near St. Petersburg, where she died in 1910, utterly forgotten by the world over which she had queened it for so long.

The Schouvaloffs also played an important part, and had considerable influence, during the reign of Alexander II.— influence which, in the case of Count Paul at least, continued under his successor. They were nobles belonging to the proudest in Russia, who had always ranked among favourites of the Sovereign. In the latter part of last century this old family was represented by two brothers, Count Paul and Count Peter Schouvaloff, who were among the most influential personages of the Empire. Count Paul married, in his early youth, a Princess Belosselsky, the sister of the celebrated Princess Lison Troubetzkoy—so well known in Paris during the first years of the Third Republic, when she passed for being the "Egeria" of M. Thiers. He followed a military career, and was in command of the Corps de la Garde when the Turkish War broke out. Against the wish of the Emperor, who would have liked him to stay in St. Petersburg, where his corps remained, Count Paul volunteered for a command at the front, where soon he obtained immense popularity and won great distinction. He was an extremely pleasant and cultured person, a man of the world, full of tact, and gifted with singular diplomatic instincts.

When relations between Russia and Germany became strained after the Berlin Congress, and the two Ambassadors who had been sent there, M. d'Oubril and M. Sabouroff, had failed to improve them, Prince Orloff was asked to leave Paris in order to try to mend matters. He was well known to Prince Bismarck, who had expressed the desire to see him appointed to the German Court; but Prince Orloff, when he reached Berlin, was already attacked with the illness, to which he succumbed a few months later, and the post was vacant once more.

It was felt on all sides that upon the judicious choice of a successor to Prince Orloff depended the continuation of good relations between the two countries. The old Emperor William expressed the wish that a general should be appointed. The difficulty was to find one. It was then that Alexander III., with his usual common sense, said: "Let us send Paul Andrieievitch; he is a real soldier and a thorough gentleman."

This choice was entirely successful, and Count Schouvaloff very soon made for himself quite an exceptional position in Berlin. He was a *grand seigneur* of that old school in which William I. had himself been brought up; he had tact, and he knew how to hold his own, as well as maintain the dignity of his Court and of his country. During the long years that he remained in Germany he made for himself many friends, and managed to come with honour out of many a difficult situation. He was generally respected and liked in all circles, military as well as diplomatic, and when he was recalled and appointed Governor-General of Warsaw and the Polish provinces there was general regret at the departure of Count and Countess Schouvaloff.

The latter, a Mademoiselle Komaroff, whom the Count had married as his second wife, is still alive, and Mistress of the Household of the widowed Grand Duchess Vladimir. As for the Count, very soon after his appointment in Warsaw he was struck with apoplexy, and thenceforward dragged out a sad existence, incapable of moving, and yet retaining all the clearness of his intelligence and all the vivacity of his mind. He died one year later, and was generally mourned as one of the last gentlemen of that apparently bygone time, when gentlemanly deportment was considered before everything else to be indispensable.

His eldest son, who had married a daughter of Count Worontzoff Dachkoff, the present Viceroy of the Caucasian provinces, fell a victim to the Nihilist movement, being murdered in Moscow, where he held the position of Governor. He was a charming young man, who promised to follow in his father's footsteps, and his tragic end created a great sensation at the time.

Very much like his brother in appearance, and yet totally different in disposition, was Count Peter Andrieievitch Schouvaloff, whose career was even more brilliant. He was a very superior man, more of a statesman than Count Paul, and with larger views, a keener sense of the importance of events, and with more independent opinions. He had, moreover, a quality very rare in Russia, that of not hesitating to take the responsibility for his actions, and of caring nothing for the judgment passed upon them by the public. He had been for years at the head of the famous Third Section, or secret police of the Empire, and it so happened that during his administration of that department the Nihilist troubles began. Actually he had been accused of having caused them by his extreme severity and acute sense of autocracy. I do not think that this accusation was a just one. If Schouvaloff kept the flag of absolutism aloft in Russia it was because he sincerely believed that it was the only way to prevent all the forces, known or unknown, which the reforms of Alexander II. had let loose from bursting out in an unreasoned, wild revolt against Society in general. In his difficult position he had shown admirable tact, and on several occasions had been an efficacious intermediary between the Throne and the people. Many a delicate affair had been confided to him, and many a social scandal had been avoided or hushed up through his intervention, which had ever been tactful and wise. But when a wave of Liberal ideas apparently swept away the remnants that were left of common sense in the entourage of Alexander II., the days of Count Peter Schouvaloff became numbered. The Emperor had to yield to the public feeling that would have it that the Count had served his day and epoch, and that his removal from the post of head of the Third Section was a necessity. But as it was out of the question to deprive the State of the services of so useful a man, he was appointed Ambassador to the Court of St. James's, where a Russian Princess, the Grand Duchess

Marie Alexandrovna, the only daughter of the Emperor, was about to take her place as the wife of the second son of Queen Victoria.

This was the turning point in Count Schouvaloff's career. After he left England he filled the place of second Russian plenipotentiary at the Congress of Berlin, and then disappeared altogether from the political arena. He had allowed himself to be outwitted by Lord Beaconsfield upon the question of Cyprus, and in the opinion of the Russian public, as well as of the Russian press, had not upheld sufficiently Russian interests during the Congress. He was made by an unjust public the scapegoat for all the mistakes of others, which he could neither foresee nor repair. Gifted with an exceedingly keen perception, he had realised that Russia had not the means whereby to retain the advantages of the war; and when he yielded to the necessities of the situation, it was with the knowledge that this would not be forgiven to him, but as a real patriot he had the moral strength to accept the responsibility for evils which he had not personally brought about.

His position in Berlin had been most painful and difficult. He was, as it were, between two fires. On the one hand he had to fight against the quiet but firm determination of Lord Beaconsfield, who would have gone to war rather than allow Russia to occupy Bulgaria and annex that province, and, on the other, he had to follow the instructions of Prince Gortschakov, whose extreme vanity blinded him to the difficulties of the situation. No one knew better than Count Peter Schouvaloff the state of public opinion in Russia; no one understood more thoroughly that after he had signed his name at the foot of the Berlin Treaty, he would never more be called upon to serve his country, but would end his days in an undeserved ostracism. Yet he did not hesitate, and courageously assumed the responsibility of an act that no one deplored more thoroughly than he did himself.

After his return to Russia he lived in St. Petersburg, and there continued to see his numerous friends, but never again took part in public life. Even when he died attacks against him did not cease, and I never remember more bitter criticisms uttered over a newly opened grave than those that were showered upon him.

It would be difficult to find a pleasanter man socially than was Count Peter Schouvaloff; not only was he liked by all those who had the privilege of his acquaintance, but he had many successes with women, who were quickly won by his chivalrous manner and the courtly grace with which he approached them. He had married a widow, the Countess Orloff Denissoff, but the marriage did not turn out so successfully as the courtship that preceded it, and the Count and Countess lived as much apart as might be without a formal separation. Physically, Count Peter Schouvaloff was extremely handsome; he had most aristocratic features and a wonderful bearing. I shall never forget him during the Berlin Congress, when he certainly was the most picturesque figure there, with his *allures de grand seigneur*, and a certain regality of manner that made everyone step aside to allow him to pass whenever he entered a room. Altogether, though I have met more intelligent men than Count Schouvaloff in the course of my life, I have not seen a more remarkable one.

CHAPTER VII

ST. PETERSBURG BEFORE THE WAR OF 1877-8

WHEN, after several years of residence abroad, I returned to St. Petersburg, early in March, 1876, I found that during my long absence a considerable change had taken place in Society. For one thing, people talked more and discussed more freely upon subjects which had been merely whispered before I had left the banks of the Neva. They had got into that habit during the period when the projected and half-accomplished reforms which had heralded the new reign had been the subject not only of conversations, but also of discussion, an unknown thing at the time of the Emperor Nicholas. The Government itself had invited criticism by appealing to the country and asking it to express its opinions by the voice of the *zemstvos*, or local county councils in every Government.

This establishment of the zemstvos had been received with a general joy. Young men belonging to the best families of the Empire had expressed not only their willingness but even their earnest desire to be appointed members of these assemblies, in the hope that they would thus be allowed to participate in the administration of the country. For a short time everything had gone off brilliantly, just as the introduction of the *juges de paix*, or *mirovoy soudias*, as they are called in Russian, gave universal satisfaction. However, very soon the Administration became alarmed at the independence showed by these zemstvos, and began to try to eliminate the independent members, who worked not from necessity, but from conviction that by doing so they were making themselves useful to the country in general. Governors of the different provinces, who in Russia are always taken out of the class of the regular functionaries, or *Tchinownikis*, as one calls them, were given secret instructions, which they but too gladly followed, of watching the deliberations of the zemstvos and of hindering any attempt made by these assemblies to bring about local self-government, which was particularly dreaded in Court circles, where the system of centralisation of the Government in the hands of the few is to this present day strongly supported and established. But the upshot of it all was that these men—who in the enthusiasm of the first moment had eagerly embraced the opportunities which they imagined had been given to them to serve their country otherwise than by wearing a uniform—returned to St. Petersburg, and began to relate all that they had seen or heard, and thus their talk accustomed the public to hear discussion on questions that had slumbered before. Then the Universities began to move, and the Liberal papers abroad controlled by the Russian political refugees—who by an admirable feeling of patriotism had kept silent in order to allow the Emperor to have a free field for his projected reforms—began to get tired of waiting for a change that never came, though it had been pompously announced; and they once more assumed the task of enlightening the public as to what in their opinion ought to be done. In a word, it was felt that the new system had failed, because no one had been found to carry on loyally the experiment which might have led to something, had it only been tried long enough.

One satisfactory result accrued, however—that of accustoming people to talk and to discuss, and to give up the sleepiness under which Russia had suffered for the previous twenty-five years, although people who were experienced in the political conditions of other countries were soon aware of a certain incoherence of thought and aim in the discussions, which resulted more often than not in confusion and even in absurdities. But one fact was evident, and that was that conversation was no longer confined to Society gossip, but turned on what was being done, or would be done, by the Government.

This did not quite please the Emperor. He did not like to know that his actions were discussed. He could not well say so, but he made his Ministers feel that such was the case, and they, desirous of meeting with his approbation, attempted to bring about a return to the old order of things, and when they found this was no easy task, they looked about to see whether something else could not be found to engross public opinion and form the subject of its conversations.

It is to this cause, and to this alone, that the war with Turkey, which broke out in 1877, can be attributed. It was engaged upon against the wishes of the Sovereign and the desires of the country, simply because an outlet had to be found for the ebullitions of public opinion, weary of waiting for an indefinite something which did not materialise, something which all wanted, but which no one could explain beyond saying that "it had to come." What was implied by this expression was precisely what nobody knew.

Just at this moment, by ill chance, broke out the insurrection in Bosnia and Herzegovina. Immediately a campaign, on purely religious lines, was begun in Russia against the Turks. The press began saying that Russia had a mission to perform in the Balkans, that it was her duty to help the Orthodox subjects of the Sultan, persecuted in their faith as well as in their nationality. The Slavophil party was started, and God alone knows the harm that it has done to the country.

At first it enjoyed high and even august protection in St. Petersburg. The Empress Marie Alexandrovna, very pious, almost inclined to fanaticism, put herself unofficially at the head of the movement, with which it soon became known that she was thoroughly in sympathy, and it was her lady-in-waiting and intimate friend, the Countess Antoinette Bloudoff, who, with an energy worthy of a better cause, came forward to lend the weight of her name and of her position to the promoters of the liberation of the Slavs from the Turkish yoke.

I must digress for a moment to refer more particularly to the Countess Bloudoff. She was a most remarkable woman. Many statesmen might have envied, and few of them have possessed, the clarity of her often mistaken view as to political events and their consequences. She was the daughter of one of the leading members of the Government during the reign of the Emperor Nicholas I., Count Dmitry

Andrieievitch Bloudoff, for many years Procurator of the Holy Synod, and invested with the entire confidence of the monarch, who often used to say: "Bloudoff is the only man who will always do what I wish, in the way I want it done." He was a man of strong principles, of stronger convictions; often passionate, sometimes unjust, but never mean, never above owning himself to be in the wrong when it was proved to him to be the case, and with a loyalty such as is no longer met with. He was possessed of independence, even with his Sovereign, and was known to have opposed Nicholas on grave questions where he thought him to be wanting either in prudence or in justice. He had plenty of adversaries and but few enemies, which latter he disdained. He died as he had lived, a faithful servant of the Crown, and his daughter inherited the favour which he had enjoyed. She was very much like him in character and even in appearance. Beauty she had none, yet she did not lack charm; while intelligence she possessed in no small degree. She was the only great lady who held a *salon*, such as was understood by the term in France under the old regime, and that *salon* was at one time of immense importance. It was there that the idea of sending volunteers to Servia was first broached, and it was she who assured these volunteers that the Emperor would shut his eyes to their departure. It was she who kept the standard of public opinion at a high level; she who persuaded some leading men in Moscow, such as Ivan Aksakoff, to organise these volunteers, and to begin in his paper a campaign in favour of the Orthodox brothers of Holy Russia, done to death by murderous Bashi Bazouks.

Altogether the Countess Antoinette was an enthusiast, an exalted patriot according to old Russian ideas, when nationality and religion meant the same thing. Still her zeal outran her discretion upon many occasions, and she came later on—after the failure of those hopes which she had been the first to raise and the last to give up—to regret the energy which she had expended in trying to realise a programme which was not in accord either with the needs or the desires of her country, and which only brought upon it disaster, both moral and material. She was compelled, much against her wishes, to be convinced that neither Bulgarians, nor Serbs, nor Greeks were worthy of interest; that the majority of them—at that epoch, at least—were grabbing, money-loving, unscrupulous people, full of ingratitude, who never for one single moment thought of admitting Russian influence, which they rejected just as much as they had opposed Turkish rule.

But at the time to which I am referring the Countess Antoinette was in the enthusiastic period of her life and of her political activities. It was to her one went to receive the latest news as to the development of Eastern affairs. She kept up an active correspondence with General Ignatieff, at that time Russian Ambassador in Constantinople; sharing alike his ambitions and his desires to see the Crescent replaced by the Cross on the minarets of St. Sophia. Continually she made reports to the Empress as to what she had heard, and used to explain to that Sovereign that it was her duty to influence her husband not to reject the great mission given to Russia—that of driving back to the confines of Asia Minor the Turk who had dared to raise his tents in the city founded by Constantine the Great and destined by him to remain the bulwark of the Christian faith in the East.

Alas, alas, for all these dreams! Poor Countess Bloudoff survived them, and when she ended her days, long after all of them had been forgotten, she might well have felt all the bitterness of a life's disappointment. But this was not the case—at least outwardly. She was far too clever not to admit her defeat, but she maintained that her failure had been due to circumstances only, and that one day Russia would fulfil the mission which she had been given by the Almighty. She remained ever the same bright, clever woman, always deeply interested in politics, in literature, in art, even in current gossip, though in a most kindly way. For she was indeed kind—that small, short woman with the piercing eyes and the quick flash of sympathy in them, which made them glisten every time that she was being told something that interested her. Easy to move, she never refused a service, and at the time when her very name was a power she tried always to do good, to bring to the notice of her Imperial mistress every case in which the latter could help, either by a word spoken in season or by money given just when and where it was needed. Towards the end of her life she grew very infirm, and could hardly leave her arm-chair; but she loved seeing people, though her rooms were no longer thronged as during the time when she was all-powerful. She had kept a small circle of old friends, who came to see her almost daily, and through them she remained in touch with that social world in which she had been a leader.

Countess Bloudoff had one *bête noire*, and that was the famous Mme. Olga Novikoff. Poor "O.K." never guessed the antipathy which she inspired, and always imagined that her activity in favour of the Slav cause, and her influence over Mr. Gladstone, were highly appreciated by the Countess Antoinette; but the latter had too keen a sense of humour not to feel that Mme. Novikoff was making herself ridiculous, and, what was worse, was involving in that ridicule her country itself. "*Je déteste ces ambassadeurs volontaires en jupon*," she used to say, and she was not far wrong. The rôle played by the too celebrated Princess Lieven needs a very great lady, and one with a very large fortune or a great position, not to give rise to calumny and to ironical smiles and comments, and "O.K." had none of these advantages. It is still a question whether the Princess Lieven could to-day have made for herself a position such as the one she enjoyed in London and in Paris. Society was different then, and fewer outsiders had entered its fold; people well born, and belonging to the upper ten thousand, could still pretend to influence, simply by reason of their being within that charmed circle. Now that classes are mixed, a person like Mme. Novikoff, who is merely a gentlewoman, runs a great risk of being considered in the light of a simple journalist in need of copy, and such only wield that measured influence which they delude themselves into believing they possess. Countess Antoinette knew all this well, and she disliked intensely women of the style of her famous compatriot, about whom she once made the most bitter remark I ever heard her utter against anyone: "*Cette femme là fait de la politique*," she said, "*comme une saltimbanque ses tours de passe passe*."

These reminiscences have caused me to diverge far from the subject of this chapter. What I wanted to say was that the war of 1877-8 was the natural result of the activity which the ill-executed reforms of Alexander II. had awakened in the country; an activity which a certain circle of St. Petersburg Society, headed by the Countess Bloudoff and the little coterie of the Empress Marie Alexandrovna— in which her confessor, Father Bajanov, was a leading figure—helped to divert from the channel towards which it had been directed: that of the internal administration of the country. The Government, that never for one single instant admitted the possibility of defeat, secretly encouraged this diversion, and, thanks to all these circumstances, the

Emperor, who was the only person who sincerely wished that peace might not be disturbed, found himself drawn into a war the consequences of which were to be the disastrous Treaty of Berlin, the extraordinary development of Nihilism, and finally his own assassination. Dark days were about to dawn for Russia, and when again I left St. Petersburg I was far from anticipating the changes that its Society would experience between the day of my departure and that of my return to the capital, when everything was different and another Sovereign upon the Throne.

CHAPTER VIII

THE EASTERN WAR AND AFTERWARDS

I DO not think that the Eastern War of 1877 was so popular as people were fain to represent, even at its beginning. The Slav movement, which had sent thousands of volunteers to Servia to help the Christian subjects of the Sultan against their oppressors, was very popular at the moment of its inception, but as soon as the volunteers began to return home and the public heard something about "these Slav brothers" it had been eager to defend, there was a violent reaction. People began to ask what good it was to sacrifice Russian blood for the needs of people who turned out to be not only cowards but brigands as bad as the Bashi Bazouks of whose cruelties they complained. Had the Emperor declared war during the summer of 1876, before the battle of Alexinatz had been fought and lost, the enthusiasm certainly would have been great; but by April, 1877, public opinion had had time to cool, and serious people were apprehensive as to the result of what, after all, was nothing but an adventure unworthy of a great nation.

The army itself, that for months had been kept at Kichinev on a war basis, was beginning to tire of its armed inaction; and, what was worse, the incapacity of those in command had already become evident, demoralising the troops and breeding discontent among them. The Grand Duke Nicholas, who was in supreme command, had never been very popular, and the measures he had taken in view of the approaching campaign were severely criticised. One wondered why men with a serious military reputation— such, for instance, as Todleben, the defender of Sebastopol —had not been called upon to give at least their advice as to what should be done. The officers, more competent to form an opinion as to the *morale* of the soldiers than the

Staff of the Grand Duke, knew very well that their men did not believe in the walk-over that was promised to them, and they knew also that the many refugees who had crowded to the Russian camp from Bulgaria and Servia had made anything but a good impression as to the qualities of their nations on their would-be liberators.

When, therefore, the war began in earnest, it was with far less enthusiasm among the army than was confidently expected and had been promised to the Emperor. When the Imperial manifesto was read announcing that war had been declared, and concluding with the words: "We order our faithful troops to cross the frontiers of Turkey," it was noticed that the hurrahs that greeted them proceeded more from the officers than from the ranks, where they were but faintly echoed. It was only after the Danube had been crossed that anything like animation became evident in the army. To stimulate it a religious propaganda was started, and all the old legends concerning Constantinople and the mosque of St. Sophia, destined to become again a Christian church thanks to the efforts of Russia, were revived. That was a mistake of which the future was to prove the abysmal extent.

At length came the first battle of Plevna. It was there that Skobeleff, "the White General," "Ak Pasha" as the Turks called him, won immortal fame. The mention of his name always recalls to my mind that sad and bloody day of the 30th of August, 1877, when the fortress was stormed for the third time in response to the mad idea of the Grand Duke Nicholas to present it as an offering to his brother on his name-day. It was a beautiful summer morning, with the roses blooming in the fields, and a clear blue sky lighting up what was so soon to become a scene of horror. The Turkish town lay in a valley, all surrounded by hills, each of which was a redoubt whence the enemy's artillery was directed against our troops. They were ordered to storm it, and valiantly did they attempt to do so at three different times through that morning. As each regiment rushed to the attack, it was decimated by the deadly fire of the Turkish guns, thousands of men being mown down like ripe corn. At length the Bender Regiment was told to advance. It was commanded by the veteran Colonel Panioutine, to whom Skobeleff himself gave the orders to march. Panioutine looked up at the fort, which he knew that he could not by any possibility hope to wrest from the enemy, and simply answered with the classical word of the Russian soldier, "*Slouchaious*" (I shall obey); then he took off his cap and made the sign of the Cross. In dead silence the whole regiment took off their caps and crossed themselves, following the example of their commanding officer.

Skobeleff turned towards his staff and said: "If Panioutine is repulsed, I will myself lead the troops to the attack."

He did lead them forward—led them to their death and to his glory. To his soldiers he appeared "the true god of war," as Archibald Forbes justly described him. The troops followed him with an enthusiasm which made them forget their own danger, and the Turkish bullets whistling in their ears, and their old commander falling on the field of honour before their eyes. Skobeleff was the only object of their regard; and they seemed to be asking him in mute supplication to show them the way to conquer or to die.

When all was over, when the shades of night had fallen, and the sun gone down upon the scene of carnage, the "White General" turned his steps towards an ambulance where he had been told that one of his friends had been carried wounded unto death. When he gazed upon Panioutine lying on a straw couch, awaiting the eternal dawn, the hero, who unmoved had seen men fall around him stricken by the bullets of the enemy, lost the calm with which he had confronted death, and, bursting into sobs, exclaimed in a broken voice, "And to think that all this has been in vain, all in vain."

The war continued, and at last Plevna fell, not, however, before old Todleben had been called to the rescue; the veteran of Sebastopol, who had been considered too old to be any good, was, when all seemed lost, asked to come and repair the mistakes and follies of others. Then came the day when Osman Pasha gave up his sword, and the fortress which he had defended so stubbornly fell into Russian hands. It was a bleak November day, with a cruel wind blowing from the Balkans, freezing men's souls as well as their bodies. The Grand Duke Nicholas went in an open carriage to meet the vanquished Turkish general, greeting him with the respect and courtesy which his bravery had deserved. The Russian troops, seeing the old warrior sitting by their commander's side, burst into acclamations, which were but homage to the courage of their vanquished opponents.

Then followed the passage of the Balkans, the battles of Shipka, when General Raiovski so bravely crossed the murderous passes of these famous mountains, and finally San Stefano, which we did not have the courage to defend against Europe, incensed at our successes, and the treaty to which General Ignatieff and M. Nélidoff were to put their names.

Much has been written about that famous treaty, but now that years have passed since it was signed we may well ask ourselves whether our occupation of Constantinople would have been so dangerous to the peace of the world as was thought at the time, and what result a war with England would have had for us. Our diplomats were too weak either to understand our position or to see farther than the needs of the moment. The Emperor felt himself bound by the declaration which, in an unguarded moment, he had made to Lord Augustus Loftus, that he did not seek territorial compensations in the Balkans. He also did not like it to appear that he had abandoned the chivalrous position he had taken up when he declared that he had only gone to war to free from the Turkish yoke the Christian subjects of the Sultan, and not for his own personal satisfaction. The Emperor, indeed, carried this vanity—for it was nothing else—so far that he sacrificed to it the interests of his own people, and the desires of his army. Less of a politician than Prince Bismarck—who had so well understood in 1870 the importance of giving satisfaction to the wishes of the troops and to the *amour propre* of the nation by insisting upon the Germans entering Paris for a few hours at least—Alexander II. thought it beneath him to take his soldiers before St. Sophia, and to allow some of the regiments quartered at San Stefano to enter Constantinople. He had neither the consciousness of his own power nor a just comprehension of the recognition which everybody, be they individuals or nations, must have for accomplished facts. He allowed himself to be bluffed by Lord Beaconsfield, and did not understand that when England threatened it was because she knew that she had—at that time at least—no other means than threats of enforcing her wishes. Much later, during the Berlin Conference, I asked the English Prime Minister what he would have done had we not heeded his menaces and entered Constantinople. He replied to me in the following memorable words: "I would have achieved my greatest diplomatic triumph in getting you out of it without going to war."

Alexander II. did not realise this, and when it was pointed out to him upon his return to St. Petersburg from Bulgaria, before the Treaty of San Stefano had been signed, he said that he could not run any risk—as though risks were not the only means through which nations can accomplish their task in history!

Perhaps no war has been so disastrous to Russia as this unfortunate Turkish campaign, disastrous in spite of the victories which attended it, because it sounded the knell of our influence in the East, and gave birth to the Bulgarian, Servian, Montenegrin, and Roumanian kingdoms. These small States are destined one day to be absorbed by the strongest and most cunning among them, who will reap the benefits of our efforts and bring the Cross once more over the minarets of St. Sophia, thus entirely destroying the old tradition that it was Russia who was destined to erect it and to replace the Greek Emperors upon the throne of old Byzantium.

San Stefano reminds me of Count Ignatieff, and I will say a few words concerning him. He had great defects, but at the same time he possessed what so many of our politicians lack—a keen sense of duty to keep both the Russian flag and Russian prestige well aloft. He was a patriot in the full sense of the term, and would never admit the possibility of returning along a road once entered upon. He wanted other nations to fear Russia, and he well knew that, in Turkey especially, the moment that one did not domineer over one's colleagues of the diplomatic corps, one was lost in the eyes of the Government to which one was accredited. Throughout the long years during which he was Russian Ambassador in Constantinople, Russian influence was paramount. The Embassy was a centre not only of social activity, but also of political power.

The Turks were very well aware that Ignatieff would never have hesitated to take the most energetic measures if one of his countrymen had been made the object of an indignity of any kind. In that he followed the example of England, who always maintains the interests of her citizens abroad. In Russia, on the contrary, it seems almost a fundamental principle for diplomats to show themselves as disagreeable as possible to those of their countrymen who happen to get into difficulties abroad, and to refuse them either aid or protection. One has only to see what happens in Paris, where both Embassy and Consulate treat worse than dogs Russians who apply there for assistance, and instead of protecting them, seem to do all that is possible to make their position even more unpleasant.

Count Ignatieff was the only Russian Ambassador who made it his duty to show not only every civility, but every protection to Russians in Turkey, and he thus sustained the prestige of his country. He had, what only great politicians have, a gift of foreseeing the future, and realising the consequences of even the most insignificant events. His conceptions of the results which the Berlin Treaty was bound to have were quite extraordinary, and it would be curious, if his family ever publishes the interesting memoirs which he has left, to read the note which he addressed upon that subject to Alexander II. In this he clearly proved that an autonomous principality of Bulgaria would inevitably become independent, and transform itself into a kingdom that would claim the succession to the Greek Emperors, to which Russia had all along aspired.

It is a great pity that the genius of Count Ignatieff was marred by a deplorable love for intrigue that had become, as it were, a second nature to him. Long accustomed to dealing with Asiatic natures—to whom a lie more or less is of no consequence—and with whom he had, when quite a young man, concluded a treaty which was to prove most advantageous for Russia; and still more used to Turks and to the various political trickeries for which Constantinople was ever famous, he seemed to think that similar tactics could be employed with success in European diplomacy. He apparently thought he could hoodwink Western diplomats as he had hoodwinked the Ministers of Sultan Abdul Aziz. Of course he made a vast mistake, and did not realise that in view of the reputation which he had acquired on the Bosphorus, his only chance was to keep a rigid guard upon every word he uttered. Hence, at the very time he was staying at Hatfield House, he incensed Lord Salisbury by entering into an intrigue against him with Austria.

It was thought that the failure of Russian diplomacy at the Berlin Conference would put an end to the career of Count Ignatieff, but to general surprise Alexander III. recalled him to power in the responsible position of Minister of the Interior, after he had parted with his father's Liberal councillors under the influence of M. Pobedonostseff. In that capacity Ignatieff again gave a proof of his political foresight, and at the same time of the mistaken nature of the methods he employed to realise his conceptions of Government.

This occasion arose, I should say here, after the assassination of Alexander II. had struck terror all over Russia, and when everyone felt that only a strong hand could stay the spread of the revolution. At the same time, it was also felt that an outlet had to be given to the impatience of certain circles of society, who were clamouring for a change, and screaming that the promulgation of a Constitution was the only means to save Russia from disaster. Ignatieff was too clever not to see that, sooner or later, such a Constitution would have to be granted, and perhaps granted under conditions and in such circumstances that it would appear to have been snatched by force instead of bestowed voluntarily. He then evolved the idea of reviving the old Russian institution called the *Zemski Sabor*, which existed before the iron hand of Peter the Great had transformed into an autocracy the old monarchy of Ivan the Terrible. He thought that under a wise Sovereign such as Alexander III. this calling together of the clever and honest men of each Government—especially if this choice of men was left to the Emperor—might have a beneficial influence over the destinies of the country. In this attempt, however, he failed, for he found armed against him not only the chief counsellor of the Tsar, the redoubtable Pobedonostseff, but also the Sovereign himself, who feared that by accepting the proposal of Count Ignatieff people would be led to think that he departed from these principles of absolute government which he had made up his mind to maintain. Ignatieff was sacrificed, and had to tender his resignation, and this time his political career came definitely to an end.

Many years later I discussed with him the circumstances that had attended his fall, and he explained to me what had been his idea. Events had crowded upon us; Alexander III. was no more, and the disaster of Tsushima—in which the Count had lost a son—a disaster indeed such as Russia had never suffered before, had taken place. Everything was changed in the country, and the first Duma called together by Nicholas II. had just been dismissed. I asked Ignatieff his opinion of the general political condition of the country. He then began to talk of the time when he was Minister of the Interior, and expressed his regret that his plan of calling together the *Zemski Sabor* had not met with success: "I am sure that it would have proved a safety valve for the country," he said. "You see, we were bound to come to some such solution, and it would have been infinitely better for Russia had people got accustomed to take part in political life under a monarch who had enough authority to direct that necessary adoption of Occidental forms of Government, which we could not escape *à la longue*. Under a weak Sovereign—and who can deny that Nicholas II. *is* weak?—a Duma can very easily assume the shape of a Convention such as the one that sent Louis XVI. to the scaffold in 1793. It only requires one energetic man to do that, and what guarantee have we that such a man will not be found?"

I have often thought of these words, and wondered whether they would ever come true—whether they were the utterance of a discontented politician, or revealed the foresight of a real statesman.

CHAPTER IX

THE BERLIN CONGRESS AND ITS CONSEQUENCES

I DO not propose to write a history of the Berlin Congress. First it would be painful; then again, to a certain degree, it has lost its interest. But I will say a few words as to some of the plenipotentiaries to whom was entrusted the task of drawing out the famous Treaty, which is certainly discussed to the present day, yet is no more understood than at the time of its conclusion.

Russia was represented at this celebrated assembly by Prince Gortschakov, Count Schouvaloff, and M. Oubril, at that time Russian Ambassador at the Court of Berlin. To tell the truth, it was the second of these gentlemen, together with some officials from our Foreign Office, such as M. de Jomini and Baron Hamburger, who did all the work. M. Oubril was a mute personage, whose rôle was entirely passive; while, on the other hand, Prince Gortschakov, who believed himself to be the leading light of the Congress, only hindered others from coming to a practical solution of the many difficulties that rendered the situation so strained. Had he not been there, it is probable that Russia would have obtained better conditions than those that were imposed upon her, and certainly she could have made more out of the Convention which Count Schouvaloff had concluded with the Cabinet of St. James's before his departure from London to attend the Congress.

It is to be questioned, indeed, what could have been done to satisfy the inordinate vanity of the Russian Chancellor, had not Baron Jomini been there to smooth matters with his unfailing tact. Very few people in Russia realise what the country owes to Baron Jomini, to his capacity for work, his conscientious way of looking at facts, the clearness of his mind, which allowed him always to marshal things in their right order, to view them with common sense—the quality which our diplomacy most lacks —and his perfect knowledge of diplomatic traditions, as well as the character of his immediate chiefs. He also was the most perfect French scholar in the department of Foreign Affairs, and, indeed, of all the plenipotentiaries assembled in Berlin, with the exception, perhaps, of Lord Odo Russell; and this advantage allowed him to give certain turns to certain phrases which made them sound less offensive to the parties concerned than would otherwise have been the case.

Baron Hamburger was a very different type from Baron Jomini. He was supposed to be a great favourite with Prince Gortschakov, and had a rather indifferent reputation. But he, too, was a good worker and, moreover, a modest man, who never put himself forward on any occasion, but was, nevertheless, suspected of sometimes pouring oil on a fire which perhaps would have gone out of itself had it not been for his intervention.

The chief attention of the Congress was concentrated upon the English plenipotentiaries and upon Count Andrassy, the Austrian Minister for Foreign Affairs. The latter was supposed to rank among Russia's principal foes, owing to his position as a Hungarian noble, and the part he had taken in the rebellion of 1848, which had only been subdued by the intervention of the Emperor Nicholas and Russian troops.

Count Andrassy was said to be a very clever man; I think he was more than that—a clever politician. Nevertheless, he was no statesman. His was the narrow view which the French call *la politique de clocher*, or the politics of "the parish pump," as the English have it. All his thoughts were concentrated upon Hungary, and all his judgments were Hungarian—not even Austrian. Profoundly ignorant, as is generally the case with the aristocracy in the realm of the Hapsburgs, he had all the insolence of the *grand seigneur* that he undoubtedly was, as well as the obstinacy of a narrow mind that believes itself to be a great one. He had all the prejudices of his class, all the arrogance of the Austrian character, and all the unscrupulousness that has always distinguished Austrian politicians.

Andrassy had arrived in Berlin with only one fixed idea, and that was to humiliate Russia, as much as was humanly possible, and to make her expiate the crime of having obliged the rebel Gyorgyi to lay down his arms before the Russian army. Had it not been for that circumstance, he might have proved more tractable. As it was, he had sworn to his countrymen to return to them with triumph over the hated foe, and he used unmercifully the advantages that circumstances gave to him.

Prince Bismarck had need of Andrassy, and consequently lent him assistance that he would not have extended under different circumstances; but the German Chancellor well knew that the one inevitable result of the Congress would be a coolness in German relations with Russia, and the resentment of the latter country against the Berlin Cabinet and the leaders of its policy. He also was well aware that certain circumstances had got beyond his control, and so all his efforts were directed towards bringing the work of the Congress to a close, whether successful or not, at any rate to a close that would not damage German interests. He played the part of the "honest broker," as he had called himself, and in a sense he succeeded. He did not, however, attain a tangible result with regard to the establishment of a *modus vivendi* between Vienna and St. Petersburg, and the fault of it lay entirely with Count Andrassy; the latter's haughtiness and narrowness of mind unfitted him for the work of diplomacy.

In comparison with the impatience of Count Andrassy, the dignity of the English plenipotentiaries stood out as something quite unique and wonderful. Lord Salisbury, that worthy descendant of Elizabeth's great Minister, imposed the weight of his powerful personality, and every single word he uttered was pregnant with the earnestness which pervaded his whole character. Never aggressive, courteous even when it was necessary to oppose or contradict those with whom he was discussing, he showed firmness without insolence, and amiability without weakness. There was no meanness about this truly great man, great in every sense: in his convictions, his resolutions, the knowledge of which he never boasted, but of which he knew very well how to make use when he found it necessary to do so.

Lord Beaconsfield was a perfect contrast, not only to his English colleagues, but to everyone else in Berlin. His was the figure that was scanned with the greatest amount of curiosity, and his strongly marked Oriental features contrasted with his suave manners, that reminded one of the days of the old French Court of Louis XV. He was perhaps the one man who thought the most during all the deliberations of the Congress, and his thoughts were as much for himself as for his country.

He was also the only one who could afford to laugh at the anxieties with which other people were watching the turn of events. He alone knew the amount of bluff that had been needed to persuade the world that England had come to the Congress with the firm intention of going to war if her wishes were not granted, or her interests unconsidered. He was the only one who feared that Count Schouvaloff's perspicacity would see through the comedy which he had been playing, and advise his Sovereign to disdain British threats; and as I have already said, he was meditating upon the best way to drive the Russians out of Constantinople in the event of their entering it, without having to fire a single shot.

One evening, at a party given by the Austrian Ambassadress, the Countess Karolyi—who, later on, was to create such a sensation in London—Beaconsfield began talking with me, and grew quite animated in explaining how satisfied he felt at the success of his policy. He then told me the following amusing story: "When I was a little boy I loved sugar plums, but was strictly forbidden to eat any. My schoolfellows, who knew this, were constantly teasing me about it and the severity of my parents. One day I became angry and made a bet that I would bring some of these cherished sweets and eat them before the whole school. The bet was accepted, but I found it was not so easy as I thought to win it. I had no money to buy sugar plums, and those I asked to make me a present of some refused, saying that my parents would not like it. I did not know what to do, when suddenly the thought occurred to me to use some imitation sweets which I had found among my toys. I therefore brought them triumphantly to school, and, nasty as they proved to be, ate them in public, so as to show that I had been able to get what I wanted. I was horribly ill afterwards, but this little adventure was a lesson to me for the rest of my life, and I made up my mind always to appear to succeed even when such was not the case. The world never asks you whether you eat real or imitation sugar plums; it only notices that you have got the plums, and admires you for having had the pluck to take them."

Lord Beaconsfield did not speak any other language than English, and this, in a measure, placed him at a disadvantage with the other plenipotentiaries. Most of them, it is true, understood English, but nevertheless he would often have been embarrassed had he not been most ably seconded by his colleague, Lord Odo Russell.

The latter was certainly a unique personality. Few people have been gifted with more tact, more gentle but firm urbanity; few men have possessed such strong common sense allied with such bright intelligence, such keen sense of humour, and such statesmanlike views. He was a *persona grata* everywhere, with Queen Victoria as well as with her Ministers, no matter to what party they belonged; with Prince Bismarck, as well as with that section of Berlin Society that was opposed to the Iron Chancellor. Together with his clever and charming wife, the daughter of the late Lord Clarendon, he had made his house in Berlin a perfect centre of all that was clever, interesting, and amusing in the German capital. He was trusted by the Crown Prince and by the Crown Princess of Germany, and nevertheless contrived never to fall under suspicion of a political intrigue of any kind, which would have been more than easy, considering the gossip that rendered life so very difficult in Berlin. He did not commit a single indiscretion during his long diplomatic career, and never was guilty of a blunder. His knowledge of humanity was amusing because of its accuracy, and the quiet, dry remarks in which he sometimes indulged revealed the wit that had given them birth. He certainly contributed in no small degree to the success of the Congress from the social point of view. It was impossible to resist his politeness and amiability, and under their pleasant influence most bitter adversaries of the Conference would be conciliated whilst dining or having tea in the hospitable rooms of the British Embassy after the most desperate differences a few hours earlier. Without Lord Odo Russell, the Congress might not have ended so quickly, and certainly not so well. He knew how to elude difficulties, to pass over painful subjects, and to show the best points in every question. At his death England lost her most brilliant diplomat.

Lord Odo was sometimes very amusing in the anecdotes which he related, or the remarks which he made. One that he told me concerned the late Lord Salisbury, who, as everyone knows, shared with the rest of his family the defect of being rather *négligé* in his dress and general appearance. One evening Lord Odo and I were chatting about this—not ill-naturedly, for it is doubtful which of us had the greatest admiration for the remarkable statesman in question—and he laughingly mentioned to me his surprise when, one day after the dinner-bell of the Embassy had been ringing, he found Lord Salisbury, who was living there, still busy at work in his study. "He rushed out," said the Ambassador, "and before I had had time to put aside the papers on the table, literally in *three* minutes was back again ready for dinner. Now in that time he could not even have washed his hands, yet there he was in his evening clothes! I was so thunder-struck that I felt compelled to ask him how he managed to dress so quickly. Do you know what reply I got?—and the Ambassador's mouth showed a malicious smile: 'Oh, my dear Russell, changing one's coat is done at once, and I had black trousers on already.'"

Another hit of Russell's was made apropos of the famous Princess Lison Troubetzkoy, the friend of Thiers, who had played an important part at the début of the Third Republic, when her salon in Paris was supposed to be a *succursale* of the Elysée. This enterprising lady, who lived only for politics, and who had made herself so thoroughly ridiculous in St. Petersburg, had arrived in Berlin, fully persuaded—Heaven knows by whom other than herself—that the Congress could not get on without her, and that her presence and knowledge of politics were indispensable to Prince Gortschakov. Someone said in presence of Odo Russell that it was extraordinary how a clever man like Thiers could have been taken in by the Princess, who did not even possess the instinct for intrigue, but was only a very vain woman desiring to pass for what she was not.

"It is very simple," Russell replied. "Princess Lison has always been envious of the position which the Princess Lieven at one time occupied in Paris society, Thiers was always jealous of Guizot; they both imagined that by imitating their friendship for one another they could replace them in importance. But, you see, they forgot that one must have also *le physique de l'emploi*. Guizot was a tall and dry old man, and Madame de Lieven a thin, hard, old woman, whereas Thiers is small and bright and Princess Troubetzkoy short and lively. So you see, that though things may be the same, *c'est pourtant plus petit*," he ended in French, with an inimitable twinkle in his eye.

France had sent to Berlin as her first representative M. Waddington, who at the time was presiding at the Foreign Office, and the second plenipotentiary was the Comte de St. Vallier, then occupying the post of Ambassador at the Court of the Emperor William. The latter was a very remarkable man, perhaps as remarkable as his chief, and without the former's phlegmatic nature and quietness which he owed to his English origin. M. Waddington's influence was beneficial in many ways. He was a perfect gentleman, and though perhaps slow and pompous, he was a keen observer, a man of tact, and one who knew how to make the best of circumstances. He was watchful to seize every possible opportunity to raise the prestige of his country and impress others with the conviction that, though Prussia had been victorious in 1870, the defeat had not deprived France of her place in the great European concert. It was impossible to show more dignity than he did, nor to combine it with greater firmness and courtesy.

He was well seconded by the Comte de St. Vallier, who was the very first French statesman to see the possibility— nay the probability—of a Russo-French alliance as an outcome of the Berlin Congress. He had guessed that public opinion in St. Petersburg would never forgive Russian diplomacy for its failure to obtain real advantages from the war just ended, and that it would also cherish a terrible resentment against Germany and Prince Bismarck for not having assisted Russia after her neutrality had enabled Prussia to accomplish the conquest of the eastern provinces of France in 1871 and to compel that country to sign the Treaty of Frankfort. The Count realised at once the consequences of the Russian irritation, and doubtless there is still in the pigeon-holes of the Foreign Office in Paris a report which he addressed on that subject to his Government. Therein he firmly insisted that the time had come to consider the possibility of a friendly understanding with the Cabinet of St. Petersburg, and of working towards the completion of an alliance which circumstances would render indispensable to both countries, and from which both might derive enormous benefits.

Of all the plenipotentiaries assembled in Berlin, those of Turkey played the saddest part. Méhémet Ali, a German by birth, felt ill at ease in the country upon which he had turned his back, and whose religion he had spurned; Karatheodori Pasha was a Christian, and as such was not the proper person to defend the interests of Mussulman Turkey. They both felt that whatever they might do or say they could not conquer circumstance nor avert the fate that had decreed that Turkey should emerge from the conflict diminished in prestige and territory. They lived a very retired life in Berlin, seldom leaving their hotel other than to attend the sittings of the Congress.

During the month the Congress lasted, no one followed its deliberations with more interest and greater anxiety than the Emperor Alexander II. When he agreed to Germany's proposal for its assembly he hoped much from his beloved uncle, the Emperor William, upon whose gratitude he relied for the tacit help which Russia had given Prussia by its non-intervention in France after Sedan. Unfortunately for these hopes, his uncle was disabled from taking any part in public affairs at this critical moment. A few days before the opening of the Congress the attempt of Nobiling on the life of William I. took place, and the illness which followed upon the severe wound which he received obliged him to delegate the Regency to his son, and Russia was deprived of her best friend at a time when she needed him the most.

I have said already that Alexander II. was very vindictive. He had not enough political sense to distinguish between foreseen and unforeseen events, and not enough shrewdness to fix responsibility where it really belonged. He became bitter, not only against Germany generally, but against the Prussian Royal Family, and though he afterwards met his uncle at Skiernievice and Alexandrovo, their relations were never so cordial as they had been before. Alexander II. never visited Berlin again, though he once sent his son the Tsarevitch with his wife on a courtesy visit, in return for his uncle's attempts to re-establish the old family ties which the Berlin Congress had so rudely shattered.

CHAPTER X

ALEXANDER'S LOVE AFFAIRS

ALEXANDER II. was always susceptible to feminine charms. From his early youth women had exercised a great attraction for him, and the recipients of his favours were many. When quite a young man, and long before his marriage, he had been in love with Mademoiselle Sophie Dachkoff, a maid of honour to the Empress Alexandra Feodorovna, and his attentions became so marked that Society began to talk about the matter. The young lady, however, displayed a strength of will rare at her age—she was scarcely eighteen—and sought an explanation with the Grand Duke, when she told him plainly that as she could not be his wife his attentions were not desirable. She then married Prince Gregory Gagarine, the nephew of the celebrated Madame Svetchine, and for a number of years settled with him abroad. Prince Gagarine was a distinguished man, a great artist, who subsequently became Director of the Academy of Fine Arts in St. Petersburg. When he returned to the capital with the Princess she had already passed her first youth, and the history of her romance with the then Emperor was nearly forgotten. She lived to an advanced age, extremely respected by all, and held in high esteem by the Imperial Family. At the Coronation of the present Sovereign she was appointed *Dame à Portrait*, the highest feminine distinction at the Court of Russia, and enjoyed for some years the advantages attached to that position.

Some little time after his marriage Alexander II. sought companionship with persons better able to enter into his interests and to comprehend his thoughts than the Tsarevna, who was too timid and too cold even to attempt to exert influence over her husband. Later on when she became Empress, and especially after the death of her mother-in-law, Alexandra Feodorovna, she began to assert herself, but it was too late; and though the Emperor always showed her in public the greatest respect, he had become accustomed to live his life without her. Later still, when the influence of the Princess Yourievsky became stronger, he failed even in the outward marks of deference to his Empress.

So long as Nicholas I. lived, however, the conduct of the Tsarevitch in public left nothing to be desired. He had flirtations without number, but no one could accuse him of having a *maîtresse en titre*.

One whom he held in high esteem was a daughter of the noble house of Dolgorouky, the Princess Alexandra, later on to become the wife of General Albedynsky. The Princess Alexandra was the daughter of a most clever, intriguing mother, who had from the first decided to use the beauty of her children as a stepping-stone to their fortunes. The Princess Dolgorouky was at one time a very considerable personage in St. Petersburg Society. She was clever, unsparing in her criticisms, and she managed to inculcate in all her family a spirit of solidarity such as one rarely meets with nowadays. This quality enabled them to make themselves very prominent people indeed. So long as their mother lived she ruled them with a rod of iron, and insisted on their coming to her for advice, even in the smallest of matters. When she died she had seen the fortunes of her numerous children established on quite an unassailable footing.

Her eldest daughter, the Princess Alexandra, helped her in that task to the utmost. She was an unusually intelligent and at the same time extremely kind woman, whose quiet manner and soft low voice impressed others most favourably. She was on very friendly terms with Alexander II. and was consulted by him on many occasions when faced with embarrassing questions. She always gave her opinion in a fearless, honest way, and considered his advantage above everything. She was the instrument of her husband's career. He, though an extremely ordinary individual, reached the highest dignities, became *aide-de-camp général* and Governor of the Polish provinces. Madame Albedynsky reigned a veritable queen in Warsaw for a considerable time, where she succeeded in making herself liked in spite of the strong prejudices that existed there against Russian functionaries. When she became a widow, she lived for some years in St. Petersburg, and at last settled abroad for the benefit of her health. During the whole of Alexander II.'s lifetime, whenever she wanted to see him or to speak to him about some important matter, she used to drive to the Winter Palace and have herself announced by the valet-in-waiting without any further ceremony. The Empress herself often had recourse to her influence to obtain things that she did not dare to ask for herself, and all the entourage of the Sovereign held her in awe, but also in esteem.

Of her three brothers, one—Prince Alexis—settled in England, where he married, and is a well-known figure in London Society. The eldest, Prince Alexander, wedded a rich heiress, Countess Schouvaloff, and died recently, having reached the position of Grand Marshal of the Imperial Court. He was known to his friends by the name of Sandy, and was perhaps the handsomest man of his day and a great favourite. His influence was great, and he kept in favour through three reigns, and died at the zenith of his power.

His youngest brother, Prince Nicholas, "Nicky," as he was called, was scarcely less handsome than he, and enjoyed the special favours of Alexander II. He, too, reached the highest dignities. He was for some time attached to the person of the German Emperor in Berlin, where he did not succeed in making himself liked, was sent as Minister to Persia, and later as Ambassador to Rome, where he died in April, 1913.

Madame Albedynsky had three sisters. They were all beautiful, and all of them at one time leaders of the smart set of St. Petersburg. The eldest, however, the Countess Marguerite Steinbock Fermor, who died not so very long ago, had very delicate health, and retired from Society after the marriage of her two daughters. The second one, Princess Annette, was wedded to perhaps the richest man in Russia, Prince Soltykoff, and has recently been widowed. She was without doubt one of the loveliest women of her time.

Her sister, the Princess Marie, was also unusually handsome. She, however, had a more eventful life than any other member of her family. She was married in her early youth to a cousin, also a Prince Dolgorouky, and when he died some years afterwards, to Count Benckendorff. Her husband was appointed Head of the Household of the present Emperor, and she was made a Lady of the Order of St. Catherine. So much for having been, as the old French proverb says, careful in the choice of one's parents.

But however much Alexander II. might have been in love in his early years, he was destined to fall the victim to a stronger passion, and one which was to lead him upon a path which might have compromised his crown had fate and Ryssakoff's bomb not interfered. I refer to his love for the Princess Catherine Michailovna Dolgorouky, whom he was to make his wife after the death of the Empress Marie Alexandrovna.

She and her elder sister were the daughters of Prince Michael Dolgorouky, who had been brought up together with the sons of the Emperor Nicholas, and who upon his death-bed had confided his two girls to the care of Alexander II., who had just then ascended the Throne. He accepted that charge, and had the little girls sent to the Institute of St. Catherine for daughters of the nobility, recommending them specially to the Lady Superintendent. Now the Sovereign was always fond of visiting the various educational establishments of the capital. He liked to see children crowding round him, and used to caress them as if they were his own little ones. He often called to his side the little Dolgorouky girls and examined them as to their studies and their doings, and admired them for their beauty. At length, when the eldest was eighteen, he appointed her one of the maids of honour to the Empress, and took her to live at the Winter Palace.

It was not long before gossip was rife, and it must be said in justice to St. Petersburg Society that its sense of decency and honour was revolted at this forgetfulness of a most sacred trust by the Emperor. Some representations, indeed, were made to him upon the subject, amongst others by Count Adlerberg and Count Schouvaloff, whose position, as Head of the Third Section, brought him in touch with all that was being said concerning the Emperor Alexander II.

About two years afterwards the younger of the Dolgorouky girls, Catherine Michailovna, in her turn appeared at the Imperial Court, and her arrival there sounded the death-knell of her sister's favour. Prince Mestchersky, an aide-de-camp of the Emperor, was persuaded to marry Mary Dolgorouky. The Emperor gave her a large dowry, and as a wedding present a lovely house on the English Quay.

Prince Mestchersky was killed during the Turkish War, and his widow afterwards married the nephew of the Viceroy of Poland, Count George Berg, one of the most charming men in St. Petersburg Society. She had kept upon excellent terms with her sister, and they both settled later in Nice, where they lived together in the same villa. The Countess Berg died some four or five years ago.

Princess Catherine Dolgorouky was a tall, fair, placid looking person, with lovely blonde hair, a slight figure, with unmistakably graceful movements and the best possible taste in dress, a quality to which Alexander II. was particularly susceptible. Intelligence she had little; tact even less; but she had enough sense to know that on this road which was to lead her towards the Throne of All the Russias she needed the help of someone more intelligent than herself, and with more knowledge of the world. That person she found in a distant cousin, Mademoiselle Schébéko.

The latter was one of those master minds that at once recognise the weak as well as the strong sides of every position. She directed her batteries with consummate skill towards the aim she had in view. She persuaded Catherine Michailovna to play the part of the woman capable of giving everything up for love, of resigning herself to any misfortune, and to any humiliation rather than being parted from the man to whom she wanted to devote her life. No one could have played that difficult part better than did the Princess, under the guidance of Mademoiselle Schébéko, and when it came to asking anything from the Emperor, it was always the latter, and never Catherine Michailovna, who did so. She used only to accept with astonishment, and with a gratitude that apparently savoured of pain, all the presents with which the Emperor loaded her, and she always complained that he was doing too much for her.

By and by the two ladies exercised such an influence that Ministers began to take it into account and to ask themselves where it would lead to. Politics, which at first had played no part in the alliance, became a prominent matter of discussion, and the Emperor began to meet people at the Princess's house whom it was inconvenient to receive at the Winter Palace.

Every afternoon the Emperor used to go and visit Catherine Michailovna at the house which belonged to the Princess Mestchersky, her sister, and in which she lived together with Mlle. Schébéko. There he used to spend hours, and there it was that the three children of the Princess Dolgorouky were born. Their birth only consolidated the ties between the parents. When the Emperor travelled to Ems the Princess followed him there, and once stayed at the Russian Embassy in Berlin, much to the indignation of the Empress Augusta of Germany. Later on, when the Nihilist movement became so terribly active, and it became unwise for the Emperor to drive about in the streets alone, Princess Dolgorouky removed with her children to the Winter Palace. Her rooms were situated exactly above those of the dying Empress, who could hear the clatter of little children's feet over her head.

When at length Marie Alexandrovna expired, it was with no one by her side to close her eyes, save her devoted daughter the Duchess of Edinburgh, who had arrived from England to be with her mother during the last days of her life. Owing to the indignation of the Duchess at the presence of the Princess Dolgorouky in the Palace, the latter removed to Tsarskoye Selo, whither the Emperor followed her, and where he was still when the Empress breathed her last.

Forty days after the death of the Empress, Alexander II. married Catherine Michailovna Dolgorouky, and created her Princess Yourievsky.

The little popularity which remained to the Emperor disappeared after this mad act. St. Petersburg was incensed, and discontent was openly expressed at this outrage on the conventions of life.

Catherine Michailovna, nevertheless, had her partisans. All the Liberal element in the country turned to her, and expected through her influence to obtain the promulgation of a Constitution. Count Loris Melikoff, M. Abaza, and all their friends thought the moment favourable to persuade the Emperor that the time had come when it was his duty to put the topstone to the reforms for which his reign had been remarkable, by granting the blessings of Constitutional government. They explained to him that such a measure would do away with the discontent that his marriage had raised, that the nation would bless the woman to whose influence liberty had been given to it, and would see with pleasure that woman raised to the rank of Empress.

Among the Imperial Family discontent prevailed. The Heir to the Throne and his wife openly put themselves at the head of the party of those who repudiated every possibility of a further triumph of Catherine Michailovna. They had to see her every Sunday at mass, where she appeared and stood near the Emperor, in the chapel of the Winter Palace, but beyond that official meeting they paid no attention to her. The Emperor was furious, and in his turn began to be as unpleasant as he possibly could towards his children and his family; and it is matter for surmise whether a revolution of a different character would not have taken place had not the tragic event of March 1st destroyed the hopes of those who had played their last card on the strength of a woman's influence.

Count Loris Melikoff was the staunchest friend of the Princess Yourievsky. He it was who advised and encouraged her to persuade the Emperor to enter upon the road to the most important of all the reforms of his reign. He it was who told the Sovereign that Russia would admire his courage in raising to the Throne an Empress who was a Russian, and thus following the example set by the old rulers of Muscovy, who had looked for wives among the daughters of their great nobles. He it was who had already issued orders for the coronation of the wife of Alexander II. in the Cathedral of the Assumption at Moscow, after the first anniversary of the death of the Empress Marie Alexandrovna had passed.

But alas for human wishes and human plans! Sophie Perovska and Ryssakoff took upon themselves the solution of the problem that had agitated so many minds, and with the murder of Alexander II. the ambitions of his second wife were extinguished.

The new Sovereign showed infinite tact in his relations with his father's morganatic widow. All the wrongs which he had suffered at her hands were in appearance forgotten by him. He paid her an official visit of condolence, had a beautiful house bought for her to retire to, after she had left the Winter Palace, and settled an enormous allowance upon her and her children. If ever the "Vanity of Vanities" of the Preacher was exemplified in human life, it is in that of Catherine Michailovna Dolgorouky, Princess Yourievsky, who but for an unforeseen crime would have had the crown of a Russian Empress placed upon her brow.

CHAPTER XI

ASSASSINATION OF ALEXANDER II.

BEGUN so brilliantly, the reign of Alexander II. ended in sorrow and sadness. All the bright hopes which had greeted it had been shattered, and the love of his people for the person of the Emperor was shattered too. It was realised that he was a disappointed, vindictive man, more irresolute even than he had been in his youth, and who whilst always wanting much from others, yet gave too little himself, or even took back what he had already granted. His reign had not given satisfaction to a single party, nor quieted any discontent. It was evident everywhere that after a whole quarter of a century had passed nothing useful had been done, and that everything would have to be begun over again. The old fear of offending the Sovereign which had formerly existed in Russia had vanished, and unfortunately the respect for his person was gone too. People, moreover, had got into the habit of discussing, and had forgotten how to work, and for a nation there is nothing worse than unnecessary or idle discussions.

After several attempts upon his life had followed in quick succession, Alexander II. became more and more disgusted —and in a certain sense rightly so—at what he considered ingratitude against himself, and against the good intentions with which he had ascended the Throne. He knew quite well that mistakes without number had been made, but he could not determine exactly what these mistakes were. He called one person after another to explain to him what ought to be done to repair these mistakes, but no one could tell him anything definite or seriously worth listening to. On the one hand, the Conservative party was urging him to return to the old system of repression under which Russia had been great and peaceful, and, on the other, minds more clear and more imbued with Occidental ideas of Government told him that it was impossible to go back on the road upon which he had entered, and that the country would only be restored to order when it should be given a share in its administration.

Political and Court intrigues surrounded the unfortunate monarch. His wife, who hoped to obtain from the Liberal party the recognition of that title and dignity of Empress after which her whole soul hungered, used to explain to him that if he granted a Constitution, Nihilism would disappear, robbed of its very *raison d'être*, and that at least his life would be safe. On the other hand, he was well aware that his son and successor, who would be called upon to bear the brunt of any false step which he might make, strongly disapproved of any concession to what he called "the exigencies of the mob." Feeling, perhaps, that his days were numbered, he hesitated to saddle his inheritance with new difficulties and new duties. But at length, as is usually the case, feminine influence conquered, and Alexander ordered Count Loris Melikoff to draw up a scheme for a Constitution.

Count Loris, by one of those freaks of Imperial favour which can only happen in Russia, had found himself one fine day the foremost man in the country and a veritable dictator, without having done anything to justify that appointment. He was an Armenian by birth, who had distinguished himself during the Turkish War. He was a favourite of the Grand Duke Michael, the Emperor's youngest brother, who had recommended him to the Sovereign as a capable and energetic man. Later on he had been sent to the Government of Astrakhan when the plague broke out there, and had succeeded in quieting an exasperated mob. This success had created the impression that he was a resolute character who would show no hesitation in fulfilling his duties or executing whatever orders he received. But, as is usual in Russia, where one puts a man *à toute sauce*, and believes that if he can sweep a room well he can also furnish it, and that one can transform a servant into a statesman, he had not one of the capacities indispensable to the position to which he had been raised. He had all the qualities of his race, a spirit of intrigue, acuteness, and a *finesse* that did not hesitate at the means to be employed, or the wilful disguising of the truth. He began by promising all kinds of things which he could not perform, and with that shrewdness which is a characteristic of the Oriental mind, he thought that by simple diplomacy he could appease the revolutionary movement in the country, completely overlooking the fact that it was anarchical, and that the shedding of blood was the only solution which it believed to be acceptable, and with which it would content itself.

Loris Melikoff knew very well that he was intensely disliked by a certain portion of Society, as well as by the party that was headed by the Heir to the Throne. He had even at the time of his greatest favour felt himself to be in an insecure position; and when he heard applied to himself that odious expression *wremientschik* (i.e. favourite of the moment), which from time immemorial in Russia has designated the temporary favourites of the Tsars, he could not honestly think that it was misapplied in his case. He therefore sought to make friends with the one person whose protection could help him in case of need—the Princess Yourievsky. Thus, from the union of these two interests, that of an ambitious, vain woman and of a grasping, clever, and cunning man, came the scheme upon which the welfare of the nation so much depended.

In view of these facts, one must consign to the limbo of fables the rumour that at one time was universally believed, that Count Loris had asked the Princess Yourievsky to persuade the Emperor not to go out on that fatal Sunday, March 1st. In view of the importance of the events then impending, it is more than likely that had the Minister really suspected danger of any kind he would not only have taken measures to prevent it, but also that his warning would not have been disregarded, either by Alexander II. or by his wife.

The latter was quiet and content. She was beginning to feel the ground firmer under her feet. The violent outcry raised at the time of her marriage had begun to subside. The Emperor had tried to bring her into contact with several people belonging to the most select Society of the capital. Ladies had still been chary of meeting the Princess, but men, who could not very well refuse Imperial invitations, had been asked to dine with the Sovereign and his wife. For her part, she was beginning to practise her rôle as Empress, and, thanks to the advice of her cousin, Mademoiselle Schébéko, she was performing it with tact and discretion.

On the eve of the day which proved to be his last, the Emperor had had a few friends to dinner, among whom were old Admiral Heyden and M. Abaza, Minister of Finance at the time. The party had been kept up until a late hour, and Alexander had told his guests that the next morning, after the usual Sunday review, he was going to lunch with his cousin, the Grand Duchess Catherine. He told M. Abaza to come to him in a day or two to discuss together with Count Loris several points of the manifesto which he was going to issue to the nation. Princess Yourievsky advised him not to tire himself, as he had been suffering from a slight cold. He put his hand caressingly upon her shoulders, and said in French to his guests: "*Vous le voyez, messieurs, je dois obéir, et me retirer.*" They were the last words which these two were ever to hear from him.

The next morning dawned bright and sunny. The Emperor, as usual, attended mass in the private chapel of the Winter Palace. His children were all there, save the wife of the Grand Duke Vladimir, who, being a Protestant at that time, did not attend the Greek services. It was noticed that when the Tsarevna came up to her father-in-law to take leave of him after mass was over, he rudely thrust her aside with the words "*Dites donc adieu à la Princesse,*" and he indicated the Princess Yourievsky. The Heiress to the Throne made a profound curtsey to the Sovereign and silently withdrew, after merely bending her proud little head in the direction of Alexander II.'s morganatic wife.

This angered the Emperor, and it was afterwards remarked that during the review, which took place every Sunday in the riding school known as the "Manège Michel," he appeared in a bad temper and spoke but little. However, he drove to luncheon with his cousin, and there seemed to recover his spirits, remaining with her longer than was his wont.

In consequence of the numerous attempts that had been made against his life, the Emperor was always escorted on his drives by a squadron of Cossacks, and, as a further precaution, the head of the St. Petersburg police—at that time General Dvorgetsky—drove in advance in an open *droschky* on the fatal Sunday. The close carriage in which Alexander II. was sitting was driven by an old and trusted coachman, and upon leaving the palace of the Grand Duchess Catherine—since converted into the Emperor Alexander III. Museum—he took the road by the canal that leads to the Nevski Prospekt and to the Winter Palace. The carriage had scarcely turned into it when a shot was fired and a bomb exploded in front of the vehicle. A terrible moment of confusion followed, several Cossacks were seen to fall from their horses, and the *droschky* in which the Head of the Police was riding was overturned, the General himself being thrown wounded upon the road. Alexander commanded his coachman to stop. The latter begged and implored him to allow him to go on, swearing that he would take him in safety to the Palace; but the Emperor would not hear of it, and got out to see after the wounded members of his escort. Some passers-by had noticed that a young man was standing on the ice on the canal with something in his hand; they threw themselves upon him. It proved to be Ryssakoff who had thrown the first bomb.

He was led before the Sovereign, and then uttered these memorable words, which ought to have been taken more seriously than they were by the listeners. The Emperor, in reply to an anxious question of one of the officers of his escort as to whether or not he was hurt, had said, "No, thanks be given to God," when Ryssakoff exclaimed, "It is too early yet to say 'thank God.'"

At that very moment the second explosion took place, and Alexander II. fell mortally wounded.

He was taken back, still alive, to the Winter Palace, followed by his brother, the Grand Duke Michael, who had also lunched with the Grand Duchess Catherine, and, hearing the first explosion, had hastened out with the presentiment of a misfortune. He arrived upon the terrible scene too late to see anything else but the bloody body of the Emperor, and to hear his last words, "Take me to the Palace ... to die there."

Two hours later the doors of the dead Tsar's rooms were thrown open, and the new Sovereign came out, with his Consort leaning on his arm. He gravely saluted the members of the Household and military authorities that had hastily gathered there, and passed into an inner room to give vent to the emotion that was overpowering him.

His brothers and uncles followed him, and a few hasty resolutions were taken. The troops of the St. Petersburg garrison were ordered at once to swear fidelity to the new Emperor. Count Loris, despairing and silent, was simply wringing his hands, and by the body of the murdered man remained only the Princess Yourievsky, weeping and despairing, and his faithful valet, who was tearing his hair in his grief.

At that moment Mademoiselle Schébéko approached Catherine Michailovna.

"The manifesto," she said; "where is it? Have you taken it? It is already signed, and it may be of use."

The Princess rushed to the writing-table which was in the room where the dead body of the Emperor was lying. With a trembling hand she was about to open the drawer when, upon the threshold, appeared the huge figure of the Grand Duke Vladimir, the eldest brother of the new Sovereign. He slowly went up to his stepmother and took the key from her hands; he turned the lock, and then in courteous tones asked her to leave the room whilst the last duties were rendered to the remains of the murdered monarch.

That same night a conference was held between Alexander III., his two eldest brothers, and one trusted adviser in whom the Emperor had the utmost confidence; then, beside the body of his murdered father, he opened the drawer which had attracted the Princess Yourievsky, and took out the topmost document. It was the manifesto granting the Constitution of which people had talked for so long a time. He was going to read it, when the friend to whom I have referred approached him, and, taking the document from his hands, tore it into a thousand fragments.

"Now, your Majesty," said he, "you can punish me, but at least it cannot be said that you stepped upon the Throne of Russia with tied hands."

Thus began the reign of Alexander III.

CHAPTER XII

ALEXANDER III. AND HIS CONSORT

THE Empress Marie Alexandrovna had been heard to say, during the last years of her life, that she bitterly repented of having allowed herself to be entirely absorbed by her affection for her eldest son to the detriment of her other children, and that God had punished her for it by taking that son away from her. There was a certain amount of truth in the remark, for it is an unmistakable fact that the care and attention bestowed upon the Grand Duke Nicholas Alexandrovitch had not been given either to the education or training of his brothers. The Grand Duke Alexander had felt this very much when he became unexpectedly the Heir to the Throne, and suffered from it in proportion to his extreme sense of duty to his country.

He was in his own odd way a most remarkable man; not brilliant by any means, perhaps not even clever, but extremely intelligent, and gifted with a sound common sense that made him rarely commit mistakes in important questions. He had tried as much as he could to perfect his defective education, and had studied as much as his military duties would allow him, when he found himself faced with new duties and future grave responsibilities. His greatest quality was frankness, united with an honesty such as is rarely met with. Once he had given his word, nothing could make him break it. He was a great patriot, and "All for Russia" became his motto. He differed from his father in that he always knew what he wanted, and never hesitated in doing what he considered to be right. He asked his Ministers to tell him the truth even in cases where it might be unpalatable, and he realised that there was yet time for a strong hand to save Russia from the chaos into which she had fallen. That strong hand he possessed, and he used it with tact and kindness, but with a perfect understanding as to the needs of the country and the necessity for replacing the indecisions of yesterday by the firmness of to-day.

He did not often speak in public, but whenever he was compelled to do so it was to the point, in a few short words that never left any doubt as to their meaning. His address to the peasants gathered in Moscow on the occasion of his Coronation was a notable example of his directness of utterance, and it at once disposed of the rumours spread by the anarchists that the Sovereign contemplated taking away lands from the nobles to distribute them to the peasantry. Alexander III. distinctly explained to the representatives of the rural classes that he would never sanction such spoliation, and that he meant to have the rights of property respected above everything. After that, everything was quiet, and the danger of an insurrection of the peasantry was entirely averted.

The nation got to love the simple, earnest, quiet, conscientious man, who never forgot the duties that Providence had put before him, and who tried in all humility to be the father of his people. His views on politics and government were straightforward, as his whole character was straightforward. He read every document that was brought for his signature; he tried to understand it, and when he did not succeed, then he had it explained to him by responsible people.

When he ascended the Throne, it was with a deep sense of the horrors of war, born of his experiences in the Balkans, where he had commanded an army corps and seen the sufferings of the soldiers as well as the mistakes of the officers. His first thought, when he found himself in a position to realise his plans, was to work at the reorganisation of the Army, to ameliorate the conditions of the soldier, and to try to develop the industries and trade of Russia. He had a programme of his own, and he meant to be master, and to do what he himself considered to be right. Strong as was his character, it was devoid of vindictiveness and obstinacy. He brought his common sense to bear on decisions he gave, and it rarely failed him. He succeeded in making Russia a great nation, feared and respected by all, and that without the firing of a single shot during the thirteen years that he occupied the Throne.

He believed in autocracy, but was not an autocrat by nature. With all his unusual strength of character, he had no tendency to tyranny, and he made himself feared simply because everybody knew that what he meant to do he would do, and that thoroughly and well.

His children adored him, and all who approached him professed for him a feeling akin to reverence. Everybody believed in his justice, and though during his reign Nihilism was entirely crushed, yet very few were those who suffered for their political opinions. After the leaders of the conspiracy that led to the murder of the Emperor Alexander II. had paid the penalty of their crime, the execution of political offenders—that had been almost a daily occurrence during the former reign—was not heard of.

Alexander III. was essentially Russian. Sometimes he called himself in jest the "first *moujik*" of his empire. He had something of the strength of the moujik in his appearance, which was commanding, but exceedingly good-natured. He had also the simplicity of the moujik, and his humble faith in God and the Saints. The Emperor was a great believer, and his trust in Divine Providence was sincere and touching in the extreme.

Strange as it may appear, there was a time, when he was still Heir to the Throne, when Alexander III. held Liberal tendencies, of which he did not care to be reminded in after life. A curious anecdote throws a light on that side of his character. The celebrated Russian historian, Bilbassoff, whose work on the life and reign of the Empress Catherine II. has become a classic, began his career as Professor at the University of Kieff. The authorities noticed that he entertained close relations with some Polish noblemen known for their anti-Russian opinions, and he was forced to resign his position. He then came to St. Petersburg and became editor of the *Golos*. It was owing to his efforts and to the relations which he entertained with Count Loris Melikoff and with the Heir to the Throne, that the paper, which later on was suppressed by the orders of Count

Tolstoy, became so famous. When its existence was threatened, Bilbassoff, fearing that his own position would be compromised, wrote to the Emperor Alexander III. to ask his protection, and in his letter used the phrase: "I have had until now the happiness of enjoying the favour of Your Majesty." The Tsar returned the letter to Count Woronzoff, after having written in pencil across it: "Unfortunately this is true."

I have already referred to his early romance and his subsequent marriage with the Princess Dagmar of Denmark. The patience, the grace, the winning nature, and the many endearing qualities of the young Grand Duchess did their work, and conquered the heart of her spouse, until he came to love her with all the strength of affection that was in him, to trust her entirely, and to find in her not only a devoted companion, but also a wise counsellor and a true friend in the difficult and serious moments in his life.

Marie Feodorovna was once called by the Emperor "the Guardian Angel of Russia," and in that, as in everything else, he spoke the truth. Few queens have grasped to the extent which she did a queen's power of doing good. Few have possessed her gift of mercy and the desire to be merciful and kind. No prayer found her indifferent, no misery was brought to her notice without being instantly relieved. Her lovely smile, the gentle look of her eyes— those great, luminous black eyes, that seemed to read into one's very soul—brought more friends to her husband than millions spent, or years of effort, would have done. Whenever she appeared, whether it were in a ball-room surrounded by Imperial pomp and adorned with the Crown jewels, or in a humble cottage, wherever one saw her, she took with her light and joy and consolation. Unceasing were her efforts in the cause of charity, innumerable the evils she contrived to repair, and the good deeds she performed, all without ostentation, and moved thereto by the gentleness and sweetness of her charming nature. As wife and mother, as Empress and woman, Marie Feodorovna was an example to all. From the heights of the Throne upon which she sat with such dignity, she instilled into the Russian nation a respect for the private life of its Sovereigns that hitherto had been unknown. Political influence over the Emperor she possessed to an enormous extent, and yet no one ever guessed it, so cleverly did she hide from the world that she ever mixed up with politics.

The Empress was intensely fond of society and of dancing and pretty dresses. Alexander III. hated parties, but, desirous to please his wife, he not only good-humouredly consented to her giving all the balls she wished during the winter season, but also accompanied her to receptions given in their honour by various hostesses in St. Petersburg. Marie Feodorovna danced to her heart's content, and by going about in this way not only imparted animation to the season, but also helped to make the Sovereigns popular and acquainted with Society. I have never seen a prettier sight than a ball at the Winter Palace during those years, with the crowd of lovely women, the glitter of magnificent jewels, the artistic gowns, and, above all, the enjoyment that was visible everywhere.

The Emperor used to play a rubber of whist whilst his consort was waltzing or going through a quadrille. Sometimes, when the hour was late, he would quietly order the musicians to leave one by one, until there remained but one to play a last tune; then the Empress, laughingly remarking that it was time to go to bed, took leave of her guests.

CHAPTER XIII

THE IMPERIAL FAMILY IN 1881

At the time of the accession of Alexander III. the Imperial family consisted of his uncles—to whom I have already referred, and who, with the exception of the Grand Duke Michael Nicolaievich, were to disappear entirely from both the political and social horizons of St. Petersburg—and of his four brothers and only sister the Duchess of Edinburgh. I do not mention the Grand Duchess Catherine and her children, nor the Leuchtenberg and Oldenburg families, as they were more distantly related to the new Sovereign. The children of the Emperor's uncles were too young at the time to be of any importance, but his brothers were to give him more trouble than he expected.

The Grand Duke Vladimir, who was the eldest, had always, even when he was a mere boy, been considered the most intelligent member of the Imperial Family, thanks to an impudent pertness which prompted him to put in his word upon every possible occasion. He was undoubtedly clever, with that cleverness which consists in appropriating other people's ideas or repeating other people's words as if they were one's own; but at the same time he was in reality very ignorant, ambitious, and intriguing. His memory was good, his wit and conversation brilliant, but it was all superficial, and he was a perfect illustration of the old proverb "*Grattez le russe*," etc. He was considered to be possessed of a forceful character, whilst he was only brutal, as being *empressé* and *galant*, towards women, whilst he was nothing but vicious. He had mastered one of the secrets of success nowadays, the art of self-advertisement, and he never missed an opportunity to apply it.

At the same time the Grand Duke Vladimir was capable of generous actions, especially when the honour of his ancestors was in question. As an example of this fact, I mention the following: When Count Adlerberg had to retire from his position as Minister of the Imperial Household, he was heavily burdened with debts. Alexander III. would not agree to do anything for him. A friend of the Count's, whose position enabled him to approach the members of the Imperial Family, went to Vladimir Alexandrovitch and asked him to speak to the Emperor, and to plead the cause of Count Adlerberg, adding that the Count had rendered such important services to Alexander II. that he ought not to be left in the precarious position brought about by his dismissal from office. The Grand Duke instantly replied that not only would he speak with the Emperor, but that if the latter refused to grant his petition he would pay the debts himself, and induce his other brothers to help him do so. The debts were eventually paid out of the private purse of the Sovereign.

When his father was murdered, and the Grand Duke Vladimir saw his eldest brother, who in the schoolroom had always been under his influence, step to the Throne, he at first imagined he could go on leading him, and become thus in reality the first man in the Empire. He less than anyone expected that Alexander III. would suddenly develop a spirit of independence and shake off the bonds of diffidence. In the first moment of confusion, after Alexander II. was brought back dying to the Winter Palace, the Grand Duke Vladimir assumed a certain authority and issued directions concerning the immediate swearing-in to the new Sovereign of the troops of the St. Petersburg garrison, of whom he was the commander; he retained his presence of mind in that trying hour to a remarkable degree, whilst his brother, overcome by the sudden burden so unexpectedly thrown upon his shoulders, sat quite overwhelmed and unable to think of anything else but grief for his father's death.

A change soon occurred, however. On the evening of that same eventful March 1st, Alexander III. returned to the Anitchkov Palace—where he continued to reside until the end of his life—in an open sledge, with the young Empress sitting by his side, and without any escort. An immense and respectful crowd greeted him and lined the whole way. Scarcely a shout was raised, and a grim earnestness pervaded this first meeting of the new Tsar and his people, but there were few dry eyes among those who watched the scene.

At the Anitchkov Palace all his household was waiting for him in the hall, and an old valet, who had attended the Tsar from his babyhood, presented him with the traditional bread and salt which is always offered in Russia upon such occasions, and asked him in a few broken words to be the "Little Father" of his people. Alexander's blue eyes kindled with a hitherto unknown light, and he gravely replied, "Yes, I will try to be the father of my people."

The very next day he started upon that task. When he appeared in the chapel of the Winter Palace, and stood in front of his brothers, he did so with all the air of a Sovereign of long standing, and not of one of yesterday, and he issued his orders with a quietness and comprehension of what he wanted that astonished everyone, and no one more so than the Grand Duke Vladimir.

The Grand Duke endeavoured to resist this unexpected independence of Alexander III., and even went so far as to oppose him in certain dispositions he had made. The Emperor looked at him, and merely said, "I want this done in the way I have said." That was all; but from that moment none of the Grand Dukes attempted to contest the will of the Emperor.

In a measure, that will was opposed to them. The young Sovereign had been witness during the war of 1877 of many abuses and mistakes committed by his uncles, and he had made up his mind to raise a barrier between the Grand Dukes and the affairs of the State. He held the Oriental idea that the younger members of every Royal House are the first to dispute its authority and rise in rebellion against it, so he decided to keep his relations strictly in their place, and to make them feel that they had above them an authority it was not wise to thwart.

This infuriated the members of the Imperial Family, but none more so than the Grand Duke Vladimir and his wife, who from that moment started a policy of opposition to the Government, and especially to the Sovereign and his wife, to whose influence they ascribed the many unpleasantnesses that became their portion. The first of these was the issue of a new Family Statute which considerably reduced the rights and income of the relations of the Emperor—one of the first acts of his reign.

The Grand Duchess Vladimir, by birth a princess of Mecklenburg-Schwerin, was thoroughly German in tastes, and entirely devoted to German interests. She was not popular in Russia, partly on account of her having refused to enter the Greek Church, as until then had been the rule for all princesses who married into the Imperial Family. At the present day the matter would not be deemed of importance, but in 1874, when the Empress Marie Alexandrovna was still alive, the question was a burning one.

The Grand Duke Alexis was a very different man from his brother. A *bon vivant*, fond of cards, wine, and women, he had nevertheless more *tenue*, more earnestness, and especially a greater indifference to the actions of others. In his early youth he had fallen in love with the daughter of his father's tutor, and he had married her in defiance of the Emperor's orders, though the marriage was subsequently annulled. The Grand Duke, however, did not again contract the marriage tie.

At the outbreak of the Japanese War the Grand Duke Alexis was Commander-in-Chief of the Fleet, an appointment he received from his brother the late Emperor, and it was publicly said that he had no control whatever over the department of which he was head. Though it is certain that carelessness may be imputed to him, he cannot, I think, be held altogether liable for the disaster of Tsushima. His hands also had been tied, and the Navy, like the Army, was no more ready in 1904 than it had been ten years earlier, at the time of the Emperor Alexander's death.

The Grand Duke was an extremely handsome man, with a great likeness to his brother the Emperor; he had dignity when he liked, was a great admirer of art in every form or shape, and had made a remarkable collection of old silver, tapestries, and other articles. His greatest failing was that terrible love *de faire la noce* that so many Russians possess. But when necessary he could put on his grandest airs, and could represent his country to perfection when called upon to do so on State occasions. He was fond of reading, and knew his classics well.

The Grand Duke Sergius, almost immediately after his father's death, married his cousin, the lovely Princess Elizabeth of Hesse, and became a person of importance when his nephew, the present Emperor, ascended the Throne, in view of the fact of his having married the sister of the new Empress. But even during his brother's lifetime he acquired more importance than other Grand Dukes, through his appointment as Governor-General of Moscow. That appointment was due to the dismissal of Prince Dolgorouky, who had held the post for more than forty years, and was so popular that it was feared his removal would excite the anger of the ancient capital, already too disposed to look askance at everything that came from St. Petersburg. In the hope of making some measure of atonement for the removal of their beloved Governor, it was decided to replace him with a member of the Imperial House, and as just about that time the Grand Duchess Elizabeth had declared her conversion to the Greek faith, it was thought that this appointment would appease the Muscovites.

The plan was good, and it succeeded so far as Elizabeth Feodorovna was concerned. She very soon endeared herself to all classes in Moscow, but with regard to the Grand Duke it was another matter. In Society he was a very charming man, cultured, clever, and of all the sons of Alexander II. he was the one who was most like his father. Unfortunately, however, he was under the influence of officials who abused their power, and he was called upon to execute measures—such as the expulsion of the Jews from Moscow—for which he was not responsible, but which brought him into unpopularity with a very powerful party.

The Leuchtenberg family was composed of the three sons of the Grand Duchess Marie Nicolaievna and her two daughters. The elder daughter had married a Prince of Baden, and paid but rare visits to Russia; the second, Princess Eugénie, was wedded to Prince Alexander of Oldenburg, and was one of the most cultured and amiable women that could be met with. She was a universal favourite. Her *salon*, where a few chosen friends used to meet, was a centre of literary, philanthropical, and scientific activity from which charity was not excluded, for it is due in part to the initiative of the Princess Eugénie that the Red Cross Society has been developed in Russia and established with such perfection. She was a very learned woman, and one who kept herself constantly *au courant* with every manifestation of science or art in the world. She did not go out much, partly through delicate health, but she liked entertaining in a quiet way at home, and was intensely popular. Her husband, Prince Alexander, was also a clever man, who in all questions of education followed in the footsteps of his father, the late Prince Peter of Oldenburg.

As for the Grand Duchess Catherine, she was a lady of the old type, who had endeavoured to sustain the *salon* of her mother, the Grand Duchess Hélène Pavlovna, but she had not the latter's activity of mind or spirit, and her parties were extremely dull. Nevertheless she was a personality, and one felt oneself in a royal atmosphere the moment one had passed her doorstep, and when she died a whole epoch was buried with her.

The Duchess of Edinburgh, the only daughter of Alexander II., in spite of her marriage and the years which she spent away from Russia, retains her affection for the land of her birth to a remarkable degree. She was, and is, in a way a very remarkable person, clever without being brilliant, extremely well read, and gifted with a strong amount of common sense. She was her father's favourite child, and an amusing story is related of her childish days. The little girl was, it must be owned, indolent by nature, and tried by every means possible to avoid her lessons. In order to escape from these she used to run into the Emperor's room even whilst he was working with his Ministers. He loved the child, and, taking her on his knee, would keep her there. At last the Countess Tolstoy, who was entrusted with the education of the Grand Duchess, seeing that she could do nothing, spoke to the Empress, who begged her husband to send Marie Alexandrovna away when she invaded his room. This was done, very much to the sorrow of the spoilt child.

Countess Tolstoy was the best person who could have been chosen to guide the education of the Emperor's daughter. She was kind in the extreme, just, and absolutely unselfish. She knew how to appeal to the best instincts of her pupil, and inspired her with a strict feeling of duty, compassion for the miseries of the world, truth, soundness of judgment, and love of occupation, which was perhaps the greatest triumph of all, as she had in her nature the laziness inherent to the Romanoff family. The present Dowager Duchess of Coburg never forgot her old teacher, and so long as the latter lived used to go and see her every day whenever she went to St. Petersburg. Gratitude was amongst the qualities which the latter had taught her.

Marie Alexandrovna remained upon good terms with all her family, and especially with the Dowager Empress Marie Feodorovna. She is full of tact, a really great lady, and a princess of the old school, with whom allegiance to the head of one's House is considered a paramount duty.

CHAPTER XIV

THE FRIENDS AND MINISTERS OF ALEXANDER III.

ONE of the foremost qualities in the character of Alexander III. was that of knowing how to choose his friends. Of all whom he honoured with his confidence, or called upon to share with him the burden of government, few turned out to be failures, and perhaps with one exception all were gentlemen and men of honour. He held that those who came of good stock, with honourable ancestors, and who belonged to the upper classes, ought to be employed in preference to any others, and though of course there were some exceptions to this rule he had laid out for himself, still among his personal and private friends there was not one who could not boast of a name well known in the annals of the Russian nobility.

That nobility was the object of the Emperor's special care; he viewed with distaste that rising tide of democracy which during the last years of his father's reign had invaded all departments of the Government. He was indignant, too, at the evident decline of the good old Russian *dvoranstvo*, or nobility, which had followed upon the emancipation of the serfs, and he did all in his power to raise it from its fallen state. His creation of a bank for the nobility was a great scheme, which averted disaster from hundreds of homes which, but for it, would have fallen under the hammer of the auctioneer. He refused, whenever it was possible, to invest with Court dignities men who did not belong to the old and well-known families. In a word, "*Il protégeait la noblesse seulement,*" as was once said by one of his detractors, who was stopped by the lady in whose house this was told, just as he was going to add, "*et au détriment des autres classes*," which would have been entirely untrue. Before his accession the Emperor had not many friends, but his position then had been rather peculiar. He knew he was suspected by his father of entertaining political views opposed to those of his advisers, and, always respectful of his father's wishes, he had refrained from any active expression of opinion, and tried to avoid any appearance of opposition to the official party. His one great personal friend was Count Woronzoff Dachkoff, who, as soon as Alexander ascended the Throne, was to replace Count Adlerberg as Minister of the Imperial Household.

Count Woronzoff belonged to one of the oldest families in Russia, whose name was written almost upon every page of its history. He was enormously rich, perfectly independent, not a mere courtier, but a man who had the courage to say what he considered to be right, and never to hide the truth from his Sovereign. His reputation was blameless, and his moral character stood so high that no one even dared to question it. Though his qualifications as a statesman were not great, his sound common sense—so greatly appreciated by the Emperor because it tallied with his own—never allowed him to go far wrong. In all the high posts which he occupied, he always showed himself to be a real *grand seigneur* of the old school, incapable of a mean action or of petty revenge. His nature was indolent, his love of his own comfort perhaps excessive, his indifference to praise or blame sometimes carried too far; but he was the best friend a well-intentioned, straightforward monarch could have had.

Count Woronzoff was a perfect man of the world, with a rare tact and most polished manners. He sincerely loved the Emperor, and his devotion to him was unbounded and has never been questioned. He remained at the head of the Imperial Household the whole time Alexander III. reigned. In that delicate position he had sometimes to run counter to members of the Imperial Family, who became incensed at the authority with which, in the Emperor's name, he reproved them. He seldom went into Society, living for the most part at home in his own family circle; but whenever he visited he was always welcomed with respect and eagerness—an eagerness due not so much to his position, as might have been suspected, but to his own personality.

After the Coronation of the present Tsar, Count Woronzoff retired from his position of Minister of the Household—a step upon which he had decided when Alexander III. died. Soon afterwards he was appointed Viceroy of the Caucasian provinces, an office which he still holds. He is very much liked in Tiflis, and though some criticise him for lack of energy, yet it is very much to be questioned whether anyone else could or would have displayed more, and it is certain that if he retired scarcely anyone would be found in the whole of Russia who could replace him.

Count Woronzoff married the Countess Schouvaloff, one of the greatest heiresses in Russia, sister to pretty Madame Balaschoff, whose husband inherited the vast domains of the last Prince Paschkievitch, son of the field-marshal who crushed the Polish mutiny in 1863.

Beside Count Woronzoff, Alexander III. had another intimate friend in the person of the late General Tchérévine, who, as chief of the political police and the *Okhrana*, or personal guard of the Sovereign, was perhaps the most powerful man in the Russian Empire. Occupying a position which was as dangerous as it was delicate, he yet secured a wide circle of friends, and made no enemies. He had been on very friendly terms with the Tsarevitch and his wife, and he had for the latter a chivalrous affection, of which he was to give her the most devoted proofs until the end of his life. Extremely clever, with more statesmanlike qualities than Count Woronzoff, he was perhaps more popular among the Society of the capital than the latter. He had, above everything, a cool, quiet courage, combined with a certain element of fatalism in his character which made him face death and danger with the utmost indifference. Twice his life was attempted, and on both occasions he disarmed the would-be murderer with an ease which astonished even those who knew him well. Few people have been more universally liked than General Tchérévine. His political adversaries respected him, and knew very well that once he had given his word he would keep it, notwithstanding any difficulties which might arise. During the period he held office Nihilism was entirely subdued, and that without resort to the rigorous measures that had been so distasteful during the last days of the preceding reign.

General Tchérévine never left the Emperor, save for two weeks' annual holiday in the autumn. In St. Petersburg he rented a modest flat in the house now occupied by the Austrian Embassy, but at Gatschina or Peterhof he lived in the palace. There he dined every day with the Imperial Family, amusing the Empress with anecdotes which he related with much humour, and with stories as to what was going on in town; but he was never known to have repeated a single item of ill-natured gossip. He knew better than any man alive how to keep a secret, and to baffle any inquiries made of him. He did good all around him, and did it without any ostentation, being as modest as he was clever.

He was always consulted whenever any important political decision was to be taken. Alexander III. valued his political abilities, and his clear outlook on events, as well as his dislike of every kind of intrigue. When Count Ignatieff had been obliged to leave the Ministry of the Interior, Tchérévine had not hesitated to say that the step was indispensable; not that he cherished any animosity towards the Count, but because he shared the Sovereign's opinion that the day had not dawned when a *Zemski Sobor*, which was but a Duma in disguise, could be summoned.

It is probable that had he lived he too would have resigned his functions after the Coronation in virtue of the old saying that a Sovereign's favourites never get on with his successor; but death claimed him a very few months after Alexander III. In him Russia and the Imperial Family, especially the Empress Dowager, lost a truly devoted friend and servant.

The most remarkable among the politicians who governed the Empire during the reign, however, were M. Pobedonostseff, Procurator of the Holy Synod, and Count Dmitry Andrieievitch Tolstoy. The former had been the tutor of the Emperor. He was of clerical origin, had studied law, and was considered one of the best jurisconsults in Europe. His great work on Roman Law has become classical. In appearance he was a lean old man, with a long nose, and sharp eyes half hidden under spectacles. He could be very pleasant, was a most agreeable talker, and was wonderfully learned and well read. He was a Russian of the old school, who saw no salvation for the country outside of absolutism, autocracy or orthodoxy, but he was not the narrow-minded individual he has been so often represented. He hated democracy, and used to maintain that its growth was particularly dangerous in Russia, where education had not had time to influence in any marked degree the intelligence of the masses. He would have liked to augment the number of elementary and village schools, and held strongly the opinion that the number of students accepted for the higher schools and Universities should be restricted, and in that he showed a singularly keen knowledge of the country and of its moral and intellectual condition.

When Alexander III. ascended the Throne, he found in power men of the most Liberal opinions, such as Count Loris Melikoff, at whose instigation the famous Constitution which Alexander II. had signed on the morning of his death had been drawn up; M. Abaza, not less Liberal than his chief; and Count Milioutine, who, though in a less degree, was of the same opinion as his colleagues, that the time had come when some kind of liberty ought to be granted to the country. At first the new Emperor tried honestly to work with them; but when he found that their opinions were incompatible with what he considered to be the right course to follow, he called in his old tutor M. Pobedonostseff to assist him. The latter drafted the famous manifesto in which were clearly announced the intentions of the Emperor to rule according to the strict principles of autocracy, of which he believed himself to be the responsible guardian.

The Ministers at once sent in their resignations, and then it was that Alexander called in Count Ignatieff, who had lived in semi-disgrace since the Eastern War. Unfortunately, the two men did not agree. Ignatieff had an intense admiration for the Emperor, and considered him the ideal of what a Russian Sovereign should be, but at the same time he had lived too long abroad not to have become imbued with European ideas; and he, too, thought that the people of a great empire ought not to be left without some knowledge of the way in which it is governed. He therefore prepared a scheme of reform which he hoped would please the Emperor and appease the democratic party, but the Emperor saw in it an attempt to weaken his rule as an autocrat, and angrily dismissed Count Ignatieff.

The man who was to succeed him was probably at the time the most unpopular in the country. He, too, was a great noble, a perfect gentleman, and a man of strong character. For many years he had held the post of Minister of Education, and exercised such an iron rule in that capacity that he had raised against himself a perfect storm of hatred. His name stood for a system of repression which crushed every intellectual aspiration of the people. He had been compelled to retire from this position through the general indignation against him, and a hymn of praise had been sung when this had taken place. And this was the man, whom it was thought had vanished for ever from public life, who was called back to take a leading position in the government of a nation that had nothing but execration for him and his methods.

It required the strong will of the Emperor to face this indignation, but he never flinched. In my opinion he was right. No choice could have been wiser than that of Count Tolstoy to restore order out of chaos. He was an honest man, one who could listen to reason, a statesman by nature and by education. He had what so many lacked in Russia, a plan of government, a clear insight as to the necessities which were paramount to the welfare of the country; he knew that in order to make it powerful it ought to be quieted, that the revolutionary instincts of the peasants ought to be checked, the spirit of revolt in the Universities subdued, and the Army and finances strengthened. When he expressed these opinions to the Emperor, he is credited with having told him that he must not expect a glorious, but a useful reign, and that if he succeeded in this, he would deserve the gratitude of the country more than if he won a hundred battles.

Alexander III. could understand and appreciate this, and these two men planned, thought, and worked together, and succeeded in raising the moral standard of Russia until it became a Great Power, and its Sovereign looked upon as the arbiter of Europe. It was a great work, done in a very short time, if we consider that the reign of Alexander lasted only thirteen years, and that Count Tolstoy preceded him to the grave.

It was a work for which posterity ought to be grateful to them, even though in great part its effects have been effaced by the misfortunes of the Japanese War and of the Revolution that followed upon it.

The Empress, too, had friends with whom she shared sorrows and joys, and she also was fortunate in her choice of them. I have already referred to the Countess Woronzoff, and in addition to her I may mention the Countess Apraxine, who had been the first lady-in-waiting to welcome the young Tsarevna upon her arrival into her new country, and who later on became the Princess Vladimir Obolensky. The Princess was a sure and faithful friend to her Imperial mistress, whose favour she enjoys to this day. Her husband was for many years at the head of the private household of the Heir to the Throne, and remained in that position after the Emperor's accession—until his death, indeed, which occurred in the Crimea three years before that of Alexander. Then there were Count and Countess Sergius Scheremetieff, worthy representatives of the old class of Russian *boyars* that have made the country great; and then again there was Madame Scheremetieff, by birth a daughter of the mighty house of Strogonoff, whose mother had been the Grand Duchess Marie Nicolaiena, the sister of Alexander II. The two principal figures of the Empress's Court, however, were Prince John Galitzine and the Princess Hélène Kotchoubey.

Prince John Galitzine was perhaps the most popular man in St. Petersburg Society. Few have been more amiable, more charming to receive as guests in one's house, and more discreet to have for one's friend. No one knew more than he about all the scandals of St. Petersburg Society, and no one was ever more silent concerning them. He had manners recalling those of the old French Court, was conversant with all questions of ceremonial, had most remarkable diplomatic qualities, and was for the young Empress not only a devoted friend and servant, but also a sure guide in all social questions. He it was who used to tell her about the people who were presented to her; who prevented her from falling into error as to what she ought to say to them; who replied to all inquiries, and who smoothed away, with never failing tact, all the little difficulties which crop up in a Court where rivalry and jealousy are keen.

The Princess Hélène Kotchoubey was one of the remarkable women of the nineteenth century. She was twice married: first to Prince Belosselsky, by whom she was mother of the present Prince of that name, of the Countess Schouvaloff, and the Princess Lise, or Lison, Troubetzkoy. By her second husband she had one daughter, who was one of the leaders of St. Petersburg Society, and was married to a millionaire, General Dournoff. The Princess Hélène had in her youth played an important part in the social world of the Russian capital; she was clever, not exactly beautiful, but possessed, even in extreme old age, a wonderful charm, and was one of the most admired women of her day. Her enormous riches had allowed her to keep open house and dispense a semi-royal hospitality to her friends. Her palace on the Nevski Prospekt—which ultimately became the home of the Grand Duke Sergius and his wife—was the scene of most splendid balls, which rivalled even the Imperial entertainments.

The Princess Hélène had travelled more than was usual among Russians at that time; she had visited every Court in Europe, was everywhere welcome, and knew etiquette like that Duchesse de Noailles whom poor Queen Marie Antoinette had nicknamed "Madame l'Etiquette." No one could uphold the dignity of a Court in the way that she did, and no one could walk with such majesty of bearing, or enter a room with such authority. When one saw her, one understood the part played by the old aristocracy in the times of the French kings, when it was considered a privilege and an honour to be in attendance upon the Sovereign.

The Princess Kotchoubey, during her long journeys abroad, had become a friend of Queen Louise of Denmark. When the Princess Kourakine, who had been Mistress of the Household of Marie Feodorovna, died—an event that happened just after the accession of the Empress—the Queen recommended to her daughter the Princess Hélène Kotchoubey for that difficult position, who, as she well knew, was the one woman who could win for the new Sovereign of Russia the sympathies of the Courts and reigning Houses of Europe. This choice was one of the most successful that could have been made. The Princess Hélène was for the Empress a sure guide in all social and Court matters; she signalled to her the people she ought to see, and brought to her notice every fact to which her attention ought to be drawn. When foreigners arrived in St. Petersburg she knew who they were, and whether they ought to be received or not, and was a stickler for etiquette such as Russian Society had never seen. Her knowledge of the *Almanach de Gotha*, which she had learned by heart, prevented her from ever making a blunder; and whilst she lived the dignity of the Court and of the Imperial Household was managed and maintained with something that was akin to art. No one who saw her at a State function could ever forget her. It was a poem to watch her enter a room, or to precede or follow the Empress; she was quite small, and yet appeared taller than many tall women, for not only had she a perfect carriage, but an elasticity in all her movements that at once attracted attention.

With a soul above intrigue, she yet gloried in the exercise of influence, being always ready to tell the Sovereigns what she thought it was necessary for them to know, and free in her language with them, yet perfectly respectful; very diplomatic with those with whom she came in contact, she was often entrusted with missions abroad, especially in regard to the old Emperor William, who had a very high opinion of her abilities. Her receptions were attended not only by all the élite of the capital, but also by the crowds of people from the provinces who flocked to St. Petersburg every winter. It was there that one could admire the tact and knowledge of the world which the Princess possessed. She knew exactly every *nuance* with which she ought to receive either this or that person; she showed each individual the right chair he was to occupy, and the moment he sat upon it, the friends of the Princess Kotchoubey became aware of the importance in which she held him. When she had to administer rebukes, she did so with such tact that no one could be offended, and yet they were sometimes very bitter. I shall always remember one afternoon when a young officer, who was introduced to her for the first time, and who, as he belonged to a family worthy of her attention, she had seated next to herself, did not rise for an old general who arrived a few moments later. The Princess, seeing that the young man did not move, and that the general had humbly appropriated another seat, rose, and taking a small chair, carried it next to him, and began chatting, leaving the offending youth solitary on his sofa.

Another amusing episode of Princess Kotchoubey's career at Court occurred when the daughter and son-in-law of Baron Alphonse de Rothschild, M. and Madame Ephrussi, arrived in St. Petersburg. They came on a financial mission, for it was just at the time when a new foreign loan was in question. Madame Ephrussi, a lovely woman, knew a good many Russians, who had been warmly welcomed in her house in Paris, but, alas! her husband was a Russian subject, and as such had not the privilege to be admitted to Court or invited to an Imperial ball. Nevertheless, the invitation was sent without the knowledge of Princess Kotchoubey, who rose up in arms against it. She stormed, she raged, and at last declared, with pinched lips, that she would not present Madame Ephrussi. Prince John Galitzine tried in vain to persuade her to yield, and she finally declared that she would rather give up her position than consent to such a breach of ceremonial, which it was her duty to respect. "*Sa Majesté peut faire ce qui lui plait,*" she repeated; "*mais moi je ne présenterai pas Madame Ephrussi.*" Prince Galitzine at last, in despair, went to consult the Empress, who in her turn was terribly embarrassed, as she did not like to offend the daughter of the mighty Baron Alphonse, and, on the other hand, she was afraid to act contrary to her Mistress of the Robes. At last she thought of a way out of the difficulty.

"*Voilà ce qu'il faut faire,*" she said. "*Vous me nommerez Madame Ephrussi, dans une porte lorsque je la traverserai.*"

And it was done in the way suggested. With the greatest of trouble, the amiable and tactful Prince Galitzine hustled Madame Ephrussi between two doors, and whilst the Empress was passing, stopped her with the words, "*Madame, voici Madame Ephrussi.*" The Empress bowed, and murmured a few words; and the thing was done to the relief of everybody.

With the death of Princess Kotchoubey the old traditions of a *dame d'honneur*, such as it was understood in the Royal Households of older days, came to an end. She has never been replaced. After she died her position was given to the Countess Strogonoff, and at the Court of the present Empress the post was filled first by the Princess Mary Galitzine, and is now held by Madame Narischkine, who has tried to revive its glories, but in vain. Times have changed, and the old Court ceremonial and etiquette have been relegated, with much else, to the lumber-room of forgetfulness.

CHAPTER XV

ALEXANDER III IS CROWNED

I<small>T</small> was with a certain amount of apprehension that the public in Russia prepared itself for the Coronation of Alexander III. March 1st was not yet forgotten, and though little had been heard of Nihilists or anarchists in the two years that had elapsed, yet everyone knew that the movement still existed, and that the danger of yesterday might easily become the peril of to-day. One person, perhaps, in the whole country had no apprehension, and that was General Tchérévine, who was very well aware that the precautions which he meant to take would be sufficient, and that the person of the Emperor was in no danger whatever. These precautions, indeed, were so well planned that the numerous people who arrived in Moscow for the memorable event suffered far less inconvenience from the police measures inseparable from such occasions than those who thirteen years later were to attend the Coronation of Nicholas II.

When it is necessary to do so, no Court in the world can display more pomp and splendour than the Russian, but it must be acknowledged that the magnificence of the sight witnessed in Moscow during the month of May, of the Year of Grace 1883, surpassed all expectations. The pageant began with the solemn entry of the Emperor and Empress into Moscow, previous to the Coronation ceremony. I witnessed it from the window of a house overlooking the famous chapel of the Iverski Virgin, the patron saint of Moscow. We sat from nine o'clock in the morning until nearly one before the procession began to appear, but no one thought for one moment that he had waited too long, so intensely interesting was it to watch the crowd which filled the streets behind the soldiers that lined both sides of it. From time to time a superior officer was seen on horseback, passing from one place to another, and saying, as the occasion demanded, a word or two to another officer on duty. Then, again, a member of the high clergy appeared, and, robed in cloth of gold, entered the chapel, from the steps of which he was to welcome the two Sovereigns. Or, again, a Cossack of the escort in his red uniform went to and fro, looking for somebody who was not to be found, or a Court official, with a cocked hat decked with white plumes, and in his hand a stick surmounted by a knot of pale blue ribbon, disposed the various deputations massed at the entrance of the chapel, or gave a direction to the choristers standing in their long tunics of raspberry red, braided with gold. It was a never-ending pleasure to look upon this varied sight, so quaint and so unlike anything one had ever seen before; and when at length the first gun was fired announcing that the cortège had left the Petrovsky Palace outside the town, where the Emperor had passed the night, expectation became so intense that it was almost painful.

Another gun, and then another, and three more in quick succession; and then, after another half-hour, appeared in the distance the first troops that heralded the approach of the procession. One regiment after another filed before the sacred chapel, the officers saluting it with their swords, and took up their position beyond its gates on the big square opposite the Kremlin. Then came the Gentlemen of the Imperial Household on horseback, in their gold-laced uniforms; then again masters of the ceremonies, in gilded carriages lined with red velvet, and then troops again; deputations sent from the Asiatic dominions of the Tsar, also on horseback, in most original Eastern costumes, among which the head-dress of a Buddhist Lama attracted great attention. It was a kind of gold cap, reminding one in its shape of the historical coiffure of the Venetian Doges. The Emir of Bokhara, with his suite, also on horseback, came next, and at length, riding a small white horse, surrounded with a brilliant staff, and followed by his brothers and all the foreign princes present in Moscow, appeared the Emperor. He rode slightly in advance of the others, and when he arrived in front of the chapel he stopped his horse. Endless hurrahs greeted him whilst he slowly descended from his steed and waited until the heavy gilt carriage, drawn by eight milk-white horses, in which the Empress was riding, accompanied by her little daughter, drew up. Alexander himself opened the door of it, waving back the equerry who was about to do so, and helped Marie Feodorovna to alight. For one moment she stood there, dressed all in white, a big diadem of brilliants on her head, innumerable diamonds round her neck and on the bodice of her dress, clothed in cloth of silver and with a cloud of delicate white lace enveloping her graceful figure, the loveliest of smiles playing round her mouth, whilst tears of emotion were glistening in her sweet eyes. With one of those impulses which made her always do the right thing, even when it was not imposed by the ceremonial, she turned round and saluted the crowd that was staring at her, lost in admiration before her beauty. Then together with the Emperor she advanced towards the chapel, her train held up by pages, and listened with reverence to the few words of greeting of the bishop who, with cross in hand, was waiting to bless the Imperial pair on the steps of the chapel. They entered the chapel for a few moments of silent prayer, and then the Emperor helped his Consort to re-enter her carriage, himself remounted his horse, and the procession started again.

It was an imposing sight, in spite of the narrowness of the way to which it was confined. The carriage of the Empress was the chief object of attraction; a heavy coach, dating from the times of Elizabeth of Russia, with her monogram in diamonds on the doors; it was lined with pure white velvet, and through the glass sides the figures of the Empress and her little daughter could distinctly be seen. Then came other carriages just as magnificent and imposing, in which rode the Grand Duchesses and other princesses, all in magnificent dresses and Court trains and splendid jewels. Then other vehicles not so gorgeous, perhaps, but still gilded and glorious with red velvet and golden laces, which contained the ladies of the Imperial Court, foremost among whom was seen the *kokochnik*, or old Russian head-dress embroidered with pearls, of the Princess Hélène Kotchoubey. Then troops again, the Cossacks of the private escort of the Emperor in red tunics, the *chevaliers gardes* in their golden cuirasses and big helmets surmounted by the Imperial Eagle with outstretched wings, and the big guns of the artillery; and finally a timid little boy who had followed the procession from the very gates of the Petrovsky Park accompanied by a small black dog, that seemed just as lost in bewilderment at all that was happening as was his master.

The boom of the last gun had advised the crowd that for that day at least the pageant was over, and the Emperor had reached the Kremlin Palace. Everything had passed off to perfection without a single incident to disturb the splendour of the ceremony; and now came three days of waiting, until that fixed for the Coronation dawned.

It was a rainy morning to which, unusually early, we awoke, for one had to be in the cathedral by eight o'clock. All Moscow was in a fever of expectation, and I believe very few people slept that night. Inside the Kremlin itself the excitement was intense. The whole of the pavement of the inner courtyard in which stand the three cathedrals, with that of the Assumption in the farther background, and the palace with its famous so-called "red staircase" in front of the belfry of Ivan Weliki, was covered with scarlet cloth, and tribunes were erected around it. On each step of the staircase was stationed alternatively a Cossack from the private escort in red tunic, and a *chevalier garde* with his shining gold cuirass. A crowd of chosen representatives of the merchant and peasant classes was standing in that open space and examining with curiosity the occupiers of the tribunes, all of them people belonging to the highest society of the two capitals.

The sky was grey, and a drizzling rain was falling at intervals. Inside the Cathedral of the Assumption were gathered the highest military and civil officers of the Crown, ladies of high rank and the heads of the foreign embassies. A common excitement, such as no one had experienced before, prevailed among all these people, the one anxiety being as to how the ceremony would proceed. At last the clergy left the cathedral in solemn procession to sprinkle with holy water the path which the Sovereigns were to tread from the Kremlin to the church. Then one saw slowly approaching the foot of the staircase a heavy canopy held by officers belonging to the higher ranks. It was stationary for a few minutes, and then a long train of gentlemen-in-waiting issued from the gallery which leads from the inner apartments of the palace to the "Red Staircase." They were followed by chamberlains, masters of the ceremonies, and at last by a procession headed by the Queen of Greece, Olga Constantinovna, first cousin to the Emperor, walking with a young boy, in whom everyone recognised Nicholas Alexandrovitch, the Heir to the Throne, arrayed in the full uniform of Chief Ataman of the Cossack army. They were followed by all the foreign princes and princesses, and the members of the Russian Imperial Family, and entered one after another the precincts of the cathedral to await the arrival of the Emperor and the Empress.

Another few minutes of almost breathless silence, and then shouts and acclamations announce the coming of the

Sovereigns, and on the top of the staircase they appear together, he with bared head, in full uniform of a general; she in a white gown all silver and lace, but with nothing on her head, whence lovely curls and locks of hair fall on to her neck; Alexander III. leading by the hand Marie Feodorovna. He is calm but very pale; she, on the contrary, looks extremely agitated, and her lovely eyes seem full of tears, whilst red spots upon her cheeks testify to her emotion. Slowly they descend together the long flight of stairs, and slowly also, under the big canopy with its ostrich plumes hovering above their heads, proceed to the cathedral. On the threshold of the ancient church, the Metropolitan of Moscow, surrounded by his clergy, awaits their coming. For a few minutes they stand thus face to face, the Head of the State and the Representative of the Church, and then all this splendour disappears within the gates of the oldest of antique Moscow's shrines.

As they proceeded to their seats, clergy, high dignitaries, and Sovereigns, the choristers burst forth into a chant of joy, at first subdued, then breaking out into a sound of triumph, and thunder their welcome to the Tsar of All the Russias.

Then the imposing ceremony began. At first the Metropolitan read prayers, and then the Crown was brought to him—that great Imperial Crown, the very sight of which inspires terror to the onlookers, so perfectly does it represent the weight of responsibility which rests upon its wearer. The clergy blessed it, and then Alexander III. stepped forward and with firm hands took it and put it upon his head. The sun then shone for the first time on that eventful morning, and its rays lit up the big diamonds and the fair, massive head beneath the beautiful diadem. Then the sound of the guns broke the silence, proclaiming from their iron throats to all the world that the Chief of the House of Romanoff has assumed the Crown which his ancestors had first won in that ancient city of Moscow. One after another the reports fall on the ears of the crowds outside the cathedral, and they too shout "Hurrah!" and "Hurrah!" until the walls of the Kremlin ring with the echo.

Whilst the choristers intoned with their sweet voices the *Te Deum*, generals approached the Sovereign, bringing the Imperial Mantle in cloth of gold heavily embroidered with black eagles and lined with ermine, and tied it around his shoulders; he took the Sceptre in his right hand and the

Orb in his left, and then the whole assembly fell upon their knees, whilst he alone remained standing, arrayed with all the attributes of his Imperial power, and a prayer for him was read; and after all the people assembled to witness his triumph had prayed for him, he, the Tsar, began in his turn to recite aloud the Nicene Creed, which has never varied since the day it was first composed, and which is treasured by the Orthodox Church as the fundamental stone of its whole edifice. When one looked at him there, with the Crown shining upon his head and the Sceptre grasped in his firm hand, one was reminded of those beautiful lines by Longfellow:

"Dost thou see on the rampart's height

That wreath of mist, in the light

Of the midnight moon? O hist,

It is not a wreath of mist;

It is the Tsar, the White Tsar,

Bayuschka! Gosudar!"

Then, in her turn, the Empress advanced and knelt down at the feet of her Imperial spouse, with the folds of her silver dress falling around her, its white shimmer adding brilliancy to her whole figure. He, the mighty Emperor, slowly took a pretty small crown of diamonds, and carefully, with loving movements, set it on her bowed head. At that moment the Empress raised her beautiful, expressive eyes towards his face, and one could see that between the two there passed one of those fugitive minutes of intense emotion which occur but once in a human life, and which are sufficient to fill up the rest of it, with its remembered joy. He raised her in his arms, and, forgetful of the world around them both, pressed her close to his heart in one long and passionate embrace. And the choir chanted once more the words of a hymn of thankfulness, a *Te Deum* of reverent gratitude.

After the Empress in her turn had been robed in her Imperial mantle and received from the hands of the Metropolitan the blue ribbon of the Order of St. Andrew, a solemn thanksgiving mass was celebrated; and when that was over the doors of the cathedral were thrown open, and the Imperial procession appeared once more upon the threshold. This time Alexander wore the Crown and stepped alone under the canopy, his regal mantle trailing behind him, and, followed by the Empress, whose hands are joined together as if in prayer, he passed before his subjects, on towards the ancient Cathedral of the Archangels, and to the other churches of the Kremlin. The bells rang, and the belfry of Ivan Weliki sent forth its grave, solemn tones, and all the guns posted on the other side of the river added their vociferation to that of the crowd, and the hurrahs with which it greeted its crowned Sovereigns. The sun that had remained hidden, save for some few minutes, at length broke through the clouds, adding its splendour to the magnificent scene. Alexander III. appeared before his people, splendid in appearance, the image of that mighty Empire at whose head he found himself, which he was to lead on to peace and to prosperity, such as no one had even dreamt of on that sad day when he ascended his bloody throne.

Festivity upon festivity followed through the succeeding three weeks, and then came the sensational moment of all, when the Emperor declared to the assembled peasants, come to greet him with the traditional bread and salt, that they were to return to their homes, and say that he would always care for their welfare, but would never consent to a new distribution to them of the lands belonging to the rural proprietors. To this firm speech can certainly be attributed the quietude which Russia enjoyed with regard to agrarian questions, until the Revolution which followed upon the reverses of the Japanese War opened the era of new troubles, of which we have not yet seen the end.

CHAPTER XVI

ST. PETERSBURG SOCIETY FROM 1883 TO 1894

DURING the winter that followed the Coronation, Society in St. Petersburg began to settle down, and to assume the aspect which was to continue during the whole of the reign of Alexander III. As usual, the Court took the lead, and the programme of the season's festivities was generally drawn up to accord with that approved by the Empress for the Winter Palace; this, as a rule, varied only in exceptional circumstances, but depended upon the time of the year at which Easter was celebrated.

After his father's murder it was deemed advisable for the new Emperor not to reside in St. Petersburg. Alexander hated Tsarskoye Selo—where the Princess Yourievsky had queened it for the previous ten years or so—and Peterhof being uninhabitable in winter, it was decided that the Court should reside at Gatschina, a magnificent but totally isolated palace, which boasted of an immense park and many discomforts.

The latter did not prevent the Emperor from liking the place, which he considerably improved, and where he resided for the greater part of each year until his death. He was able to enjoy there a certain amount of liberty, which was impossible for him in St. Petersburg; he could take the exercise indispensable to his health without being disturbed, and have some mild shooting without going out of his park. He really loved Gatschina, and so did his children; but it cannot be said that this affection was shared by his Household, who were always sighing whenever they returned to it, and rejoicing when the month of January took the Court back to St. Petersburg.

Life at Gatschina was very quiet, and more like that of a private country squire than that generally supposed to be led by a Sovereign. The Ministers used to come in turns to present their reports to the Emperor, after which he generally kept them for lunch. Officers of high rank, functionaries called upon to present themselves to the Sovereign, were also received in the morning; but these did not enjoy the favour of sharing his meal. In the afternoon Alexander generally took a long walk of some two hours, accompanied either by one of his sons or by the Empress, and in the evening a few members of the suite dined with the Imperial couple, after which the Emperor remained for an hour or so in the small drawing-room of his Consort, chatting pleasantly and smoking a few cigarettes. He then retired to his study, where he worked until very late in the night.

Such was the life that went on day after day with but very little variation. Whenever anything of importance occurred in the capital, and to every regimental feast—of which there are so many in Russia—the Emperor and Empress went to St. Petersburg. The latter, kind and considerate as she always was upon these days, used to receive at the Anitchkov Palace the ladies desirous of presenting their respects to her, and also before the beginning of each season the débutantes of the year, together with their mothers, so as to save them the tedious journey to Gatschina in winter. At Christmas there are generally Christmas trees lighted for all the members of the Household, and also for the soldiers of the regiments quartered at Gatschina, as well as for the children of all the Imperial servants, from which presents were distributed by Marie Feodorovna with her own hands. On New Year's Eve the Imperial Family removed to St. Petersburg to remain there until the beginning of Lent.

On New Year's morning, after mass, there was a great reception in the Winter Palace. Everybody that was anybody was present, and though it was most trying for ladies to dress in full Court dress and trains at the early hour of ten o'clock, yet not one of those who composed the élite of St. Petersburg would have missed it. They were all but too eager to present their good wishes to their beloved Empress, who always received them with a beaming smile and the kindest of welcomes. Generally, immediately after mass, she received, with the Emperor, the members of the Corps Diplomatique, without their wives, as only Russian ladies were admitted to the Palace upon that day; then Marie Feodorovna passed into another room, where she smiled her New Year's wishes upon her own feminine subjects. It was a long and trying day for her, but never did she show the slightest sign of fatigue or weariness, and she generally left everyone who had been allowed the happiness to approach her upon that morning, delighted with her kindness and affability.

On New Year's Day the official rewards for the year were granted, and it was amusing to watch the faces of those that had received some sign of Imperial favour, and the disappointment of the less honoured ones. The Winter Palace, indeed, on the morning in question, afforded to students of psychology a wonderful opportunity to study human nature; whilst the simple observer also could amuse himself by watching the display of pomp that this unique reception presented. It is still held, and once more is regularly attended, for Marie Feodorovna again presides at it, owing to the continued ill-health of the young Empress.

On January 6th there was another reception at the Winter Palace, without ladies this time, for the blessing of the waters of the Neva. This sight was also viewed by the members of the Diplomatic Corps, with their wives and daughters, and the foreigners of distinction present in the capital, who were introduced by their respective Ambassadors or Ministers. After the ceremony there was a luncheon, the honours of which were undertaken by the Mistress of the Robes to the Empress, and the ladies-in-waiting. It was not until after these two functions that the official winter season was considered to have begun.

The first ball of the year generally took place on or about January 10th. It was essentially an official function, inasmuch as invitations were sent only to personages belonging to the first four classes of the *Tschin*, as it is called, or to members of the Imperial Household, with their wives and daughters, and to ladies who before their marriage had borne the diamond initial of the Empress and the rank of maid of honour. There were generally some seven or eight thousand invitations distributed for this festivity, at which the most extraordinary figures appeared, who only showed themselves upon that one day, whilst many smart people, whose presence was an ornament at all the small balls of the Empress, were absent from this particular one, owing to their not having the necessary rank to be admitted to it. Provincials arrived in town for the occasion; governors of distant countries, functionaries who would not have been admitted to any smart drawing-room, mustered in full force. It may have been they were more attracted by the supper, which was always the feature of this particular ball, than for the pleasure of seeing the Sovereigns, who, owing to the immense crowd, could not possibly be seen by every one of the numerous guests at this extraordinary function. Marie Feodorovna literally blazed with diamonds when she entered the ball-room with the Emperor, for on her slender person were displayed all the Crown gems. She was generally dressed in white satin or velvet upon that day, with the blue ribbon of St. Andrew across her shoulder, and an enormous diadem, the middle stone of which was a huge pink diamond. The Grand Duchesses followed her, but the Imperial Family did not dance much on this occasion beyond the one official quadrille, in which the Ambassadors and their wives were invited to participate.

I have referred to the supper served at this ball. The menu of it was classical, and spoken of in all those inferior circles of St. Petersburg Society for whom asparagus and lobster represented the *ne plus ultra* of luxury. Each of these figured upon the menu, and were supposed to be brought fresh from Paris at great trouble and expense. The expense, of course, is less now than when the custom was inaugurated, but the tradition remains, and how often have

I heard one or other of the remarkable old ladies who, with their feathers and flounces, came out of their retirement to attend the ball of the "Salle Nicolas," as it is called, remark, *"Mon cher, il y avait des asperges fraiches pour tout le monde."*

Though asparagus might be there for everybody, it is certain, however, that there was not enough room for this heterogeneous assembly, and that the crush at these receptions surpassed everything that could be imagined. There was hardly elbow room, and to enjoy oneself was quite out of the question.

With the ball once over, the Empress was free to receive her friends in the way she liked best, and generally three, or sometimes four—according to the time left before the beginning of Lent—receptions were given in what was called the "Concert Room" of the Winter Palace. These balls were certainly unique from every point of view. They were never crowded, as rarely more than eight hundred invitations were issued, and the supper was served in the Nicholas Hall, a splendid apartment which was transformed into a winter garden. Each small table was laid for eight to ten people, having in the middle of it a big palm tree, at the foot of which was a parterre of roses and other flowers. Under the portrait of the Emperor Nicholas I., which hangs in the centre of one wall, was a kind of parterre of hyacinths, mixed with tulips, opposite which stood the supper table of the Empress, to which were invited, apart from the Grand Duchesses, the Ambassadors, and some other important personages, and which was literally covered with the most splendid exotics. The Emperor never sat down to supper, but used to walk round the different tables, speaking a word here and there to the people whom he knew, and seeing to the comfort of his guests, as any other master of the house would do.

These balls were the great feature of the St. Petersburg season, and the brilliance of the dresses and jewels displayed at them was quite remarkable. The Empress used to dance every dance, and contrived in the intervals to speak with her friends, or give a word of encouragement to young débutantes, who were always the object of her special care, and whom she loved to see enjoy themselves.

In addition to these balls at the Winter Palace, Marie Feodorovna gave small dances at the Anitchkov Palace. To those she invited only her most intimate friends, to the number of three hundred at the most; and, with the exception of the Danish Minister, no diplomat was ever seen there. It was quite a private reception, and it lasted generally until the small hours of the morning. Another small ball, the invitations to which were confined within a very narrow circle, was the one given at the Hermitage, where supper was served in the brilliantly illuminated picture gallery, where one could admire the many *chefs d'œuvre* which this famous collection contains, whilst talking with one's partner.

Finally, on the last Sunday in Carnival, there was a reception at Court, which was generally held in the Yelaguine Palace, on the island of that name. Luncheon was followed by dances, which lasted, with an interruption for dinner, until twelve o'clock, when the Empress took leave of her friends until the next season, and left immediately for Gatschina, whither the Court returned that same night.

With a few exceptions this programme was carried out regularly during the thirteen years of Alexander III.'s reign. The Emperor and his Consort used also to attend the receptions and balls of foreign Ambassadors, as well as those of some members of the Russian aristocracy, such as Count Scheremetieff, Prince Volkhonsky, Count Woronzoff, and M. Balashoff, and Count and Countess Steinbock Fermor. The last-mentioned gave one ball which to this day is remembered in St. Petersburg Society, so very magnificent was it. Then there were the receptions of Prince and Princess Menschikoff, which were always graced by the Imperial presence, as well as those of Count Orloff Davydoff and of the old Prince Youssoupoff.

Lent was generally spent in Gatschina, and for Easter the Imperial Family returned to town for a few days. In June they moved to Peterhof, on the Baltic Sea, and in July made an excursion to Finland on their yacht. In August the great summer manœuvres took place, after which the Emperor and Empress generally went to Denmark with their children. That was the time which Alexander III. considered his real vacation. There he could live quite like a private person surrounded by congenial people; there he could for a few solitary moments forget that he was the Tsar of All the Russias, and enjoy life in the way that he liked best.

Of course, there were some variations to this yearly routine. Visits to be paid to or received from foreign monarchs, or journeys into the interior of the Empire; but, generally speaking, the description I have given represents the existence led by the Imperial Family at that time.

Naturally St. Petersburg Society was influenced by all this. It underwent a certain change from its established customs of the former reign. For one thing it danced more, and for another it criticised less. Salons belonging to what one would call in England the Opposition gradually closed their doors. Somehow, it was felt they were out of place. Social scandals were for the most part discussed only among the coterie of the Grand Duchess Marie Pavlovna, or in reference to that coterie. Politics ceased to interest the public, because it was felt—without its having been ever said—that this was a subject which the Sovereign liked to reserve to himself. Of course, people talked—this can never be prevented—but with one difference: when blame was heard anywhere, it was always connected with this or that Minister, and never attributed to the Emperor, whilst in the time of his father it had been the contrary: it was the Monarch who was criticised or taken to task, and his Ministers held blameless.

Morals also underwent a transformation. Ugly scandals became rare, and I cannot now remember one of flagrant character. Among the leaders of Society at the time were the Countess Olga Lewachoff, the Countess Marie Kleinmichel—noted for her political proclivities—a reputation which she shared with Madame Nélidoff. The latter was sister to General Annenkoff, who constructed the Transcaspian Railway, and cousin to the late Russian Ambassador in Paris. Count and Countess Pahlen were also very considerable personages in the social horizon of St. Petersburg. He had been Minister of Justice during the reign of Alexander II., and she was a *Dame à Portrait* of the Empress. They represented the German element at Court, but were highly esteemed and very much respected by the Emperor. The Countess Strogonoff, Mistress of the Robes in succession to Princess Hélène Kotchoubey, was a great lady who, before her appointment, had always lived a retired life, and retained her provincial tastes and manners. She was very timid, and took a great deal of time to get used to her position. Her receptions, given in a most magnificent house, were dull to the extreme, but very decorous; she never knew who attended them, and rarely could recognise anyone. The attention of Society was forcibly drawn to her the first time that she appeared in St. Petersburg after her appointment as maid of honour. It was at a performance at the French theatre, and a rude young man, rather the worse for drink, Prince V——, seeing an old frump sitting modestly in a corner of a box, went up and put out his tongue at her. One can imagine the scandal that followed. The hero of it was nearly turned out of his regiment, and probably would have been had not the good-natured Countess herself pleaded for his forgiveness. She was a kind woman, very stiff, very prim, but full of good qualities and intentions.

Another maid of honour, of more social consequence than the Countess Strogonoff, was the Princess Elizabeth—or Betsy, as everybody called her—Bariatinsky. She was a really great lady, who knew her place, and filled it to perfection; her receptions were visited by the best people of St. Petersburg Society, whom she welcomed with a quiet dignity.

I cannot take leave of my old friends among these ladies without mentioning the Princess Lise Volkhonsky. She was the wife of Prince Michael Volkhonsky, whose father had taken part in the conspiracy of December 14th that nearly cost Nicholas I. his throne. Prince Michael was born in Siberia, whither his mother had elected to follow her husband, and at his majority was restored to his title and rank in the *noblesse*. He had risen to a very high position, and had married a cousin—the Princess Volkhonsky—beautiful, clever, charming, with exquisite manners and most attractive personality. She frequently used to receive the Emperor and Empress, and though she seldom visited at other houses, yet she received a number of people in her own. Before her death she fell under the influence of the philosopher Vladimir Solovieff, and, partly owing to that influence, she was converted to the Roman Catholic faith. The event was not made public until her death, when difficulties ensued through the fact that Prince Volkhonsky wished the funeral to be conducted in accordance with the rites of the Orthodox Church. M. Pobedonostseff, the Procurator, interposed, and decided that since the Princess had seceded from Orthodoxy, the funeral ceremony must be conducted by the ministers of the religion she had adopted. A violent discussion ensued, the end of which was that the Procurator of the Holy Synod was severely blamed for the so-called "fanaticism," which, after all, had only secured what the Princess Volkhonsky would probably have herself preferred.

Among the most exciting social events of the period was the matrimonial venture of the Grand Duke Michael Michailovitch. When the young Grand Duke began his social career it was thought that his marriage would take place with a certain beautiful and accomplished young countess, but to the surprise of everyone he went abroad, whence it was announced he had wedded the young Countess Merenberg.

Society talked extensively, of course, and the excitement was intensified by the news of the sudden death of the Grand Duchess Olga at Kharkoff, on her way to the Crimea. The Emperor deprived the Grand Duke of his rank at Court, and in the Army, and forbade him to return to Russia. He settled with his wife in Cannes, and she received from the Grand Duke of Luxemburg the title of Countess Torby. The present Emperor has, however, forgiven them, and Michael Michailovitch is sometimes seen at Court festivities in St. Petersburg.

CHAPTER XVII

THE FOREIGN POLICY OF ALEXANDER III.

ONE of the questions that occupied public attention, both in Russia and abroad, when Alexander III. succeeded his father, was as to the policy he would adopt with regard to foreign affairs. Prince Gortschakov was still alive and officially at the head of the Ministry; but its real leader was M. de Giers, who was to remain in control of it until his death. In appearance he was an insignificant little man, walking with a peculiar droop of one of his shoulders, and with as mild a manner as diplomat ever bore. He was supposed to foster German sympathies, and to be strongly inclined towards an anti-French policy. The Emperor, on the other hand, was known to be antagonistic to Teuton influences, and it was wondered what direction the Cabinet of St. Petersburg would take under the new regime.

A strange little incident helped to excite the curiosity of St. Petersburg Society. It is nearly forgotten by now, but I must mention it because it had an undoubted influence on the spirit of distrust which Alexander III. entertained until his death towards Germany and its intrigues.

It was well known that the Grand Duchess did her utmost to give prominence to everything German, and to try to give the policy of the Russian Government an inclination towards Berlin. She was also believed to have personal communication with Prince Bismarck and to keep him *au courant* of everything that was going on in St. Petersburg. She had been a great favourite with Alexander II., and was the only member of the Imperial Family that had condescended to visit and be upon good terms with the Princess Yourievsky. This last circumstance gave her an opportunity to keep herself well informed concerning the foreign policy pursued by the Government, and it is certain that she tried her best to smooth down the differences that had arisen between the Cabinets of Berlin and St. Petersburg subsequent to the Congress of 1878.

When Alexander II. was murdered the position of his daughter-in-law underwent a change. The new Sovereign was the last man capable of consulting or confiding in a woman on matters of State. The Grand Duchess found herself thrust aside, and experienced from this inevitable change a keen feeling of disappointment and of anger.

It would appear that one day she wrote fully upon these matters to Prince Bismarck, mingling in her letter not only complaints, but also bitter criticisms directed against the Emperor, his views, opinions, and future plans, such as she imagined them to be. Now comes the tragic side of the story. The letter fell into the hands of an aide-de-camp of the Grand Duke Vladimir, Count C——, but how was never told. The Grand Duchess openly accused him of having stolen it, whilst he replied that he had found it in a place where it had no business to be, and had thought it his duty to appropriate it. I leave the reader to judge whether this explanation was justifiable or not; it is certain that the letter was placed by the Count in the hands of the Minister of the Imperial Household and was submitted by him to the Sovereign. The scandal was great, and, for a wonder, was not hushed up. The Grand Duchess was the first to speak about it, and to complain of the indelicacy of her husband's aide-de-camp. In this it has always seemed to me that she was right, for there is no excuse for such a mean thing as stealing a letter. The Count was dismissed by the Grand Duke, but immediately received the appointment of aide-de-camp to the Emperor, which set tongues wagging with more energy than ever. No one knows what would have happened had not the Grand Duchess fallen dangerously ill and been sent abroad to complete her recovery. When she returned the scandal had blown over, but its effects were not so easily forgotten. Alexander III. was disgusted to find that he had German spies even among the members of his own family, and the relations between the two Governments became more strained every day, in spite of the tact displayed by the German Ambassador in St. Petersburg, General von Schweinitz, and the military attaché, General von Werder, who were both great favourites with the Tsar. Thanks to their efforts, a kind of *modus vivendi* was established, and the public had no knowledge that relations between the two nations were not as cordial as they had been before.

It was not, however, the case, as some people have thought, that because of this breach between Russia and Germany the new Emperor at once turned his thoughts towards a French alliance. France as a country was not sympathetic to him, and he hated Republican governments almost as energetically as did his grandfather Nicholas I. Furthermore, the Tsar was not entirely convinced of the stability of the French Republic, but his was a mind which prompted him to look round and to convince himself where lay the real interests of his own beloved Russia before taking a step which would be definitive. During this interval of waiting and making up his mind as to what was to be done, a Minister such as M. de Giers proved himself to be most useful.

The aim of the Emperor was to restore to the country the quietness of which it had been deprived for some years previous to his accession. He wanted a prosperous Russia from the economical, as well as from the industrial point of view. Already he had in his mind the great scheme which will immortalise his name—the construction of the Trans-Siberian Railway, which was to unite Europe with his vast Asiatic dominions, and he well knew that in order to achieve such a gigantic enterprise peace was indispensable; that without it all his plans would be futile.

He consequently waited, making no sign as to his intentions, and he became furious whenever an untoward event disturbed his plans and shook the edifice of peace he was labouring to construct.

One can therefore imagine the anger with which an episode such as that connected with the two speeches of General Skobeleff was received by him. The comments of the German press on this regrettable incident increased the Tsar's passion, because he saw himself indirectly accused of having approved this intemperate language. It was, therefore, an imperative order which he sent to "the White General" to leave Paris immediately and report himself at St. Petersburg.

I will here mention a fact of which, I believe, very few living people are aware. When Skobeleff received this message, or rather this command, his first thought was to resist, and he wrote in that sense to a friend in St. Petersburg, saying that he would not submit to be treated like a naughty schoolboy after all he had done for the country. It was the first time that friend had heard him mention his own services, and he thought it was not the moment to do so, when a numerous and powerful party was accusing him of trying to provoke a war for his own personal satisfaction.

"Do not make any mistake," he replied to the General. "If you disobey, you will not find in the whole of Russia a single man who will not judge you harshly for so doing. It is not for one so great as you to assume the right to give others an example of disobedience to one's Sovereign and to one's flag. Come back, explain yourself, and you will find that you will thus disarm your most bitter enemies. Rightly or wrongly, you have been represented as an ambitious man, who even dreams sometimes of putting upon his own head the crown of the Romanoffs. Show them that you are made of other stuff, that before everything you are a true Russian and as such a faithful servant of the Crown. The time for military revolutions is past, never to return, and the Army is no longer a power standing face to face with the Sovereign, but a tool for the realisation of his wishes and a support for his Throne."

Whether this letter had or had not an influence over Skobeleff I cannot say, but it is certain that after receiving it he returned to St. Petersburg and on the very next day presented himself to Alexander III. What passed during that interview no one knows. Neither the Tsar nor "the White General" ever mentioned the conversation which took place between them, but Skobeleff changed considerably after this eventful journey of his; he left the capital very soon after and returned to Minsk, where his army corps was stationed. Four months later, in the very prime of life, and at the zenith of his reputation, he died quite suddenly, and in circumstances which some people persist to this day in thinking mysterious, whilst in reality they were only unmentionable. With him disappeared the last Sir Galahad that Russia will ever see—a legendary hero, whose exploits will be the subject of popular ballads which will be remembered and sung by women and children after we are dead and forgotten.

It is useless to attempt to conceal the fact that the death of Skobeleff, which was a national misfortune, caused something like a feeling of relief abroad, especially in Germany, where the conviction held that he wanted to provoke a war, and in Turkey, where he was considered to be dreaming of becoming Prince of Bulgaria at the first opportunity, with ambitions which might ultimately lead him to Constantinople. As for the Emperor, he regretted the loss of the General, but he was not sorry, if one can make such a distinction. War was far from his mind, and he could not help considering whether such a strong man, as Skobeleff undoubtedly was, would not become as dangerous in time of peace as he was useful on a battlefield.

After the Coronation the foreign policy which Alexander III. meant to pursue became more evident. People understood that it would be directed towards the maintenance of peace so long as it was necessary for Russian interests. "All for Russia" became the motto, not only of the Emperor, but also of all his Ministers. The spirit of nationalism which had been dormant for so long began to revive, and gradually the world came to recognise that Alexander would have no other consideration than the welfare of his own country, in which the interests of his neighbours would have no part. In spite of his anti-German feelings, he had too much common sense not to understand that it was essential for both nations to live in peace with each other, and even when he was most incensed with the policy of Prince Bismarck, he did not contemplate a war with Germany, from which he well knew that no possible advantage to Russia could result.

It is now the time to say one word as to those famous forged Bulgarian documents about which so much fuss was made. No one knows to this day by what channel they reached the Emperor, but it is certain that he once remarked, when talking with one of his rare friends and confidants about that strange episode and the denial of Prince Bismarck of any knowledge of the papers in question, *"Tout mauvais cas est niable."* There is no question that he entertained feelings of suspicion against the Chancellor, and never quite believed that the documents were not genuine. Perhaps this conviction proceeded from his knowledge of the person from whom he had received them, and whom he probably considered as one who would not have stooped to such a means of revenge as helping to impose upon him such a gross fabrication. Of course, he was bound to accept the explanations offered by the German Chancellor, but it is to be questioned whether he believed in them implicitly. However, he appeared to dismiss the incident from his attention, but, nevertheless, it was to lead to great results, because in the course of time the idea of a Russo-French alliance was suggested by the very people who had brought these Bulgarian papers to the Emperor and at last succeeded in interesting in their cause no less a person than the Procurator of the Holy Synod, the all-powerful M. Pobedonostseff.

It was he who convinced Alexander that, without going so far as an open and acknowledged alliance, some kind of tacit understanding might be arrived at with the French Republic, an understanding that would have for consequences a complete change in the political equilibrium of Europe, and might serve as a useful check on Austrian ambitions and designs in the Near East.

It was upon this basis that the French fleet was sent to Cronstadt and that of Russia to Toulon. The festivities which attended both occasions, and which originally were intended to be purely military in character, were transformed into manifestations of real friendship. So completely was prejudice swept away before these national displays that the Tsar at length consented to the "Marseillaise" being played in the halls of the Peterhof Palace, on the day that the French Admiral and officers dined there, and on its being sung in the streets of St. Petersburg itself.

"*Nous avions fait du chemin*," as the French say.

Whether Alexander III. would have gone to Paris is a question that would be difficult to answer. It is certain that the visit would not have been sympathetic to him; it is equally certain he would not have hesitated from it had he thought it was necessary as a guarantee of a long period of peace for Russia. That peace was his most earnest desire, and no Sovereign has ever had so much at heart the peaceful development of his nation than this mighty ruler of 160,000,000 people. If ever one earned the glorious title of "Peacemaker," it was the father of the present Tsar.

CHAPTER XVIII

ALEXANDER'S MINISTERS

ONE of the first cares of Alexander III. when he began to reign was the financial condition of Russia. It was far from cheerful at that particular moment. The expenses of the Turkish War had not been paid; taxes were coming in most irregularly; the value of the paper rouble had gone down considerably; and foreign credit was not easy to obtain. It was impossible to do without the latter, for the national deficit could not be met from the resources of the country alone. At length, after endless trouble, a loan was arranged, but under terrible conditions, imposed by the Jewish banking world of Paris and Berlin. With this loan the Rothschilds absolutely refused to have anything to do, on account of the massacres of Jews that had taken place in the south of Russia, especially in Kischinev.

The situation was serious, and needed an energetic and clever man to face it. In the year 1889 the official world of St. Petersburg was surprised to read that the Director of the Technological Institute of that capital, M. Wischnegradsky, had been appointed Minister of Finances.

If ever an "outsider" gained a foremost position, it was M. Wischnegradsky. He was unknown to the fashionable world, and hitherto Ministers had been looked for in that charmed circle. No one knew him, no one had heard anything definite about him, except that he had been Chairman of the South-Western Railway, and succeeded in re-establishing order and prosperity to that enterprise, which had far from a good reputation when he was called upon to save it from bankruptcy. He was also credited with great tact, great learning, and an excellent knowledge of financial matters and problems. He was no longer young, but full of energy and determination. Beyond these superficial facts, no one could tell anything concerning him, or even make speculations as to whether or not he was fitted for the important post to which his Sovereign had called him.

There were people in St. Petersburg who said that it was M. Pobedonostseff who was responsible for the appointment. This assertion was absolutely untrue. It was the personal act of the Emperor, who had been greatly struck by a pamphlet written by M. Wischnegradsky on the Public Debt of Russia, which had quite accidentally fallen into his hands. He sent for the author of the pamphlet, and had two long conversations with him, after which the world was stunned by the news that Ivan Alexieievitch Wischnegradsky had been appointed to the task of repairing the shattered finances of the Russian Empire.

Difficult though that task was, it was crowned with success. At least, M. Wischnegradsky put matters so far right that his successors only had to reap the benefit of his almost superhuman work. In his ideas as to the best way of restoring the credit of the country he showed himself a great statesman as well as a great financier. He overcame difficulties almost insurmountable at first sight; he induced the Rothschilds once more to smile upon a land in which their "co-religionists" were persecuted and trodden upon. He persuaded them, as well as other financial powers in Europe, that Russia had unknown resources within its limits, which only needed developing for the good of the whole of the industrial world. He above all things obeyed his Imperial master's orders, which consisted in trying to convince public opinion that so long as he reigned peace would never be endangered, and that Russia would follow a policy of industrial progress and peaceful development of her resources towards one goal, that of becoming a rich nation rather than a conquering one.

For years M. Wischnegradsky worked at this task, and he lost his health and ultimately his life in bringing it to an issue. His first care was to consolidate the value of the paper money by gathering enough gold to guarantee the redemption of any issue that the Government thought it necessary to make. When he took in hand the direction of the Treasury, the amount of gold in the cellars of the Imperial Bank was scarcely sufficient to serve as security for the foreign loans with which the country was saddled, and all payments were made in paper. When he was compelled to retire from the public service, gold was beginning to be the common currency, and now one finds more of it in Russia even than in France, and the scarcity is in paper money.

Wischnegradsky well knew that it was only a future generation that would reap the benefit of his policy, but this did not deter him from carrying out the programme which he had in his mind, in spite of his numerous enemies who howled at him because they did not perceive any immediate amelioration in the conditions which he had undertaken to transform from bad to good.

Ivan Alexieievitch was a charming man from the social point of view, full of fun and amusing anecdotes, which he freely distributed in the course of conversation. In spite of the enormous burden of work which he had taken upon his shoulders, he found the necessary time to keep himself cognisant of everything that was going on in the world, and I do not think that any remarkable work of science or of literature was published without his finding time to glance at it, so as to be conversant with its most important points. He realised that it is essential for a statesman to keep himself posted as to the state of public opinion, not only at home but abroad, so as to be able to see to the needs of his own country through the criticisms addressed to it by the foreign press. Light was the thing he most valued, and of light he never found enough around him nor around the Emperor; the latter, he used to say, ought to be spared petty criticisms and details, but should be kept informed as to the essential points of weakness in his dominions, no matter even if they became a source of painful disillusionment or of sorrow.

He loved Alexander III. sincerely, and with a devotion such as is rarely met with in a Minister. He appreciated his honesty and the straightforwardness of his intentions, and above all he respected the love for Russia which animated his Sovereign; he would have induced the Tsar to make the greatest sacrifices if only they were conducive to the prosperity of the Russian people.

When the famine of 1892 brought the population of twelve of the most fertile Governments in the Empire to the verge of starvation, it was Wischnegradsky who spoke to Alexander III. of the misery that this famine was causing and would cause to Russia. This in spite of the recommendations of the then Minister of the Interior, M. Dournovo, who had succeeded Count Tolstoy in that responsible post, and who, being above everything a flatterer, did not like to tell the Emperor the true state of things. Wischnegradsky even went so far as to have sent to the Tsar a piece of the terrible bread, made of grass and straw, that the peasants in certain localities were eating, in order to convince His Majesty of the distress; and he, who was supposed to be so very economical, insisted upon enormous credits being opened in order to relieve the stricken provinces. The burden of this arduous responsibility, and the strain of this gigantic work, told at last on the constitution of Ivan Alexieievitch, and one day in spring, whilst at Gatschina, where he had gone to submit his weekly report to the Emperor, he was stricken with an attack of what at first sight appeared to be apoplexy, and was with difficulty taken home.

It was at that particular moment there appeared upon the political scene a person who ever since has occupied a considerable position in the history of Russia, Sergius Ioulievitch Witte, now Count Witte, whose signature stands at the foot of the Portsmouth Treaty of Peace with Japan.

Count Witte, about whom so much has been written, comes of a good family of German origin, which settled in Odessa many years ago. He studied well, but through lack of means had not been able to obtain any appointment, except of an inferior kind. For a number of years he was station-master at Popielna, a small station on the South-Western Railway, not very far from Kieff. It was there that M. Wischnegradsky, at that time chairman of the railway, saw him, and was struck with his abilities, and appointed M. Witte manager of the rolling stock of the company. Once in a position from which there was a chance of promotion and distinction, Witte showed to their best his unquestionable ability and knowledge of financial matters. When M. Wischnegradsky was called to the Ministry of Finance he at once brought Witte to St. Petersburg and made him chief of one of the most important departments of the Treasury. The rest became easy, and doubtless many of the reforms carried out by Wischnegradsky were due in part to his *alter ego*, Sergius Ioulievitch Witte. Wischnegradsky continually praised his subordinate to the Emperor, saying that without him he would never have been able to accomplish what he had, and when the Ministry of Communications became vacant, he proposed to the Sovereign to appoint M. Witte to the post. On the morning of the day of that fateful journey to Gatschina, Ivan Alexieievitch had felt unwell, and seeing Sergius Ioulievitch, asked him to accompany him. It was Witte who brought back to town his former chief, and during the sad days that followed he was continually in the house helping the bereaved family and taking all the trouble he possibly could from their shoulders, so as to leave them free to attend upon the sick man.

About a week after the attack that had prostrated the Minister of Finance a letter was sent to the Emperor; it opened in a most humble tone, and with the assurance that the writer was prompted only by a sense of duty, but the interests of Russia were dearer to him even than the ties of a grateful friendship. And then it went on to state that the health of M. Wischnegradsky was such that there was no hope of his ever again fulfilling the duties of his responsible post, and that this contingency ought to be provided against, or the interests of the country would suffer. Even whilst this letter was being written the Minister was slowly mending and looking forward to the day when he would be able to take up his work again.

The Emperor showed this letter to General Tchérévine, who urged him not to take any immediate action, and offered himself to go and see how matters stood. He did so, and was able to assure the Tsar that there was nothing to warrant the assumption that Wischnegradsky would not get better, and that in any case it would be better to wait before making a decision that would certainly break the heart of the old man, who was conscientious enough to resign his duties if he saw himself unfit to perform them.

After a long illness, followed by a longer leave spent in the Crimea, Ivan Alexieievitch returned to St. Petersburg, and once more took up his duties; but the old activity was gone, and gone with it, too, was the energy, as well as the power to work, for which he had been so famed. After a few months he asked to be relieved of his duties, tired perhaps also of the many intrigues against him, prompted by the desire to see his successor installed. Before leaving his post, at a last interview with the Emperor, he recommended the appointment of M. Witte in his place. He retired into private life, and died two years later, deeply regretted by all who knew him, and leaving behind him the reputation of one of the most disinterested servants the Crown had ever had.

Even before death had claimed M. Wischnegradsky, M. Witte had become one of the foremost men in official Russia. Clever to an uncommon degree, of great intellectual ability and statesmanlike views, he knew what he wanted, and in Russia that is the quality which is seldom met with. He was ambitious; he desired power, and was one of the few men who knew how to use it. Above all, he had a keen knowledge of humanity, of its defects, and of its meannesses. Free from prejudices, he was not a man to be hampered by convention, and during the course of his career he had given striking examples of this disdain for public opinion. If not a Napoleon or a Bismarck, he was unquestionably a strong man, with the capacities, perhaps, of a Richelieu, who rose to his high position because a king helped him, and not because he helped a king.

At the present moment Count Witte is, without doubt, the cleverest statesman that Russia possesses, though it is very doubtful whether he will ever return to power with the weight of the Treaty of Portsmouth hanging round his neck.

I cannot end this chapter without saying a few words about another of the Ministers of Alexander III., who played an important part in public affairs owing to the transformation which he effected at the Ministry of Justice. Nicholas Valerianovitch Muravieff was a character out of the common. He was Public Prosecutor at the trial of the murderer of Alexander II., and had risen to fame by the very able manner in which he conducted this difficult case. When he became Minister, principally through the influence of General Tchérévine, who considered him one of the ablest of public men, he at once made his presence felt in his department, into which he brought a degree of order previously unknown. He was brilliant in the extreme, a quality which he shared in common with all the Muravieffs, and especially with his cousin, who was afterwards Minister for Foreign Affairs. After the Japanese War he resigned his position and accepted the post of Ambassador in Rome, where he died quite suddenly and in mysterious circumstances very soon afterwards. Apart from his sterling qualities, he was one of the most interesting and charming men of his time. He left some curious memoirs relative to the events which accompanied the murder of the Emperor Alexander II., and the development and crushing of the Nihilist movement. If ever these memoirs are published they will prove an interesting contribution to the history of Russia during the last quarter of the nineteenth century.

CHAPTER XIX

THE POLICE UNDER ALEXANDER III.

It is impossible, when writing about Russia, to avoid reference to the police. The general idea abroad is that visitors to the country have a policeman at their heels at every moment, and run the risk of being sent to Siberia at the slightest provocation, or even without any provocation at all. They are exceedingly surprised when they arrive in St. Petersburg to find that the police are never seen anywhere except in the streets, and that their presence is not felt in any offensive way. During the reign of Alexander III. the Russian police system, especially that of the capital, was organised to a degree of absolute perfection, but at the same time the members of it were never obtrusively in evidence.

The force was divided into three sections. The political police, to which belonged the special corps known as the "*corps des gendarmes*," was controlled from the Ministry of the Interior, and its ramifications spread over the whole of Russia. The second section confined its operations to St. Petersburg and was under the command of the Prefect of the city; and, thirdly, there was the *Okhrana*, or special police, employed in guarding the Sovereign, to which section the others were subordinate. The Chief of the *Okhrana* was General Tchérévine, to whose able care the most difficult matters connected with the organisation of these different branches of the service were entrusted, and who had the last word to say in regard to them.

The Prefect of St. Petersburg was General Gresser, a most able, trustworthy, and vigilant officer, full of energy, tact, and discretion, who not only had secured the most perfect order in the city, but was also most watchful as to any political manifestation that might occur. The *corps des gendarmes* was commanded by General Orgewsky, a personage of a certain importance, if only on account of the number of enemies he had managed to make.

General Orgewsky commenced his career in the crack regiment of the *chevaliers gardes*, and though not a favourite, yet was a prominent personage in St. Petersburg Society. He had been transferred to Warsaw as Colonel of the gendarmes at a time when Warsaw was supposed to be infested with revolutionaries and Nihilists, and had fulfilled his duties there to the general satisfaction of everybody. Further, he had married a lady honoured with the particular friendship of the Empress Marie Feodorovna, a friendship which she thoroughly deserved, being a most charming, amiable, and good woman. When the question arose of finding a suitable man to take over the command of the political police, and act as adviser to the Minister of the Interior, General Orgewsky was selected for the post.

The General was a stern man, of a harshness of character that bordered on cruelty, and he set himself to perform his duties in the most relentless way. No one could boast of having succeeded in arousing his indulgence or the slightest feeling of mercy when what he considered to be his duty was in question. He was, indeed, oversensitive on the point of duty, and jealous to a painful degree of the power which he wielded.

It was this jealousy that brought him into disgrace. About four years after the accession of Alexander III. there were rumours of a Nihilist plot against his life. The police had an inkling of it, but could not ascertain anything definite concerning it. General Orgewsky took the matter into his own hands, and wanted to send men to St. Petersburg to make investigations. General Gresser objected to this, saying that his agents were already on the track of the conspirators, and that as *he* was responsible in the city for the safety of the Sovereign, he was not going to have *his* plans disturbed by other people, who were ignorant of them. The quarrel at last became so bitter that it was carried to the Emperor, who upheld General Gresser, adding that he "could find plenty of men to fill the post of Chief of the Gendarmes, but that he could not so easily replace General Gresser as Prefect of the capital." Events justified the Emperor's confidence in the Prefect, for a few days afterwards the city police arrested all the conspirators on the Nevski Prospekt, where they were parading with bombs in their pockets, waiting for the coming of the Emperor to the Commemoration Service in the church of the fortress of St. Peter and St. Paul on the anniversary of his father's death.

After that there was no question of the supercession of General Gresser, and until his death he retained the position of Prefect of St. Petersburg in a manner that has never been equalled. He was everywhere, and saw to everything; was present at every fire, and every day drove all through the city to see that everything was in order. He knew absolutely all that was going on, even down to the private love affairs of prominent people in the capital, but never was he heard to utter a single word that could have revealed his knowledge. His discretion was supreme, and secrets secured by him were never revealed. After his death he was succeeded by General——, and it became a common saying in town that "Gresser knew everything and told nothing, while—— knew nothing and told everything."

When Count Tolstoy, under whom Orgewsky and Gresser served, was asked why he had sacrificed Orgewsky instead of Gresser, he replied, "Gresser is a subordinate who behaves as such; Orgewsky is also a subordinate who has forgotten the fact. I have reminded him of it, and that is all I have to say."

General Gresser's death at a comparatively early age was tragic in the extreme. That a man so clever, so cynical in a certain sense, who knew better than anyone the value which ought to be attached to quack medicine advertisements, should have been victimised by one of these specious charlatans is almost incredible. Yet it was the allurement of a "youth restorer" that captured this astute chief of police. The drug was administered by injection, and General Gresser submitted to several doses; blood-poisoning ensued, and he died in terrible agony in the course of three or four days.

When General Orgewsky retired from the responsible post of Chief of the Gendarmes, he was appointed a senator, and lived for some years in St. Petersburg. He was then appointed Governor-General of the Provinces of Lithuania, and some little while later died at Wilna, after terrible agony, from cancer.

The safety of the Sovereign and of his family was finally entrusted to the *Okhrana*, but after the death of General Tchérévine, which occurred during the present reign, the police arrangements were entirely changed. Whether the present arrangement is more successful than the former I do not know. One thing, however, is certain, and that is, in spite of what may have been believed abroad, there were not many attempts on the life of Alexander III. The most serious was the one to which I have already referred. All the others were either of no consequence, or were nipped in the bud by the police. The Emperor himself hated to be followed by detectives, and whenever he noticed one about him would send him away, almost rudely. He repeatedly told his Ministers that he believed in Divine Providence, and knew he would not die one hour earlier than was ordained, and that all the precautions which they took in regard to his safety only made him ridiculous.

It was, therefore, extremely difficult to combine the measures that were considered indispensable to the security of the Tsar with his own orders, about which he was very particular, getting into a passion when they were not obeyed.

An amusing instance of this occurred one afternoon when the Emperor was walking in the park at Gatschina, accompanied only by his dog. He suddenly saw a man hiding in the bushes as if afraid of being seen. Alexander went towards him, but the man ran away, and whilst the Tsar was still looking in the direction taken by the suspect, some detectives appeared, and a wild chase began, which ended in the man being caught. In view of the Emperor's orders, not one of the police officials would consent to take the culprit before him, until General Tchérévine appeared upon the scene and gave the necessary directions. It then turned out that the person who had been the cause of all this disturbance was himself a detective who had been ordered to follow the Emperor, but in such a way that the latter might not notice him. When he saw that Alexander had discovered him, his only desire was to run away. The incident caused a deal of amusement, but Alexander III. was furious, and gave vent to his rage in a few most energetic expressions that produced terror all round. For three days he would not speak to General Tchérévine, whom he said was lacking in common sense in adopting such childish measures for his safety. His straightforward nature hated all this "unnecessary fuss," as he called it, and he always used to say that Providence was his best guardian angel, whom he trusted in preference to all others.

CHAPTER XX

THE TRUTH ABOUT BORKY

Any account of Alexander III. would be incomplete without a reference to the railway accident which happened at Borky and nearly cost the Sovereign and his family their lives. Foreign papers have always attributed it to an attempt made against his person, but I can say on the authority of one who conducted the inquiry concerning it that the incident at Borky *was an accident*, but an accident due to criminal carelessness and the absurd principle that a monarch cannot be disobeyed when he gives an order, even when that order is bound to end in disaster to himself.

The manner of the accident was as follows:—

The Emperor and his family were returning from the first visit to the Caucasus that they had paid since the accession. This visit had been made the occasion of numberless ovations, and had been extremely popular. The three weeks spent by the Imperial pair in this part of their dominion formed a continual triumph, and the Empress in particular had been excessively pleased and touched by the love which had been expressed for her by the different classes of the population. Contrary to the usual practice, the entire personal suite of the Sovereigns had accompanied them during this journey, as well as all the Ministers. Among the latter was Admiral Possiet, the Minister of Public Ways and Communications, who had occupied that post for fifteen years and had been a personal friend of the late Emperor. Upon him had fallen the entire management of what was to prove a momentous journey. He it was who had given instructions as to how the Imperial train was to be watched and driven, and he had allowed no one to share with him this responsibility. The Royal train was a very long and heavy one, but its capacity was not equal to the demands of the increased entourage, and carriages had to be coupled on to accommodate them. Two engines had also to be employed, one of which was of recent construction and the other almost obsolete in its antiquity, and totally unfit to be driven at the same speed as the other. This oversight was in part the cause of the accident. It is related that when the train passed Kharkoff an engineer who happened to be at the station remarked that it would be a wonder if no accident happened to it. The train was driven very slowly, so slowly that the Emperor became impatient, and asked whether the speed might not be accelerated. Admiral Possiet gave orders to that effect, but the principal engineer of the line, who was also on the train, replied that this could not be done, and pointed out to the Minister the reasons for it. Possiet said that if the commands of the Emperor were not executed he would ask for explanations, and that such explanations would involve the blame of everyone concerned. He added that he would telegraph to the next important station ahead, ordering another engine to be ready for the Imperial train, and meanwhile nothing would happen. The engineer kept silence, but gave instructions for a slight increase of speed; and it was entirely due to his disregard of the Admiral's order for greatly increased speed that Alexander III. owed his life, for if the train had been going faster not one person would have escaped the catastrophe. At the time, the Imperial Family were sitting at lunch with the members of their suite. Suddenly there was a jerk; it was when the leading—and weaker—engine, was pushed was off the rails. At the same moment the carriages at the end of the train, being lighter than those in front, were also derailed. Before anyone could inquire what had happened the roof of the Imperial saloon had fallen in, and the whole carriage overturned, burying in its wreckage all who were in it.

The confusion which followed was indescribable. Not one of those who escaped but believed himself to be the only one left alive to tell of the catastrophe. The first person to emerge from under the broken carriage was the Emperor, who, crawling on all fours, managed to emerge from the mass of broken timber and iron that was crushing him. He called for help, and himself began to remove the wreckage in an effort to save the Empress. She was his first thought, and when at last, aided by two soldiers who had run to his assistance, he managed to pull her out from the ruins of the train, he was so thoroughly unnerved that he sat down on a stone, and drawing her to his heart, exclaimed, "Mimi, Mimi, are you sure that you are not hurt?"

In the meantime help had come, and an officer having heard the cries of a child in the field close by, had run to its assistance, and brought back the little Grand Duchess Olga, aged six, who had been thrown out of the open window of the carriage into the field. Soon the other Imperial children were found, and the survivors of this terrible accident were able to estimate its effect.

The number of victims was considerable. Imperial servants, soldiers, guards in charge of the train, cooks, maids, in all about forty-five people were killed or injured. The telegraph poles had been damaged, and it was impossible to summon medical help quickly. The Emperor's own doctor began to attend to the injured, and the Empress, forgetful of her own slight contusions, helped him with all the devotion of a real sister of charity. She carried water, made bandages with her own linen, which she tore into shreds for the purpose, spoke to the injured, and comforted them with all the sweet words that came to her lips. The Emperor, in the meanwhile, was superintending the rescue and salvage operations, and doing all he possibly could to hurry them on, and, above all, to remove the wounded men and see to their being properly attended. Then at last, after five weary hours of waiting in a drizzling rain that added to the discomfort of the situation, a relief train arrived.

The Emperor had it driven to the next station, and there summoned the village priest to conduct a service of thanksgiving for the living and of memory for the dead in his presence, during which the tears streamed down his cheeks, and when he returned to St. Petersburg it was noticed that a great change seemed to have occurred in him: he was oppressed by sadness, every sign of joyousness seemed to have departed from his nature. This unfortunate accident at Borky without question laid the foundations of the disease to which the Emperor was to become a victim. In the joy of seeing him emerge from it safely and apparently uninjured, people forgot to ask themselves whether it might not after all have harmed his constitution. He looked such a picture of health that the idea that something might be amiss did not even enter the minds of those who surrounded the Emperor—not even that of the Empress. As a matter of fact, he received an injury to his kidneys which might have been cured if it had been treated immediately, but which, neglected, was to bring him to an early grave. The weight of the wreckage under which he had been pinned had crushed some nerves in his back, and chronic nephritis ensued. Ultimately Bright's disease developed, which was only discovered when it was too late to attempt a cure. Though he had rallied immediately from the shock of the accident, the Emperor soon after began to find that he was not so well as formerly; he complained of headaches, and that he could not secure a comfortable pair of shoes, always saying that those he had were too narrow for him. This was attributed to caprice, and it did not occur to anyone that the reason for it lay in the fact that the Emperor's feet were swelling rapidly.

In January of 1894, St. Petersburg was startled by the news that its beloved Emperor was ill. It was almost on the eve of the first ball of the season, and caused great excitement in Society. The ball was countermanded, and it was officially announced that the illness was a sharp attack of influenza complicated with a touch of pneumonia. For three or four days the bulletins were rather alarming, and a celebrated Moscow doctor, Professor Zakharine, was called in. But Alexander mended wonderfully quickly, and very soon was out again. His daughter the Grand Duchess Xenia was making her début, and he did not like to cancel any of the Court festivities for which arrangements had been already made. The first Court ball was postponed for a fortnight, and then was attended by the Emperor, as were those that followed after. Apparently he was again in good health, though in accordance with his doctors' orders he worked a little less hard. He was, nevertheless, looking so ill, and his complexion had grown so sallow, that a few keen observers suspected that something was radically wrong, but, of course, did not dare to give expression to their fears. In July the Imperial Family started as usual for its annual excursion in Finnish waters, and it was during this trip that the Emperor's health took a decided turn for the worse. A young doctor who was accompanying him took upon himself to make certain analyses, and was horrified to find as a result that the Sovereign was suffering from albuminuria in an advanced stage and in an acute form.

He told the truth to the Empress, who at first would not believe him. The Court was returning to Peterhof for the marriage of the Grand Duchess Xenia with her cousin the Grand Duke Alexander Michailovitch, and it was decided that nothing should be told the Emperor, until this event was over, beyond the necessity to take certain remedies. The Tsar felt keenly the parting from his eldest daughter, and though she was not leaving the country, yet he well knew that, with her new interests, the relations between them would no longer be the same. Then, too, the betrothal of the Heir to the Throne with the Princess Alix of Hesse was a subject of preoccupation to the Sovereign. The Grand Duke had spent a part of the summer in England, where his future wife was residing at Windsor Castle with her grandmother Queen Victoria, and had been delighted with his stay there. But Alexander III., as a rule, did not care for a member of his family to remain too long abroad, and he was eager for his son to return to Russia, yet, on the other hand, he did not like to say so; and altogether he was worried more than was good for his health.

In September the Imperial Family left for the Castle of Bielowiege, in the Government of Grodno, in the centre of the vast forest which is the glory of that splendid domain. There Alexander seemed at first to rally, but afterwards the worst symptoms of his disease developed, and it was decided to summon from Berlin the famous Professor Leyden, supposed to be the greatest living authority on the disease from which the Emperor was suffering.

When Leyden saw him he recognised at once that a cure was impossible, but he applied himself to minimise the sufferings and to prolong as far as was possible the life of the sick man. His efforts were successful in bringing a little ease to the invalid, and the suggestion was made that he should go to a warmer climate than the damp one of St. Petersburg. The Queen of Greece suggested Corfu; this seemed to please the Emperor, and he laughingly remarked that in his cousin's house he should still feel at home. The King and Queen of Greece offered him the use of their lovely villa "Mon Repos" at Corfu, and Alexander accepted it with an eagerness which surprised his family, who were well aware of his dislike of living anywhere but in his own house. The plans for the journey were accordingly made, and servants and furniture sent in advance, so as to have everything ready by the end of October, when it was decided that the visit should take place. Professor Leyden was asked to accompany the Emperor to Greece, and readily agreed. Alexander seemed so delighted that apparently he began to pick up strength, and at length in the last days of September he left Bielowiege for Livadia in the Crimea on the first stage of his migration to Corfu. When he reached there he seemed so much better that the Empress began to have hopes that after all the doctors might be mistaken, and that her beloved husband would recover. But about a fortnight after their arrival in the Crimea, Alexander had a relapse, after which the thought of his being well enough to leave Livadia had to be abandoned, and his family were warned to prepare for the worst. The days of the best and wisest Sovereign that Russia ever had were numbered.

CHAPTER XXI

LAST DAYS AT LIVADIA

I⊤ was a lovely autumn afternoon, almost summerlike in its beauty, when the *Polar Star*, flying the Imperial standard, steamed into the harbour of Yalta. All the local authorities had gathered there to await the arrival of the Emperor and his family. They had not visited the Crimea for three years, and as usual whenever they arrived in their southern residence, the whole population turned out to receive them and express their delight. Livadia was more a country house than a palace. It had been built for the Empress Marie Alexandrovna—whose state of health had often obliged her to spend the autumn and winter months in a warm climate—and had been bequeathed by her to her eldest son. The Emperor, however, did not share his mother's affection for the place, and it was not often that he visited it. On this occasion it was only after great hesitation that he consented to stop at Livadia at all, for his desire was to go straight to Corfu. He seemed to have a presentiment that the place would be fatal to him, and even said so to the Empress. Circumstances and the doctors, however, proved too strong for him, and he was persuaded to see what the Crimean climate would do for him, and to try and gather there some strength for the longer journey to which he looked forward with an eagerness he had never been seen to display for anything before.

When the Imperial yacht drew up at the pier of Yalta, Alexander did not feel well enough to receive the authorities on board as was the custom on such occasions. The Empress welcomed them with her usual kindness and sweet smile, saying merely that the Emperor felt tired with his journey, but that he was ever so much better, and that she hoped a few months' stay in the lovely climate of the south coast would soon set him quite right again. She spoke with a conviction which she could not have felt, but perhaps in the effort to assure others she found comfort to herself, some lightening of the dark shadow which was hovering over her. She herself supported her husband when they landed, and did her best to dissimulate her anxiety as well as the tottering steps of the Emperor.

The change in the latter's appearance since his last stay in the Crimea terrified all those who had assembled to greet him. He looked a perfect ghost—pale, thin, and with the saddest of smiles upon his lips. He spoke a few words to the Governor and the other authorities, but seemed to be in a hurry to get home, and hastened to his carriage, in which he was rapidly driven to the Palace.

The first few days passed quietly. The invalid spent most of his time out of doors, and appeared more cheerful and more content with his condition. He watched from the terrace the blue sea spreading beyond, and the warships anchored in the harbour of Yalta, of which one, the *Pamiat Merkuria*, newly built, was the object of his special interest and attention, and he often spoke of it, saying that as soon as he felt better he would go on board and examine it carefully. Alas! it was upon this same ship that his mortal remains were taken to Sebastopol on their way to St. Petersburg for burial.

By and by the whole Imperial Family gathered in the Crimea under one pretence or another, so as not to allow the invalid to suspect that it was anxiety for his health that had brought them there. But Alexander was not deceived, and well understood the gravity of his condition. When the Empress was not present he sometimes spoke of what was to be done after he had gone, but the proposal which was made at that time to celebrate quietly the marriage of the Heir to the Throne with the Princess Alix of Hesse, in the private chapel of Livadia, did not meet with his approval. He did not think, and said so, that the wedding of the future Sovereign ought to be solemnised without the proper pomp and ceremonies inseparable from such events. He did not even express the desire to see his prospective daughter-in-law arrive in the Crimea earlier than the time which had been originally fixed for her journey, the last days of October, and yet he had not seen her since her betrothal to the Tsarevitch. It seemed as though he was afraid of exhausting his remaining strength in useless emotions, and wanted to reserve it for the last parting with the wife he loved so well. She, on her side, was heroic in the calm she displayed and the force of will with which she dried her tears whenever she entered her husband's room, so that he might not perceive her agony. She surprised everybody by her courage and Christian resignation to the will of the Almighty; never once did she allow herself to give vent to her despair.

Only when her heart was wellnigh breaking did she send an urgent telegram to her beloved sister, Alexandra, then

Princess of Wales; the appeal was responded to, for both the Prince and the Princess started the same evening for Livadia.

The Grand Duke Alexis met them at Sebastopol. The first question the Princess asked was, "Are we in time?" A mournful shake of the head was the only reply she received, and she burst into tears upon hearing it.

When the Empress saw her sister her composure gave way for the first time since her arrival at Livadia; and for the first time, too, she seemed to realise the full extent of her terrible misfortune. Her agony was piteous in the extreme to behold, and she sobbed for a long time, shedding most bitter tears when the Princess of Wales was trying to comfort her. Yet actually what could one say, what consolation could one offer for such an awful blow, when all the earthly hopes, not only of a family, but also of a whole nation, had been smitten to the ground?

Alexander III. had longed for the arrival of his brother- and sister-in-law, and often spoke of their last visit to the Crimea, which had been for the celebration of his own silver wedding. It is quite certain that the thought that they would be there to support the Empress in her trial was a last comfort for him, and though he died before they could reach Livadia, yet he found sufficient strength to write a few words of farewell to the Princess of Wales, to commend her sister to her care. He had no illusions left as to his own condition, and he kept asking eagerly for his cousin the Queen of Greece, who had always been his great favourite.

When Olga Constantinovna arrived he used to keep her beside him for hours, talking as much as his growing weakness allowed him to do, and reminding her of their youthful and childish days. The Queen's mother, the Grand Duchess Alexandra Jossifovna, joined her daughter a few days later, and she it was who suggested to the Emperor to call to his bedside the famous Father John of Cronstadt, who was venerated throughout Russia as a saint, and in whose prayers the people had enormous faith. Alexander instantly consented. The Father was telegraphed for, and when he arrived at Livadia the dying Sovereign had him brought to his room, and at once asked him to pray for him. A touching conversation took place between the mighty monarch and the humble parish priest.

"My people love you," said the Emperor.

"Yes, Your Majesty," replied Father John; "your people love me."

"And I also belong to the Russian people," said Alexander. "I too love you, and I want you to pray for me. I know I am dying, but I wish you to know that I have always tried to do my best for all—for all," he repeated. "And I am not afraid—no, I am not afraid. And I wish you to tell my people that I have no fear. Probably God thinks I have done enough that He calls me. I am content to do what He wants."

He asked that the last Sacrament might be administered to him, and after the rite had taken place he seemed more peaceful. Resigned he had always been, as well as ready to give an account of his stewardship to Him who had entrusted him with it.

While these last scenes were taking place the Princess Alix of Hesse was hastening to the Crimea. At Berlin the Emperor William came to greet her at the railway station and to exchange a few words with her whilst the train was stopping there. At Warsaw her sister the Grand Duchess Elizabeth Feodorovna met her, and accompanied her to Livadia, where already the whole of the Imperial Family had gathered. She was introduced into the Emperor's bedroom, but he was too weak to do anything else but exchange a few words with her and to bless her; but he did so with a solemnity which impressed the whole assembly, wishing her every happiness, and adding that he wished Russia happiness through her, and by her. When this was done the brave man knew that his earthly task was over, and prepared himself for death.

He lingered for a few days longer, not suffering much, save from suffocation, fits of which often troubled him. But he was even cheerful and content, talking with his doctors and thanking them for their care of him. He liked Professor Leyden, who had devised means to relieve his sufferings, and often asked him whether the swelling of his legs could not be lessened, as it troubled him much in his movements. He used to leave his bed in the afternoon, and to have his arm-chair wheeled near the window, or on to the terrace when the weather was quite warm, and he watched the landscape and the sea, and often asked for flowers to be brought to him, which he kept in his hands and then distributed to those around him. His children often came to him, and he caressed them, but seldom spoke, except to the

Empress, whom he scarcely liked to have out of his sight, as if he wanted not to lose a single one of the moments left to him to be with her. Once he was heard to say, "Poor Mimi!" but that was the only time that he seemed to give way. Otherwise his resignation was perfect, his calmness wonderful, his faith in a life everlasting entire and strong. He had cast all earthly thoughts aside, trusting to Divine Providence to take care of his family and his nation, and without a murmur was awaiting the dawn of his last day.

Through the night which preceded that fateful November 1st he was very restless, but at length, towards the morning, fell asleep. The Empress went into the next room and lay down for an hour, then returned to the dying man. At about nine o'clock he awoke, but did not move, lying on his back, supported by high pillows, and with his eyes wide open, with a cheerful expression in them, as if looking into the great unknown. Father John and his own confessor, Father Yanischeff, came to his bedside, and asked him whether he would not like to receive the Sacrament once more. He cheerfully consented, and after the ceremony was over, he had the Heir to the Throne called to him, and talked to him seriously for a few minutes; then he blessed his other children, and added a few words of thanks to his servants and to those who surrounded him. And he once more asked for the Queen of Greece. When she approached him he took her hand, and merely said, "Olga Constantinovna!" looking at her with his blue eyes that were already glazing over. The Queen knelt beside him, with difficulty restraining her tears, and he pressed her fingers with his own. Then he sank back in his pillows, as if unable to bear any more.

Towards three o'clock he had himself dressed, put in his arm-chair, and wheeled near the window, which he asked to be opened wide. The Empress came and knelt beside him, supporting him with her arms, and the family were called again. Alexander lay back quite calm, but his breathing was getting more and more difficult. He kept pressing the hand of his wife, and then, amidst a profound silence, not even broken by a sob, one last deep sigh was heard and a great light went out.

The Empress remained immovable beside him whilst the doors were opened; and the suite, household, and servants were brought into the room and defiled for one last farewell before the dead man and his kneeling wife. They reverently bent down and kissed the dead and the living hand, then retired sobbing bitterly.

A witness of this heartrending scene, Prince Sergius Troubetzkoy, then Head of the Imperial Household, made a sketch of it, which is preserved by a few chosen friends, and no more precious memento exists than that simple drawing, traced amidst all the anguish that accompanied that solemn hour.

The body of Alexander III. had not yet been placed on his funeral bed, when the ears of the inhabitants of Yalta, who through days of anguish and suspense had waited for news from the Palace of Livadia, were startled by the booming of the big guns of the *Pamiat Merkuria*; and as they listened to these minute guns they understood that all was over, and that it was the last farewell of the Black Sea Fleet to its dead Sovereign.

That same evening, on the lawn opposite the entrance to the Palace of Livadia, an altar was erected and Father Yanischeff, in golden vestments, emerged from the gates and solemnly administered to a numerous assembly the oath to the new Sovereign. Of all the pomp, the glory, the hopes, that had embellished the reign of Alexander III., nothing was left except a woman's broken heart and the tears of a whole nation.

The body of the dead Emperor was taken to St. Petersburg, and laid to rest beside those of his ancestors, in the Cathedral of St. Peter and St. Paul. For days the population of the capital passed before the bier to take a last look at the familiar features of its beloved Sovereign. How small he was, covered almost entirely with the folds of his Imperial mantle of gold and ermine—that same mantle he had so proudly worn on his Coronation day in Moscow! The expression on his face was calm and serene; he had truly entered into his rest.

All the countries of the world sent representatives to attend the funeral; the whole of Russia prostrated itself at the foot of the catafalque upon which Alexander lay. Nothing was wanted to make the ceremony an event to remember for ever. But its chief feature was that it was not a mere ceremonial time of mourning; there was displayed the genuine grief of a great nation, the cry from the heart of a people: "We have lost a Father, and there was no one greater or more virtuous than this man in the whole of Israel!"

CHAPTER I

FUNERAL AND WEDDING BELLS

IT was a cold November afternoon. The guns of the fortress of St. Peter and St. Paul in St. Petersburg were thundering their last salute to Alexander III., whose remains were being lowered into the grave by the Palace Grenadiers, whilst all the bells of the great city were tolling mournfully a solemn farewell. Round the open vault his family were kneeling, taking a last glimpse of the coffin as it slowly disappeared from their sight. Sobs were heard from the widow and her children; heartrending sobs, which merged into the low chant of the clergy, and added poignancy to the scene.

Beside the grave the new Emperor was standing, a slight, small figure, with indecision in his movements and a hunted, anxious expression in his blue eyes. When the last rites were over he escorted the widowed Empress to her carriage, which was awaiting her at a side entrance of the cathedral, and then, after another look at the tomb which was being closed, he went out of the church through the front door. He was alone, and for a few seconds paused on the steps, as if dazed by the light outside, after the half-darkness of the church.

As he appeared upon the threshold the troops massed on the large square inside the fortress lowered their colours before him for the first time since the day of his accession to the Throne of Russia, and for the first time, also, the band played the National Anthem. The Army saluted its new Chief, welcomed the new Sovereign. The reign of Nicholas II. was beginning amidst manifestations of sympathy such as rarely had been witnessed in the Empire over the destinies of which he was called upon to preside.

People pitied him for his youth, his inexperience, and for those tragic events so closely preceding his wedding. They pitied, too, his young bride, whose advent into her new country was taking place at such a mournful time. All these circumstances increased the general sympathy, so that when he entered upon his new duties and responsibilities he found everybody ready and willing to help him and anxious to make him forget that the pealing of his wedding bells was mingled with the sounds of tolling for the death of his father.

When, a few days later, the nuptials of Nicholas II. with the Empress Alexandra Feodorovna were celebrated in the Winter Palace, a sympathetic crowd again gathered in the vast halls of that historic residence. All were eager to see the young bride, whose arrival had been preceded by the reputation which she had acquired in her former country, of being not only a clever woman, but also one possessing a high moral standard and a strong character. One had heard she was kind, humane, cultivated in the extreme, and imbued with all the humanitarian ideas for which all the children and grandchildren of Queen Victoria had been so remarkable. Moreover, she belonged to that House of Hesse which had already given one Empress to Russia, in the person of the grandmother of Nicholas II. The bride had further claim on the interest of the Russians from the fact that she was the sister of a princess who had succeeded in making herself extremely popular in the country—the Grand Duchess Elizabeth Feodorovna, the consort of the Grand Duke Sergius. All these circumstances put together would have been sufficient to ensure the sympathies of the country, even if the personal appearance of Princess Alix had not been such as to command them, and her extreme beauty only added to the interest with which she was welcomed.

On the morning of that memorable November 26th which was to see the Princess Alix of Hesse united to Nicholas II., the Winter Palace early began to fill. The ceremony was fixed to take place at eleven o'clock, but long before ten had struck people poured into the residence of the Tsars. Representatives of all the different classes of society which constituted the Empire were gathered within the Palace. One could see deputations from the Army, the Navy; from the merchant and the industrial classes, as well as from the rural population; from the Cossack army and from the Asiatic populations owning allegiance to the Romanoffs. One could witness the curious spectacle of the diamond tiara of some Court beauty beside the caftan of some peasant, and the gold embroidered uniform of a chamberlain or other high official contrasting by its gorgeousness with the dark and plain tunic of a village mayor, or the neatly attired officer of the reserve forces.

All necks were stretched to catch a glimpse of the Imperial procession proceeding to the chapel, and a feverish excitement reigned amidst this motley assemblage gathered together to see a spectacle which never before had been witnessed in Russia—that of the marriage of a Reigning Sovereign.

There was a long wait, and people already began to ask themselves whether something had not happened to stop the ceremony, as twelve o'clock struck, and still no sign of the bridal procession was to be seen. The occasion was so exceptional that etiquette was for once disregarded, and discussions eagerly went on as to the future of the marriage about to be celebrated when the sounds of the prayers for the dead over the remains of Alexander III. had hardly died away.

At last the thumping of a stick was heard—that of the Master of Ceremonies, who heralded the approach of the procession. First appeared various servants and officials of the Household. Then, amidst a hushed silence and an intense emotion that brought tears to the eyes of many an old servant and follower of the dynasty of the Romanoffs, one saw the bridal couple advance.

Nicholas II. was dressed in the red uniform of his Hussar regiment, with the white dolman slung across his shoulder. He still wore the epaulets of a colonel of the Army. He had refused to assume the insignias of a higher rank, saying that he would prefer to keep those that had been conferred upon him by his father. He was leading his future Consort, whose cheeks burned with excitement, and whose trembling hand rested timidly in the one with which he was conducting her to the church.

"How beautiful she is!"

That exclamation followed her all along her path, and it is true that her appearance was positively magnificent as she stood there in her bridal array of silver cloth and old lace. Her unusual height helped her to bear the weight of her dress and set off its splendour in its best light. Her mouth quivered a little, and this relieved the habitual hard expression that was the one defect of an otherwise perfectly beautiful face, the straight, classic features of which reminded one of an antique Greek statue. The glow upon her cheeks only added to the loveliness of her countenance, and her eyes, modestly lowered, gave to her whole figure a maidenly shyness that made it wonderfully attractive. She had upon her head the diamond crown which all the Russian Grand Duchesses wear at their marriage service, and from it descended a long white lace veil, kept in its place by a few sprays of orange blossom and myrtle.

Her dress was of silver tissue, and from her shoulders descended a long mantle of gold brocade lined with ermine, the train of which was carried by eight high officials of the Court. That mantle had been the object of many a discussion. Usually the Grand Duchesses of Russia wear on their wedding day a mantle of crimson velvet, but here it was the bride of an Emperor, and it was thought that some distinction ought to be made, although there was no precedent for such an event. At last it was decided to make the mantle of gold brocade, but not to embroider it with the black eagles that adorn the Imperial mantle assumed by Sovereigns at their Coronation.

Alexandra Feodorovna wore also, on her neck and the bodice of her dress, the Crown diamonds which only the Consorts of Sovereigns have the right to assume.

Behind the bridal pair came the Empress Dowager Marie Feodorovna, who, always brave, had made this great effort to appear at her son's wedding. She was leaning on the arm of her father, the old King of Denmark. She firmly stepped on the path of duty, ever mindful of her obligations as a Sovereign; but her red eyes, and weary, despairing, tired look, told the inward struggle which she was enduring. The King was bending tenderly over her; it was a touching sight to see this old man trying to uphold the courage of his afflicted child, and to sustain her in her great sorrow.

After the Empress and her father came a long file of foreign Royalties, foremost among whom were the Queen of Greece and the Prince and Princess of Wales. The future King Edward of England had been most active during the weeks that had elapsed since the death of Alexander III. He had taken the direction of all the arrangements concerning the wedding of his nephew the Tsar. It was he who had insisted upon its being celebrated at once before the mourning for the late Emperor was at an end. It was he who had taken the part of guardian towards his niece the Princess Alix; and it was he—so it was whispered, at least—who had tried to inculcate in Nicholas II. the principles which ought to govern a Sovereign who wants to go with the age and not to keep an old regime which even in Russia had grown out of date.

It was said that owing to his efforts the old and traditional enmity which had divided the Russian and English Courts was to come to an end, and that friendly relations between them would be the result of this marriage which was going to unite the nephew of the Princess of Wales with the granddaughter of the Queen of England.

The members of the Imperial Family walked after the foreign Princes and Princesses, and the long procession was closed by the maids of honour of the Empress and the other Court ladies. Immediately behind the bridal couple were also to be seen the Minister of the Imperial Household in attendance on his Sovereign, and the Mistress of the Robes of the young Empress, the Princess Mary Galitzine, who was to become one of the most important personages of the new regime.

At the entrance to the chapel the Metropolitan of St. Petersburg and the members of the higher clergy were waiting for the procession. Holy water was presented to the Emperor and to his bride, and then the marriage ceremony began.

The chapel of the Winter Palace is quite small, and it would have been impossible for all the people assembled there to enter; but one after another those present peeped into it, just to see how things were going on, and always reported to the less fortunate ones that the bride was keeping her lovely head bowed down, and that, notwithstanding the emotion under which she was seen to be labouring, she kept quite calm, and made her responses in a firm though low voice. The bridegroom appeared more agitated, and had to be prompted by the priest. The Empress Marie was quite broken down by grief, and sobbed bitterly during the ceremony. When it was over she folded her son in her arms in one long and tender embrace, and also kissed most affectionately her new daughter-in-law. Then all the Royal and Imperial personages present came and offered their congratulations to the newly married couple, after which mass was celebrated, the procession re-formed and proceeded once more through the State rooms of the palace to the private apartments, where lunch was served for the bride and bridegroom and their family.

It was then known why the marriage ceremony had been delayed. It seems that an over-zealous police official had not allowed the *coiffeur* who was to fix the crown on the hair of the Imperial bride to enter the Winter Palace on account of his having forgotten to provide himself with the necessary entrance card. The unfortunate man protested and implored to be allowed to pass, but it was of no avail; and whilst he was discussing and protesting, Alexandra Feodorovna was sitting before her dressing-table, wondering what had happened and what she was going to do if he did not turn up.

At last he was discovered by one of the valets of the Emperor. But a whole hour had been lost, and it was past twelve o'clock when at last the bride was ready and able to proceed to church.

After lunch the Dowager Empress was the first one to leave the Winter Palace for Anitchkov, where the young people were to reside with her until their own apartments were ready to receive them. Half an hour later Nicholas II. and his bride entered a State carriage, drawn by six white horses. An immense and enthusiastic crowd cheered them as they emerged from the gates of the Winter Palace on the way to Anitchkov. The Empress kept bowing repeatedly, but she was so nervous that she appeared to move her head mechanically, and her eyes were filled with tears which she tried hard to restrain. It seemed as if she only then realised the weight of the duties and responsibilities which were henceforward to rest upon her shoulders, and, too, as if she shrank from them. Anxiety was in her countenance, her smile had lost its sweetness, but nevertheless her mien more than anything else, gave one the impression of a great dignity, and she certainly seemed fitted for the high position which had become hers.

The Sovereigns proceeded to the Kazan Cathedral, where they worshipped at the shrine of the Virgin, who is one of the patron saints of St. Petersburg. Next, they passed before the Roman Catholic church which is situated on the Nevski Prospekt, where they found standing on its threshold the Catholic Archbishop with his pastoral cross raised before him. The Emperor ordered the carriage to stop, and he accepted with reverence the wishes expressed for his happiness and that of his newly wedded Consort. That interview created a precedent, for never before had the Imperial House publicly acknowledged the existence of another religion than the orthodox one in Russia. It was freely commented upon at the time and taken as an indication of tolerance in the religious opinions of the new monarch.

A few minutes later the doors of the Anitchkov Palace were opened to the newly wedded couple. At the head of the staircase, waiting to welcome them, stood the Dowager Empress, still clothed in her white gown. She pressed to her heart her Imperial son and her new daughter-in-law, and tenderly conducted them to the rooms prepared for them, which were those the Emperor had occupied as a boy. They were quite small, and hardly fitted to be the residence of a mighty Sovereign; but, such as they were, the young couple settled in them, and there they spent the first months of their wedded life. There began the new existence of Alexandra Feodorovna; there commenced her career as an Empress, and there she became acquainted with her first sorrows and her first joys as a wife.

CHAPTER II

A CHARACTER SKETCH OF NICHOLAS II.

WHEN the present Tsar of All the Russias ascended the Throne he was absolutely unknown to the public. Unfortunately, he is almost as unknown at the present day, although nearly twenty years have elapsed since he succeeded his father. Nicholas II. is one of those timid, weak natures who nevertheless like to assert themselves at certain moments in matters utterly without importance, but which, to their eyes, appear to be vital ones. His mind is as small as his person; he sees the biggest events go by without being touched, or being even aware of their great or tragic sides.

His education had been neglected, and he was brought up as befitted an officer in the Guards, not as the heir to a mighty Empire. For a number of years after he had emerged from his teens he was treated as a little boy, and not allowed the least atom of independence. The Empress had studiously kept her children in the background, and her sons hardly ever went out of the schoolroom. When Nicholas was about fifteen he was given a tutor in the person of General Danilovitch, a most respectable man, but a nonentity, and not even a personage belonging to the upper ten, or possessed of manners or education in the social sense of the word. He was of that class of people who eat with the knife, and though he did not communicate this peculiarity to his Imperial pupil, yet he did not teach him those small conventions which

NICHOLAS II., TSAR OF RUSSIA

Photo: Boissonnas & Eggler, St. Petersburg

distinguish gentlemen born from gentlemen by reason of their official position, which latter are but too often found in Russia.

The instruction which the young Grand Duke received differed in no way from that given to cadets in military schools; he was taught obedience and submission to the will of his parents, but he was not prepared for the high position in which he found himself placed quite unexpectedly. Such a contingency had never been catered for by those responsible for his training.

The comparatively early age at which the Emperor Alexander III. died had excluded, during his lifetime, any thought of the possibility of his succession becoming open for years to come. The instruction of his children had been conducted slowly, and instead of fostering the development of their minds, it had been kept back as much as possible by their teachers. The Tsarevitch lived in two small rooms—those which he was later on to inhabit for the first months that followed upon his marriage—in the Anitchkov Palace, and he stood always in considerable awe of his parents, perhaps more of his mother than of his father. He had no companions, no friends; he had no love of reading, no artistic tastes, no interest in anything—not even in military matters.

When he was eighteen years old he entered the regiment of the Hussars of the Guard quartered at Tsarskoye Selo, and that was his first step towards independence. But he was not given as attendants people able to lead him into a path such as that which usually opens before the heir to a crown. He made some friends for himself among the youngest officers of his regiment, and it must be owned these friends were for the most part nonentities, with no ideas beyond that of eating and drinking and making merry; not one of them could either advise him or be of any use to him.

The first time he was called upon to assert himself was during his journey round the world, after his majority. He then began to realise the advantages of his position, though I doubt very much whether he understood the duties which it entailed. His companions were his brother the Grand Duke George, who, however, had to give up the journey on account of his bad health; his cousin Prince George of Greece, and a few officers from some crack regiments of the Guards, such as Prince Kotchoubey, a certain Captain Volkoff, and people of the same kind, with no recommendation except that of being nice fellows.

With all his great qualities, Alexander III. did not possess that of knowing how to direct the education of his children, and the Empress was similarly without this knowledge. She had been brought up in the simplest way possible, and could not understand that the rearing of her own sons and daughters ought to be conducted upon different lines from those under which she had been trained. It was said at one time that when a person of her near entourage asked her whether the time had not come when a governess ought to be chosen for the Grand Duchess Xenia, she replied: "But why? We had no governess when we were children."

The result was that though masters in plenty came to instruct the Tsarevitch and his brothers and sisters, they were nevertheless allowed to remain without that domestic training which alone gives to future Sovereigns, and people in high stations, the knowledge to fill their duties in the proper way, and to meet with dignity the responsibilities of their arduous position.

Again, lessons, though they teach something, yet do not instruct those who receive them if they are not accompanied by an intelligent training, and of this the Imperial children had none. They were given elementary notions of languages and arts, but I doubt very much whether to the present day any of them, the Sovereign not excluded, could write a letter in French without mistakes. The love for learning was not inculcated; reading serious books was never encouraged; the discoveries of science were only explained as things which existed, but not as things capable of further development. In a word, the Tsarevitch received quite a middle-class training, and though he was afterwards sent on a long voyage for the purpose of improving his mind and acquainting him with the world, it is more than doubtful whether he derived any real benefit from it.

As Grand Duke he was always timid, almost painfully so, and when by a strong effort of will he conquered that timidity, he came out with what he wanted to say in an almost brutal manner, which made him many enemies, often quite unjustly. He never had any opinions of his own, except in purely personal matters, and he has none to this day. His want of mind makes him always endorse the judgments of the last person he speaks to. Like every spoilt child he has no heart, not because his is a bad nature, but because he is unable to feel any woes except his own, or to understand any wants when he himself has none. He is jealous of his authority, simply because he is selfish; he tries to uphold it in a brutal manner, as in his famous speech after his accession to the Throne, when he warned his people not to indulge in senseless dreams. Nevertheless, he does nothing to make that authority respected, either at home or abroad. On the contrary, when a fit of bad temper seizes upon him he is the first one to attack the principles it should be his duty to defend. This was manifested recently when he deprived his brother the Grand Duke Michael of his rights. He is utterly incapable of grasping the consequences of his own actions, does everything through impulse, and thinks that the best argument is to knock down one's adversaries. The only strength he recognises is the strength of the fist, and unfortunately this is not a strength which one respects in a century when machinery has taken the place of the hand.

The Emperor is an exceedingly rancorous man. Instead of practising the principle which made Louis XII. of France so famous: that of not remembering as King the injuries he had received as Duke of Orleans, he thinks it his duty to chastise when he can every slight to which he considers he has been subjected either as Sovereign or as Heir to the Throne. He likes to be feared, but unfortunately he cannot even inspire respect, much less awe. He feels this, and not knowing how to fight against the lack of consideration for his person, he becomes savage in his wrath, and, though in appearance a quiet, inoffensive little man, is capable of the utmost cruelty and hardness. He has no generous impulses, none of that enthusiasm of youth which induces one to do generous actions, even when they are not quite in accordance with prudence. He lives a mechanical life, devoid of interest and indifferent to everything that does not concern his immediate person.

People have asked themselves whether the indifference he has shown in grave moments of his life has been affected or real. When the news was brought to him of that terrible disaster of Tsushima, which cost Russia her whole fleet and the loss of so many precious lives, the Emperor was playing tennis in the park of Tsarskoye Selo. He read the telegram that sounded the knell of so many hopes, and then quietly resumed his game, not a muscle of his face moving. Was it stoicism, indifference, or a strength of mind almost supernatural? The world tried to guess, but was afraid to think that it arose from inability to understand the greatness of the catastrophe. It is certain that no one has practised with greater success than he has done the famous maxim of La Rochefoucauld, that "we bear with the greatest composure the misfortunes that do not concern us." Nicholas II. probably thought that the misfortune which had befallen Russia on the day of Tsushima did not concern him personally, just as he did not realise that the catastrophe of Khodinska, which made his Coronation so memorable, and cost the lives of nearly two thousand people, concerned him too. On this last occasion he danced the whole of the night following it; on the first one he went on playing tennis. The only difference between the two lay in the kind of amusement he indulged in.

When he found himself confronted with Revolution it never once occurred to him that if he put his own person forward he might avert it. On that dreadful day in January which ended in such bloodshed, he never for one moment remembered the proud attitude of his ancestor, that other Nicholas who, on an almost similar occasion, came out of his palace and confronted the angry crowd, forcing the multitude, by the courage of his attitude, to fall down upon their knees and submit. The only thought of Nicholas II. was to flee from danger and to leave to others the task of drowning in blood these first symptoms of rebellion.

And when, later on, he called together the representatives of the different classes of his Empire, and inaugurated that first short-lived Duma, he realised neither the solemnity of the act he had decided upon nor the importance it would have in history.

I can see him, still, on that memorable day, reading his first speech in the White Hall of the Winter Palace. One could not help remembering Louis XVI., and thinking of that May morning when the *Etats-généraux* assembled for the first time at Versailles. The same pomp characterised both: ladies in Court trains and with diamond diadems; high officials in braided uniforms, gold lace, and plumes in their cocked hats; and, in their black coats, the deputies of the lower classes, those whose efforts bring about the great crises that shake the life of nations.

Did he think of this, that mighty Tsar who, in a monotonous voice, read his message to his people? Did he examine the faces of these men standing before him, and try to guess whether a Mirabeau or a Vergniaud was among them? Did the phantom of a Robespierre arise before his mind? When the ceremony was over he remarked that some of the caftans worn by the deputies from the rural classes were not new. It was all that had attracted his attention.

When travelling outside Russia I have often been asked why it was that both Nicholas II. and his Consort had made themselves so very unpopular in Russia. I must own I have found it very difficult to reply. That they *are* unpopular is unquestionable, but to explain the reason adequately would take volumes and still not initiate the outsider into the details of this difficult question. When the present Tsar ascended the throne he was surrounded by universal sympathy. People who had never seen him, nor would ever see him, were kindly disposed towards him. Great things were expected of him, and it was hoped he would govern wisely, after the example which his father had given to him.

Very soon, however, these hopes were dashed to the ground. The Emperor appeared as he really was—personal in everything, shallow-minded, weak, well-intentioned, but only in so far as it did not interfere with his own comfort, indifferent to all the necessities of his country, and governed entirely by his sympathies or antipathies without considering anything else. His was a nature which would have won for him in private life the denomination of being a "good little fellow"; but that is not enough for a Sovereign: it brings ridicule, the last thing that ought to dog the footsteps of a monarch.

Whilst Alexander III. was living people knew that they could rely upon his word, that he had opinions of his own, and that, whether these were right or wrong, they were still opinions with whom others had to count. After he had reigned a few months everyone who came into contact with Nicholas II. realised that he was the echo of everyone else's opinion except his own.

The flexibility of his mind equalled its emptiness. It was very soon found out that he changed his ideas as often and with as many people as he discussed them. Though he fully thought he knew what constituted his duties as a Sovereign, yet it can be questioned whether he could have told what they were.

The vacillation of Nicholas II. is something quite surprising, and his ingratitude for services rendered to him sometimes astounding. When M. Stolypin, struck by an assassin's shot, expired after a few days of the most horrible sufferings, the Emperor was in Kieff. Common decency would have required him to be present at the obsequies of the Minister who had laid down his life for him. People expected it, public feeling required from him this manifestation of his sorrow; but the Tsar coolly left Kieff for the Crimea, not thinking it worth while to change anything in his plans in order to follow to his grave the statesman who, whatever may have been his faults, still had crushed the Revolution which at one time threatened to overturn the Throne of the Romanoff Dynasty.

After Stolypin's death, M. Kokovtsov was appointed head of the Ministry, and when he arrived at Livadia to discuss with his Sovereign the line of action which he intended to take, he found Nicholas II. arranging some prints upon the walls and watching the effect of his work. When he saw the Prime Minister the first words that he said to him were: "Oh, I am glad that you have arrived. You can tell me whether this picture hangs well or not." And during the three days which M. Kokovtsov spent in Livadia he was unable to secure a serious conversation with his Sovereign, the latter always putting him off and at last telling him plainly that "he had come to Livadia to enjoy a holiday, and did not want to be bothered with business matters, which could be put off until he was back at Tsarskoye Selo."

Since the day when he fled from St. Petersburg for fear of the mob who, led by the too famous Gapon, had wanted to present a petition to him, Nicholas II. has not inhabited the capital. He has confined himself in his Imperial castle of Tsarskoye Selo, where his Ministers come to him with their reports, and where he leads the life of a country gentleman with a limited circle of friends. He often goes to dine at the mess of the regiments quartered there, and remains with the officers late at night, drinking champagne and indulging in the smallest of small talk. The rest of the time he signs papers, the contents of which he mostly does not understand; he shoots in his park; and he worships his son, and has him brought up in the most detestable way possible, never allowing the child to be contradicted, and insisting upon all his caprices being satisfied at once, whatever their nature may be.

During the long winter evenings the Emperor likes to turn tables, and in general is fond of arranging spiritualist séances with all the famous mediums that visit St. Petersburg. At one time a particular medium was supposed to enjoy his entire confidence, and to advise him, by means of table-turning, in the most complicated matters of State.

The relations of Nicholas II. with the different members of his family are like everything else that he does—subject to many and various changes. When he ascended the Throne his mother was supposed to wield a considerable influence over him, and though that influence is no longer as strong as it was, yet it is certain that he would not go against the Dowager Empress in anything she wanted to do.

At one time he very much liked his uncle, the Grand Duke Vladimir, but after the marriage of the latter's son, the Grand Duke Cyril, with his cousin, the divorced Grand Duchess of Hesse, their relations underwent a change and quarrels took place.

At present the Grand Duke Nicholas is *persona grata* with the Sovereign, perhaps on account of the brutality for which he is famous.

He is also supposed to like his sisters, but these are of too little importance to be reckoned with as serious factors in the general situation.

No monarch has ever led such a secluded existence as the present Tsar. Life at Court, which used to be so bright and cheerful, is now sad and dull. Festivities there are none, except one reception on New Year's Day, at which the young Empress never appears, and even that did not take place in 1913. Balls are no longer given, and foreign princes, when they arrive upon a visit to the Russian Court, are received at one or other of the country residences of the Sovereign. The Winter Palace, once so animated, has taken the appearance of a lumber room, and presents to the visitor an unkempt, forlorn, dirty, neglected sight.

No reign in Russia from the time of Peter the Great has been so unfortunate as the present one. Calamities have followed its course from the very beginning. The prestige of the country, which was so great when Alexander III. died, has been seriously impaired by the failure of the Japanese campaign and the Revolution that followed upon it. Discontent is rife and becoming stronger every day; and though the financial prosperity of the country has certainly increased and reached hitherto unknown proportions, yet it has not done away with dissatisfaction.

The most curious feature of this situation is the total lack of respect and consideration the public feels for the person of Nicholas II. and for his family. Formerly, Grand Dukes were considered as something quite apart from the rest of mankind, and as for the Emperor—one stood in awe of him, whether one loved him or not. Now, no one thinks about them at all; they simply do not exist either in the public or the social sense. Respect has gone, and familiarity has not arrived. The presence of a member of the Imperial Family at a ball or party is no longer considered as an honour, and is not looked upon as a pleasure.

No misfortune has been spared to Nicholas II., and had he only understood their importance, he would have been the most unhappy man in the whole of his vast Empire. War has humiliated his country, revolution has enfeebled it, bad and tainted politics have dishonoured it, the blood of thousands of people who perished quite uselessly cries out for revenge, the tears of other thousands of unhappy creatures who languish in prisons or in hopeless exile appeal to Heaven for the chastisement of those in authority who sent them to a living death. Danger surrounds him, treason dogs his footsteps; his nation dislikes and distrusts him; his family is hostile to him; his only brother is banished, his mother is estranged from him, the wife of his bosom is the victim of a strange and mysterious malady; his only son, and the successor to his Throne and Crown, is smitten with an incurable illness. He has no friends, no disinterested advisers, no Ministers whose popularity in the country could add something to his own. And amid these ruins he stands alone, a solitary figure, the more pathetic because he does not realise the tragedy of his own fate.

CHAPTER III

THE EMPRESS ALIX

WHEN the Princess Alix of Hesse left Darmstadt for the Crimea in order to be present at the death-bed of the Emperor Alexander III., there was one paper in Germany that dared to print what was spoken of in secret among many people, and to express some apprehension as to the fate that awaited the young bride in that distant country whither she was speeding in quest of an Imperial Crown.

Her marriage was not popular among her own country folk. The Protestant feelings of the German people revolted against the change of religion to which she would have to submit, and moreover there existed at that time a terrible prejudice in Hesse against Russia and everything that was Russian. The union which the Princess was about to contract was not popular, and, rightly or wrongly, it was firmly believed that she was being forced into it against her will; that, left to herself, she would have preferred to end her days in the peace of the little Darmstadt Court than to live among the splendours of St. Petersburg. It was this feeling that she was about to be sacrificed to reasons of

State which inspired for her a pity that was freely expressed in the article already referred to and which is quoted hereunder:—

"It is only with feelings of deep grief and pity that the German people can follow during her journey to Russia the gracious and beloved Princess Alix. I cannot banish from

my thoughts the secret forewarning that this Princess, who wept such bitter tears when she left Darmstadt, will have a life full of tears and bitterness on foreign soil. One need not be a prophet to foresee what conflict of thoughts and impressions will crowd within the heart of the august bride during these decisive weeks: Human law requires that a young girl follows the husband of her choice into the unknown.

"But the German people *cannot* consider this marriage with joy nor with the charm of things where the heart alone is in question. The German people cannot forget the old saying of the poet: 'Princes are only the slaves of their position; they must not follow the leanings of their own hearts.'

"If we cast a glance upon the Tsar fighting against the throes of death; upon the 'private life' of the bridegroom; upon the renunciation of the evangelical faith of the Princess, a faith to which she has belonged to this day, sincere and convinced as to its truth—we consider that only an heroic nature can overcome all these terrors:

"After the German people had, until the last hour, reckoned on the rupture of this union, which cannot bring any happiness for the bride, so far as it is possible to judge of these things in advance, it only remains to feel ashamed that, in the country of liberty of conscience and of convictions, one can make to political considerations the sacrifice of one's faith and of one's heart.

"One would learn with a deep joy in Germany that the Princess has found by the side of her husband real and lasting happiness. In the meanwhile we can only indulge in wishes for her welfare, and hope for the best in presence of this dark and uncertain future."

Nevertheless, in spite of the wrench which she must have undergone when parting from her country and from her family and friends, the Princess Alix was not so sorry, after all, to be married. Her life had not been a happy one in her home circle.

She had been left an orphan quite young, and when her father had died she had remained with her brother, and, so to speak, had kept house for him, spending also a good deal of her time in England with her grandmother, Queen Victoria. This unsettled kind of life had, as was to be expected, exercised an influence on the character of the young Princess, who had acutely felt the subordinate position into which events had thrust her.

When her brother, the Grand Duke of Hesse, married, she did not get on with his consort, though the latter happened to be her own cousin, the daughter of her uncle the Duke of Coburg.

All these circumstances had given an element of bitterness to a temper which from nature was haughty and not pliable. Many of those peculiarities which she developed in after life can also be ascribed to the difficult time of her early youth. Deprived when quite a baby of a mother's care, there had been no elements of softness introduced into her education, which, though carried out on strict lines, yet had not been so well attended to as should have been the case. Strong principles were instilled, but she was not taught that virtue must be amiable, especially in its contact with others and in its application to the events of existence.

The question of her marriage with the Heir to the Throne of Russia had been mooted long before this marriage became an accomplished fact. The Grand Duke of Hesse had even brought her on a visit to the Russian Court when she was beginning to go out into Society, but though at the time it was whispered that she was destined to become the bride of the Tsarevitch, yet nothing came of this visit, which, on the contrary, left bitter memories to the Princess Alix. She did not like the off-hand way in which she was treated, not only by the Imperial Family but also by St. Petersburg Society to whom she did not appeal, either by her manners or by her personal appearance, which was not then so beautiful as it became ultimately.

The idea of a German marriage was not popular in Russia, and it was hoped that the future Emperor would not choose his wife from that country. The Princess Alix was hurt at this latent animosity against her, which she felt rather than saw, and, of course, she resented it.

When the question of her wearing the Imperial Crown of the Romanoffs came to be seriously discussed a few years later, the idea did not appeal to her. The brilliancy of the position did not dazzle her, and her whole soul revolted at the thought that she would have to live in a country which had left such unpleasant impressions on her mind.

However, the advice of Queen Victoria, who was anxious for her granddaughter to accept the brilliant match thus offered to her, and the fact of the strained relations existing between her and her sister-in-law, the Grand Duchess of Hesse, with whom she was obliged to live, combined to prevail upon her, and she finally consented to become the bride of Nicholas Alexandrovitch.

At first it was intended to surround their nuptials with all the pomp and festivities which usually attend such occasions. But the fatal illness of the Emperor Alexander changed all these plans; and when the Princess Alix arrived in Russia, alone and with the utmost speed, she knew that she would not have to undergo the sometimes painful apprenticeship to the position of an Empress, which normally would have been the case, but at once would assume in her new country the position of the first lady in the land. She felt dazed and stunned by the turn events had taken. During the months that had elapsed since her engagement to the Tsarevitch she had tried to infuse some affectionate comradeship into her relations with him and to get to know him; she but partially succeeded. Both were timid, both were embarrassed in the position in which they found themselves placed, and both felt that theirs was more a union of convenience than one of affection. Their ideas were totally different, their bringing-up had been conducted on quite different lines; but they had one point in common: an exalted opinion of their own importance and their own capacities. This was to constitute the best bond between them.

When the Princess Alix first reached Russia, she had the best intentions to try to win the affections of the people who surrounded her. Her conduct during those first trying days was perfect, but she displayed no spontaneity in the care in which she performed what she considered to be her duties. She did not utter one single word that could have been badly construed; she did not overlook any of the small details of Russian Court etiquette, and she was respectful with those relatives of her future husband whose age and position commanded respect, whilst amiable with the others. But she forbore to express her private opinions, and whilst strictly polite with the people she met, she was neither frank nor familiar. The haughtiness which she did not attempt to hide was attributed to timidity, and, owing to the peculiarly sad circumstances that attended her first steps in the country which was about to become her own, the public viewed with indulgence all her actions, and were loud in their praise of her. They repeated all the kind words she was heard to utter; they admired the deference with which she spoke of the Dowager Empress and the respectful attitude she assumed towards her.

When, after the funeral of Alexander III., the arrangements for the marriage of Nicholas were discussed, and the question was broached as to where the Emperor and his bride were to live whilst the apartments in the Winter Palace were being got ready, the Princess Alix declared at once that they had better stop at the Anitchkov Palace with the Empress Mother, adding "that it was not the time when mamma ought to be left with another empty place at her dining-table." She cheerfully seemed to allow her mother-in-law to keep that first place which had been hers for so long, and in its affection and tenderness her whole demeanour towards her was touching in the extreme.

Alas, alas! these halcyon days were not to last long. The Court mourning for the late Tsar had not come to an end when the public began to criticise the young Empress, and the enthusiasm of the first months cooled down and gradually gave place to hard judgments and unpleasant remarks. Alexandra Feodorovna had not the gift to make herself lovable nor to inspire sympathy. She developed a harsh, cruel temper, with fits of caprice worthy of a spoilt child. She did not like many things which she found were usual in Russia, and she made no secret of her desire to reform them. She contrived to offend the very people she should have conciliated, and in consequence her actions, contrasting as they did with those of the Dowager Empress, were severely judged and criticised. For instance, though it is etiquette at the Russian Court for ladies to kiss the Sovereign's hand, Marie Feodorovna and her predecessors had never thought of allowing them to do so, and it was only débutantes on their presentation of whom this was required. With married ladies, however, the Empress invariably prevented them from performing that act of homage. But when Alexandra Feodorovna began to receive St. Petersburg Society, she extended her hand for the traditional kiss and seemed to impose it. She mostly granted her audiences standing and in the stiffest manner possible, never making a distinction where she ought to have done so. This incensed people against her, and all the dowagers who had come out of their retirement to be presented to her upon her marriage bitterly resented the haughty, disdainful way in which she received them. They immediately became her enemies and never spared criticism, which was the more unfortunate because there was much in her manner to be criticised.

Among other unpleasant gifts the young Empress had that of calling a spade a spade, and of giving an explanation of the reason which she thought she had for doing such and such a thing. She determined, for instance, to invite to her balls only ladies with unblemished reputations, and in order to prevent any black sheep entering her drawing-rooms she listened to every possible gossip concerning the Society of the capital. After weighing this more or less carefully, she had the list of invitations for the next Court ball brought to her and scratched out with her own hand the names of all those whom she thought fit to exclude. The result was disastrous. Only a few guests, elderly ladies, were present. St. Petersburg was incensed, and loud in its indignation. Indeed, the scandal assumed such proportions that at last the Emperor decided to allow his mother to look through, as she used to do formerly, the lists of the people invited to the Palace. The pretext given for this action was that his wife was not yet sufficiently acquainted with the ins and outs of the Society of the capital.

But this measure did not appease the wrath of the slighted ones; it only added to the popularity of the Dowager Empress, and to the dislike for her daughter-in-law, and at the next New Year's reception at the Winter Palace very few ladies, not obliged to do so by virtue of their official position, were present. The young Empress was boycotted, and nothing since has effaced that first impression which she so unfortunately contrived to create around her person.

One must, however, say one thing. Alexandra Feodorovna has had plenty of bad luck in her life. I shall relate one instance as an example. It is very well known that the Empress possesses but a very imperfect knowledge of the French language. Now French is spoken more than any other language in St. Petersburg, and the lingual mistakes of Alexandra Feodorovna were seized upon with avidity by her enemies and circulated widely everywhere. One fine day a very old dowager, who by virtue of her deceased husband's position was one of the leaders of Society and of the official world, decided to emerge from the retirement in which she had lived for a great many years, and to ask for the favour of a presentation to the young Sovereign. The latter received her standing, as she usually did; this aroused the ire of the old lady, who was further incensed when she saw that she was evidently expected to kiss the hand that was by no means graciously extended to her. With such a prelude the conversation could not be anything but stiff. At last, seeing that all her efforts at small talk met with no success, the lady asked the Empress whether she did not find the climate of St. Petersburg very trying. "Yes," replied the Sovereign, "but"—and here the phrase must be repeated in French as it was uttered, or it would lose its point—"*l'automne dernier j'ai pu me promener tous les jours dans le Crime.*" The unfortunate creature had literally translated her phrase from the German, in which the Crimea is called "*der Krim*"; but one can imagine what laughter such an utterance, repeated all round with alacrity, aroused, and how it was discussed and commented upon everywhere.

On another occasion this ignorance of the French language was to lead the Empress into trouble. One day she had to write to a certain Ambassadress, and in doing so she made several mistakes in the spelling of words. The recipient of the letter, who did not count kindness among her many qualities, showed this note to several of her intimate friends, and these, of course, carried it farther. All these things were but trivial, and had Alexandra Feodorovna succeeded in making herself liked they would have remained unnoticed; but under the existing circumstances they were made the subject of every possible kind of attack. At last it became a case of "Give a dog a bad name and hang it," and even the virtues of the Empress and her good qualities were turned into opportunities to discredit her.

She was not amiable or conciliating among her immediate entourage, and her ladies-in-waiting had to put up with a lot from her imperious temper and her cold and disdainful manner. She did not forgive them the slightest failing in their duties, and treated them with high disdain. She never allowed them to sit down in her presence, even expecting them to stand whilst reading aloud to her. They were always obliged, also, to be ready in full dress to await her commands, no matter whether she required their services or not.

One must be fair and say that the young Empress encountered many difficulties in her daily life. First and foremost among them was the subordinate position to which she found herself relegated. The Dowager Empress was intensely popular and immensely liked, and, moreover, did not like to play second fiddle where she had reigned for a number of years. She thrust aside her daughter-in-law in a most unceremonious way, and instead of drawing the latter's attention to her mistakes she magnified them and used them to keep hold of both authority and position.

Being at the head of all the educational and charitable institutions in the country, she refused to delegate the slightest part of this arduous work to Alexandra Feodorovna, who, on her part, was eager to assert herself in all matters relating to good works, and who, despairing of being able to do so in an effectual manner, tried to invent means to exercise her activity in that direction. She opened a kind of working-room for making clothes for poor children, and began by personally attending to the administration of this institution, calling upon ladies belonging to the upper classes to attend the weekly reunions of the committee, over which she presided. At first the thing took, and the new *Ouvroir*, as it was called at the Winter Palace, became a rendezvous for Society; but when the Court left the capital to settle permanently at Tsarskoye Selo, Society took no further interest in the charitable work. When Nicholas II. and his consort were crowned the unpopularity of Alexandra Feodorovna was already a recognised fact, and it came into evidence during the Moscow festivities, when the difference between the reception she received and that accorded to her mother-in-law could not but have impressed itself upon her, as it did upon all those who were present on this occasion in the old capital. At that moment the Empress, by a strong effort, might still have changed the impression of dislike which she inspired, and which was aggravated by the fact that instead of bringing into the world the much-hoped-for son, that all Russia was expecting, she had given birth to a daughter. The breach was further widened by her attitude when the Khodinsky catastrophe took place. Had she shown some heart and commiseration for the victims sentiment would have changed, but on the same day that it occurred she attended a ball at the French Embassy, and danced as if nothing had happened; and during the days which followed upon that terrible episode she never once went to a hospital to visit the sick and wounded. This apparent indifference, perhaps, arose from the fact that she did not care to appear to imitate the Dowager Empress—whose first impulse had been to rush to the bedside of the wounded—or perhaps, also, she may have felt afraid of interfering with the directions given by her mother-in-law. Nevertheless, it occasioned bitter comment among the public, and she won for herself the reputation of being a heartless woman.

It must not be supposed that this dislike was unknown to the Empress. On the contrary, she was very well aware of it, and instead of inspiring in her the wish to do something to allay it, it made her harder even than she was by nature. She bitterly resented what she considered to be an awful injustice, in view of the good intentions with which she knew she had come to Russia. This feeling that she was misunderstood inspired her with the proud resolution to have as little as possible to do with the nation who had misjudged her so thoroughly, and whose prejudices against her she was too disdainful even to attempt to dissipate.

Misfortune seemed to be her lot. Four times her hopes of giving an Heir to the Crown were brought to naught as one girl after another was born to her, adding to her blighted life the knowledge that in this respect Russia was bitterly disappointed. Her relations with her husband were affectionate, but not tender, and she never knew how to manage him, or to develop by her sympathy the best side of his nature; her manner towards him, also, was not what it ought to have been. She treated him more like a naughty boy than like a monarch whose first subject she was. In the early days of their marriage it was related that one evening, when they had a few people to tea at Tsarskoye Selo, feeling tired and desiring to withdraw, she turned towards the Emperor, and said to him in English, a language always spoken in the Imperial Family, "Now come, my boy; it is time for me to go to bed." One may imagine the stupefaction which this phrase caused among a people accustomed to all the rigidity of etiquette which had always ruled the Court of St. Petersburg. They could not understand how an Empress could forget herself so far in the presence of others as to address the Tsar of All the Russias as "my boy."

All this appears at first sight insignificant, but in reality it sounded the knell of the respect in which the monarch had been held to that day, and it destroyed a great deal of his prestige, rousing at the same time a furious indignation against Alexandra Feodorovna, among all the old adherents of the autocratic regime, which, unknown to herself, she has done so much to shatter.

The disasters of the Japanese War left a deep impression on the mind of Alexandra Feodorovna, and added to the sadness of a naturally sad disposition; she began to tremble, not only for the safety of her Throne, but also for that of the son who at last, after many weary years of waiting, was born to her in the midst of unparalleled disasters. On that child she concentrated all her affections, and for him she trembled constantly. Before he came into the world her nerves already had begun to become affected. She had unfortunately allowed herself to be drawn into a circle of people, among whom the Grand Duke Nicholas and his wife were the most prominent, who were addicted to spiritualistic practices. A medium became an important personage at Court, and succeeded in imposing his influence even on the Emperor, who went so far as to consult him on matters of State.

The Empress's nerves are certainly not in a sound condition, and this fact ought to be taken into consideration when thinking or speaking about her. The horrors of the Revolution left a deep impression upon her mind; she has no fatalism in her character, and lives in dread of seeing her children and husband murdered. Her highly strung nature takes more seriously even than they deserve certain circumstances which surround her, and she has not enough command of herself to meet with courage whatever fate lies before her. Not understanding that Sovereigns must pay with their persons for the privileges of their position in the world, she spends her time in imploring her husband to put himself and his family into safety instead of urging him to come forward and to confront whatever danger lies before him.

When it was said that the workmen of the capital were marching towards the Winter Palace and wanted to see their Tsar, Alexandra Feodorovna begged her husband to fly to Tsarskoye Selo for safety, and she has never wanted to return to the capital since that fateful day.

Owing to her nervousness the breach between the Sovereign and his people has become complete, and the estrangement that divides them has assumed proportions that can only become wider and wider as time goes by. For many people now the Emperor and Empress appear as very distant beings, something like the Mikado of Japan was before the reforms effected in that country raised it to the level of a European nation. In Society the Imperial Family serves only as a subject of gossip and nothing else, and it must be owned that never so much as at the present time has it given reason for it.

More and more the Empress shows her dislike for the Society of St. Petersburg, and whenever she can do it she flies away to the Crimea, which is the one place she cares for. She has had a new palace built there to replace the simple cottage where Alexander III. breathed his last, and she spends months in it, far from everybody, but showing herself more amiable than anywhere else to the few people privileged to see her. There also she entertains in a quiet way, and has even been known to give a dance for her daughters, which she witnessed from the door of a room near the one in which the festivity took place. She did not mix with her guests, but she looked at them, and this was already spoken of as a surprising event, so little had she been seen before. The great preoccupation of the Empress is her son; no child has ever been so spoiled as has the little Grand Duke, and no child has ever been brought up in a worse manner. Were he destined to live, it would be terrible to contemplate the future of Russia under his guidance; as it is, one can afford to pity him, and to pity his parents, for whom he represents so much. But I shall have more to say on that subject later on.

Some people say that Alexandra Feodorovna is mad, and that her madness takes an erotic direction, which accounts for the seclusion in which she is kept, and which is given out to be of her own desire. I do not believe in this rumour, which perhaps is circulated in order to account for her vagaries and extravagances of behaviour; but what I do think is that she is a woman very unfortunate in her life and in her friendships, who, dissatisfied by nature, always yearns for the impossible.

CHAPTER IV

THE IMPERIAL FAMILY TO-DAY

THE Imperial Family of Russia at the present day is in a position far different from what it was before the Revolution, and even before the accession of the present Sovereign.

Up to the death of Alexander III., Grand Dukes and Grand Duchesses were very important personages indeed. Their presence at an entertainment constituted a social event, and it was only at very high and lofty houses that they condescended to attend. Now things are changed; the Grand Dukes have lost their prestige, though they are still the subjects of sharp criticisms on the part of the gossiping public.

The present Imperial Family is no longer so numerous as it was. All the brothers of the late Tsar have died, with the exception of the Grand Duke Paul, who lives for the most part abroad, at his house in Paris, with his morganatic wife, the Countess of Hohenfelsen. At first this marriage created an enormous stir, and the Emperor deprived his uncle of his rank in the Army as well as of that part of his income which came from the Imperial domain, ordering it to be paid for the benefit of his children by his first wife, the Princess Alexandra of Greece.

Very soon after settling in Paris the Grand Duke had made for himself a brilliant position. The Countess also was not dissatisfied at the enforced exile. She queened it from the very first in Paris, where her house became a rendezvous of the Russian colony, and where she could freely see those members of the Imperial Family who came for a holiday in the gay capital, or who had settled in it permanently, like the Grand Duke Alexis, who, after the Japanese War, had preferred to retire to the banks of the Seine rather than remain on those of the Neva.

The Grand Duke Alexis had another attraction there: it was his friend Mademoiselle Balleta, a French actress. She had a very pretty house somewhere in the vicinity of the Champs Élysées, not far from the apartment which the Grand Duke occupied in the Avenue Gabriel. It was at her house that Alexis Alexandrovitch spent most of his time, and it was there he was taken ill with the attack of pneumonia that carried him off to the grave at a relatively early age.

After the death of the Grand Duke Alexis, the Emperor relented in regard to his brother, and the Grand Duke Paul was allowed to return to Russia and was restored to his former rank in the Army. He did not abuse the liberty given, and has only been seen at the Court of St. Petersburg on rare occasions, such as the marriage of his daughter the Grand Duchess Marie Pavlovna with Prince William of Sweden, and the celebration of the Borodino centenary.

Strange to say, his children are on good terms with the Countess of Hohenfelsen, whom not only do they visit but at whose house they stay during their frequent visits to Paris. The Grand Duke Dmitry Paulovitch, her stepson, is even credited with a great affection for her. He is a very nice young man, and it is openly said in St. Petersburg that both the Emperor and Empress want him to marry their eldest daughter, the Grand Duchess Olga Nicolaievna. There have even been rumours that the Tsar had the intention to change the order of succession to the Crown by issuing an ukase passing it, in the event of the death of his only son, the present Tsarevitch, to his eldest daughter and her consort, if the Grand Duke Dmitry Paulovitch.

I do not personally believe in that last rumour. Nicholas II. would hardly be able to enforce such a *coup d'état*, and from the other side the Grand Duke Dmitry himself, if we are to pay any attention to all that is said, is not at all inclined to wed the Grand Duchess Olga. If, however, such an event happened, and the order of succession was changed, serious internal troubles would be sure to take place, in which the Imperial Family would suffer.

At present, failing the little Tsarevitch, the brother of the Emperor, the Grand Duke Michael Alexandrovitch, would be the legitimate Heir to the Crown. When the boy was born a special manifesto was issued by the Emperor appointing his brother regent in the case of a minority. Until then he had occupied the position of Heir Apparent, though he had not been granted the title of Tsarevitch which his brother George had borne until his death, perhaps because the Empress had objected to it, having hopes some day of bearing a son of her own.

The Grand Duke was a meek young man, whose education had been very much neglected, who had neither the wish to lend himself to any intrigue, nor even the desire to do so. He was one of those indifferent beings who are rather sorry than otherwise to be put into responsible positions, and who, beyond all things, would like to be able to lead the quiet life of a very rich private person. When quite young he had fallen violently in love with

Mademoiselle Kossikovsky, the lady-in-waiting of his sister the Grand Duchess Olga Alexandrovna, who married Prince Peter of Oldenburg. Mademoiselle Kossikovsky was not pretty but clever and pleasant, and she gave him all her heart. The romance lasted for some time, and the possibility. A marriage between the two came to be seriously discussed in Society. But the Empress Marie, who would not hear of it, interfered, and as Mademoiselle Kossikovsky did not acquire enough influence over Michael to induce him to go against his mother's wishes, or those of the Emperor, the young lady had to give up her lover and relinquish her appointment in disgrace.

Left to himself, and not knowing to whom he could confide his woes, the miserable young man began to frequent the house of one of the officers of the regiment in which he was serving, the Gatschina Cuirassiers. That officer had a wife, who, though not extraordinarily pretty, was clever, pleasant, very cultivated, and with a past, inasmuch as she had divorced a first husband before marrying her present one. The friendship with Michael Alexandrovitch ripened, and he confided to her all his sorrows, and how badly he considered he had been treated in the matter of his affection for Mademoiselle Kossikovsky. Later on their relations became still more intimate, for the lady, having secured a second divorce, became the wife of the Grand Duke.

The scandal was immense, especially as the event occurred just at the time when the illness of the little Tsarevitch seemed again to open the question of the succession to the Throne. Every means was tried to bring about a divorce. But Michael Alexandrovitch was the soul of honour, and declared that nothing would or could make him forsake the mother of his children.

Then occurred an incident that struck the whole of Russia with amazement and dismay. Nicholas II. issued a manifesto to the nation in which he deprived his only brother of the functions of regent in the event of the future Sovereign being a minor at the time of his succession. In addition he sent an ukase to the Senate by which he made himself guardian of his brother, thus reducing Michael to the condition of a minor, and taking away from him the use and administration of his private fortune, which was placed under the administration of the private estates of the Sovereign.

This last measure would not have aroused criticism in public opinion, but the act of degrading the Grand Duke to the position of a madman or of a baby six years old was very freely commented upon. It was absolutely against the law of the land, which does not admit such an infringement of personal rights, and a reversion to an era of Russian history which all its rulers in modern times had tried to induce the country to forget.

Save a few flatterers, no one was heard to applaud this unheard-of decision.

The Grand Duke retired with his wife to Cannes in the south of France, and settled there as a private gentleman, calling himself M. Brassov, which is the name of his property in the Government of Orel. It seems that before the storm broke out he had transferred a large part of his fortune abroad, so that he is financially able to maintain his old position in Society. It is probable that very soon circumstances will induce his brother to change his mind and restore him to his former position, for it is one of the misfortunes of Nicholas II. not to persist in any action that he takes, especially in cases where his family is concerned.

The Grand Duke Cyril, cousin of Nicholas, stands next to Michael Alexandrovitch in the order of succession. Cyril, who was nearly drowned in the wreck of the *Petropavlovsk*, which cost the life of Admiral Makaroff and of so many brave officers, had been for years in love with his cousin Victoria, the daughter of the Duke of Coburg and the Grand Duchess Marie Alexandrovna of Russia. She was married to the brother of the Empress Alexandra Feodorovna, the Grand Duke of Hesse, and it was during the celebration of their nuptials that her own engagement with the Tsarevitch was officially announced to the world. This marriage of Princess Victoria did not turn out a happy one; the tempers of the Royal couple were not compatible; after some years of a stormy union they parted. After the death of Queen Victoria, who had violently opposed the idea, they were divorced. The ex-Grand Duchess of Hesse returned to her mother's house, and her husband married again, so that nothing apparently existed to prevent her from doing the same; and when the Grand Duke Cyril, after the Japanese War, asked her to become his wife, no one wondered that she accepted him, and everyone who knew her wished her joy.

But the Empress Alexandra was not of that number. It was freely spoken of in Court circles that she implored the Emperor not only not to allow the union, under the pretext that the Orthodox Church did not permit of marriages between first cousins, but, when it became an accomplished fact, to banish the Grand Duke Cyril from St. Petersburg and to deprive him of his rank and fortune. The story goes on to say that the order for banishment and confiscation was actually issued by Nicholas, but that the Grand Duke Vladimir, who was still alive, was not a character to stand any slight done either to him or to his children. Accordingly he went at once to see his nephew Nicholas, and told him that he had no right to act in the way he did, as the marriage that his cousin had contracted was perfectly honourable, and a suitable one too, adding that he would have liked to know what his father the Emperor Alexander II. would have said had he heard that his own granddaughter was refused an entry into the Russian Imperial Family, to which she belonged by the right of birth, before even she had been married to one of its members. In face of this outburst the Emperor at once retracted, restoring Cyril Vladimirovitch to all his rights, only insisting on his spending some years abroad in order to allow the scandal to blow over.

After the death of the Grand Duke Vladimir, which quickly followed his eldest son's marriage, the latter has returned to Russia and spends part of each winter in St. Petersburg, together with his wife and their two daughters. The couple are frequently seen in public places, and the Grand Duchess, being fond of dancing and society, frequents the houses of prominent hostesses of the capital, and has succeeded in making herself very popular everywhere. She has also achieved the difficult feat of remaining on very good terms with her mother-in-law, the Grand Duchess Vladimir.

The latter, about whom I have already spoken at length, has not considerably changed since the days of her youth. Her salon has retained its character, and her intimate friends are still chosen among the ranks of *le monde où on s'amuse* rather than among the old Russian aristocracy, which has never taken kindly to her. After having lived with her husband upon terms of an amicable friendship and companionship, she has developed into an inconsolable widow, and has eagerly continued the work that Vladimir had undertaken in his lifetime. By her own wish she has been appointed by the Emperor to the Presidency of the Academy of Fine Arts, and she interests herself in the artistic movements and progress of the country. She still spends part of the year in Paris, made much of among the Faubourg St. Germain, and not disdaining to frequent Society in financial and foreign circles, especially the American set that has made its home on the banks of the Seine. A little over a decade ago, when she entered the Greek Church, she had always assumed the rôle of champion of the Protestant faith in Russia. This is but one instance of her erratic nature, and in directions other than her sympathies and tastes it is displayed. She is the only Grand Duchess of the old school left, and she certainly knows how to maintain, when it is necessary, the dignity of her position, and is really *grande dame* in her manner and her way of receiving those admitted into her presence. Because of this she has won for herself a certain position in St. Petersburg, and if she is not universally liked she is still considered, and her judgments taken into account.

Besides the Grand Duke Cyril, she has one daughter, the Grand Duchess Hélène, married to Prince Nicholas of Greece, who only visits Russia occasionally, and two other sons. The youngest, the Grand Duke Andrew, is unfortunately very delicate and suspected of the possession of weak lungs, which oblige him to winter in Switzerland. The second son, the Grand Duke Boris, has given cause for a good deal to be said about him. At one time it is said that his conduct was the cause of such scandal that one wondered the Emperor did nothing to put an end to it.

Of the two sisters of the Emperor the elder one, the Grand Duchess Xenia, married her cousin, the Grand Duke Alexander Michaelovitch. They had a very numerous family, and after the accession of the present Emperor enjoyed great influence. The Grand Duke, clever, like all his mother's children, but of an intriguing disposition, managed to acquire a considerable amount of the confidence of his brother-in-law, Nicholas II.

Unfortunately, he did not know how to use it, and succumbed to intrigues directed against his person. These found food in the disorder in which everything belonging to the Navy, in which he served, was discovered to be during the Japanese War. The Grand Duke took offence at certain remarks directed against him, and, under the pretext that the bad state of his health obliged him to winter abroad, he left Russia with his family and settled in Biarritz, where he has almost continually resided since. There he became acquainted with a certain set, in which the American element predominated, and report says that both the Grand Duke and his wife live in circumstances unfettered by the exigencies of etiquette, which, although giving rise to no open scandal, nevertheless afford much food for gossip. Neither one nor the other, it is said, takes any trouble to hide his or her likes or dislikes, and they live more the life of a fashionable couple than that of members of an Imperial House.

The younger sister of the Emperor, the Grand Duchess Olga Alexandrovna, is the most popular member of his family. She is not pretty by any means, but pleasant, clever, amiable, good-natured, and very much in love with gaiety in any shape or form. She was married when quite young to Prince Peter of Oldenburg, a distant cousin. This was partly by the wish of the Dowager Empress, who wanted to keep her daughter in Russia, and partly was influenced by her long-standing friendship for the Princess Eugénie, the mother of Prince Peter.

The marriage was not viewed with favour by the public. It was known that the Prince was suffering from a chronic disease which left little hope of ever being cured. It was also felt that the Grand Duchess, without taking into account her own tastes or desires, was being sacrificed to considerations of fortune and position which were bound to bring her future unhappiness. Accordingly she was very generally pitied. But Olga Alexandrovna is one of those natures that look out for the best in every situation, no matter how trying it may be, and very soon she succeeded in arranging for herself a pleasant existence in which her husband had the rôle of a good friend and nothing else. She is the only member of the Imperial Family who lives entirely the life of a simple mortal, going out walking alone, paying visits to her friends, and never troubling about the exigencies of Court etiquette. Being extremely pleasant, she has won for herself a popularity which extends to all classes, and her merry laugh brings joy wherever it is heard. Artistic in her tastes, she paints most remarkably, and interests herself in all subjects in which art is concerned. Lately, however, an ugly scandal in connection with her has arisen; it has been whispered that, having fallen in love with an officer she used to meet at her sister's house, she wanted to divorce Prince Peter. It was also said that the Emperor, incensed at the very thought, had absolutely refused his consent to such a step, and that consequently Olga Alexandrovna fell into disgrace both with her mother and her brother. True or not, the facts were current gossip in St. Petersburg lately. They did not, however, detract from the popularity enjoyed by the young Grand Duchess.

The Grand Duke Constantine, cousin of the Tsar, lives a very quiet life, together with his wife and their numerous children. He is generally esteemed for his high moral character, and during his whole life has carefully abstained from taking any part in or even expressing an opinion on, politics or any subject concerning them. His eldest son is married to the Princess Helena of Servia, and his daughter has wedded a simple gentleman, Prince Bagration Moukhransky, the scion of a noble Caucasian family, without fortune and of no position whatever. The marriage, which was a pure love affair, is the first example of a member of the Imperial Family allying herself to one outside the Imperial circle, and when it took place it excited a good deal of comment.

The sons of the late Grand Duke Michael Nicolaievitch, also, do not impose themselves on the notice of the public. The eldest, the Grand Duke Nicholas, is an exceedingly clever man, who has written several valuable historical books. Though having in his young days afforded food for ill-natured gossip, with increasing age he has settled down into a serious personage, who occupies himself in studying the rich collection of documents which abound among the many possessions of our Imperial Family. His second brother, the Grand Duke Michael, lives chiefly abroad since his marriage with the Countess Torby, and another one, George, is the husband of Princess Marie of Greece, a pleasant little person, whose numerous frailties of conduct are rather the subject of amusement than of criticism.

I have left for the last the most important of our Grand Dukes, Nicholas Nicholaievitch. He is the only member of our reigning House who can boast of being in possession of the absolute confidence of the Sovereign. He believes that his destiny is to uphold the principle of autocracy.

When still quite young, he had been in love with a charming woman, Madame Bourenine; but later he married Princess Stanza, one of the daughters of the then Prince of Montenegro. Princess Stanza was formerly the wife of the

Duke of Leuchtenberg, but the union turned out to be a most unhappy one. Accordingly, by the influence of the Empress, it is said, a divorce was arranged between the Leuchtenberg couple, and Nicholas Nicholaievitch, who was very ambitious, saw the possibility, through marriage with Princess Stanza, the favourite of the Empress, of becoming the chief adviser of the Tsar. He became the husband of the Empress's favourite, and very soon afterwards a prominent personage among the counsellers and the intimate friends of Nicholas II. He is much given to the study of spiritualism and occultism, and is credited with first interesting the Emperor and Empress in these directions. He is commander-in-chief of the garrison of St. Petersburg, and in case of another Revolution he it is who would have the task of quieting it, or rather of crushing it. Popular belief inclines to the conclusion that, failing to learn from the lessons of history, he cannot take into consideration the change that the course of time brings into the life of nations as well as of individuals. He does not realise, therefore, that even autocracy must undergo some kind of transformation and suit itself to modern ideas and modern times. The general feeling is that, put face to face with a serious political complication, he would not be able to meet it otherwise than with the help of an executioner ready to strike all those who would not submit, or who even desired to discuss with him the best means to solve the problem. He has worn uniform all his life, and believes in the sword that can strike. Unfortunately, blows are no argument.

It is to the Grand Duke Nicholas Nicholaievitch that probably the destinies of the Empire will be entrusted by Nicholas II. in case his son should survive him whilst still a minor.

The manifesto which deprived the Grand Duke Michael of the regency did not provide for his eventual successor. The prevalent opinion is that there is expectation that this important office will devolve upon Nicholas Nicholaievitch; but manifestoes are often written for nothing. The health of the little Tsarevitch is such that it seems more than doubtful that he will ever reach manhood. He has no brother. The succession to the Throne is one of those shadows that darken the horizon of Russia. It is sure to be disputed should Nicholas II. die without a male heir.

CHAPTER V

THE ZEMSTVO OF TVER INCIDENT AND WHAT CAME OF IT

Six weeks after the death of Alexander III. the question of his successor receiving congratulations from the public bodies of the Empire on the occasion of his marriage began to be mooted.

The Minister of the Interior, at that time M. Dournovo, a man of large proportions and stature, but not of widened vision, suggested to the different deputations which were to be allowed to appear before the Sovereign, that their congratulatory addresses should be accompanied by presents and offerings. This suggestion was not kindly received by the public, and gave rise to much grumbling. However, this feeling quickly subsided, and the interest of the coming occasion dominated the public mind.

The Tsar had been credited, really no one knew why, with being inclined towards introducing more liberty in the self-government of the country, as represented by the zemstvos, or county councils, in the various Governments. These county councils, about which I have already spoken when mentioning the reforms of Alexander II., had always represented the Liberal elements in Russia, and strove hard to be allowed more independence than the Government cared to grant.

During the Nihilist troubles the zemstvos, though they had never definitely inclined towards any sympathy with that movement, yet still had attempted to make themselves heard in support of changes in the interior administration of the country.

When, however, a new reign began some members of these local councils thought that the time had at last arrived when something might be said, if not done, in this direction.

The news that the young Tsar had consented to receive these deputations was hailed with delight, although, as is usual upon such occasions, people were found to laugh at the presents which were expected to be given. I remember that a very witty man, now dead, whose *bons mots* used to enliven St. Petersburg Society, declared that the following inscriptions ought to be written upon the golden dishes presented by the various classes of Society represented by these deputations. He suggested for that of the peasants, "Give us this day our daily bread"; for that of the nobility, about the poorest class in Russia, "Forgive us our debts towards thee"; for that of the merchants, "Lead us not into temptation"; and for that of the different State functionaries and employés, "And deliver us from Dournovo," Dournovo being the Minister of the Interior through whose initiative, as I have said, all these presents had been subscribed for. The joke went round the town, and was the cause of much fun.

The first deputation which the Emperor received was one composed of the Marshals of the nobility of the various Governments. The business proceeded smoothly, but with an air of expectancy, for all were looking forward to what the Emperor would say when the zemstvos should be allowed to present their homage to him and to his Consort.

The situation will be better understood when it is mentioned that the Government of Tver had always been remarkable for its advanced ideas, and a few over-clever individuals among its local administrators thought that the moment had come to assert themselves. Consequently, when the address to the Emperor came to be dealt with at a special meeting of this zemstvo, it was drafted in a very bold, though perfectly respectful way, and expressed the hope that under the new Sovereign the zemstvos would be allowed to resume the rôle they had been allotted when they were first created by the Emperor Alexander II.: that of helping the Sovereign to govern the country well and in accordance with the principles that had made it great— until the day should come when it would be ripe enough for a system of government to be introduced in which the executive power would no longer be confined to the hands of a few. The actual text of the address may be quoted here. It is not a document of remarkable interest save to show the mildness with which, after all, the aspirations were expressed, which makes the outburst it evoked the more surprising:

"May it please Your Imperial Majesty,—In these memorable days, which see the beginning of your services in the cause of the welfare of the Russian Nation, the zemstvo of the Government of Tver greets you with feelings of fervent loyalty. We share your sorrow, Gracious Sovereign, and we hope that you will find some consolation in this sad hour, when an unexpected misfortune has befallen you, as well as the whole of Russia, in the love of your people as well as in the hopes and trust that the nation has put in you; and that you will also find in those feelings a firm support in the fulfilment of the difficult task that has been imposed upon you by Divine Providence.

"The Russian nation has listened with gratitude to the solemn expressions uttered by Your Imperial Majesty upon your accession to the Throne of All the Russias. We have also shared these feelings of gratitude, together with the rest of the nation, and we send fervent prayers to the Almighty for the success of the important task that lies before you, and for the fulfilment of the high aims you have put before you, namely, the happiness and welfare of all your faithful subjects. We allow ourselves to indulge in the hope that on the height of the Throne the voice of the nation and the expressions of its desires will be heard and listened to. We are firmly convinced that the welfare of Russia will improve and fortify itself under your rule, and that the law will henceforward be respected and obeyed, not only by the nation alone, but also by the representatives of the authority that rules it; because the law, which in Russia represents the wishes of the Monarch, must stand above the personal opinions and views of those representatives.

"We earnestly believe that during your reign the rights of individuals, as well as those of already existing representative bodies, will be protected permanently and energetically.

"*We expect, Gracious Sovereign, that these representative bodies will be allowed to voice their opinions in matters in which they are concerned*, in order that the expressions of the needs and thoughts, not only of the representatives of the administration, but also of the whole Russian nation, might reach the Throne. We expect, Gracious Sovereign, that under your rule Russia will advance on the path of civilisation and progress, as well as on the road of a peaceful development of its resources and needs. We firmly believe that in the close union of all the elements and classes that constitute the Russian people, who all of them are devoted to the Throne as well as to their country, the power which Your Majesty wields will find new sources of strength and stronger chances of success towards the fulfilment of the high aims Your Imperial Majesty has in view."

As a whole, the address breathed submissive loyalty and patriotism, but the bold passage which has been printed in italics constituted a precedent which might well excite remark, if not suspicion. Equally, on the other hand, had the words not been seized upon as an act of insubordination by a narrow-minded Minister, no one might have noticed or spoken about them except in Tver itself. A far-seeing adviser would never have spoken of the incident to the Emperor. Instead, it was transformed into a question of State. The unfortunate writer of the address was dismissed with ignominy from the public service, and an official reproof was administered to the Governor of Tver, a most upright person, who could not possibly have prevented the address being adopted, as he had nothing whatever to do with the deliberations of the zemstvo, which were conducted quite independently of the Governor, who seldom heard about the resolutions adopted until after they had become accomplished facts. The Tver deputation were refused permission to enter the Winter Palace, and it was stated that the Minister of the Interior had expressed his intention to submit to His Majesty a series of measures which in his opinion ought to be adopted in order to nip in the bud any attempt at self-government on the part of the zemstvos.

Meanwhile January 30th had been fixed for the reception of the various deputations, and on that day they were ushered into the Throne Room of the Winter Palace. Very soon the Emperor entered it, accompanied by his young wife. The latter was dressed in the deepest mourning, which at once created an unfortunate impression among the assembly, since it is not the custom in Russia to wear black when receiving congratulations upon a marriage, white being the universal colour worn on such occasions. Both took their places in front of the Throne, and the deputations were introduced one after the other, each loaded with splendid presents consisting of plate and other precious things. When the reception was over, the Emperor, who, during the whole time it lasted, had kept twisting a bit of paper that had been lying at the bottom of his cap, turned towards the assemblage, and said the following words:

"I am glad to see here the representatives of all the different classes of the country, arrived to express to me their submissive and loyal feelings. I believe in those feelings, which are inherent in every Russian heart. But it has come to my knowledge that during the last months there have been heard in some assemblies of the zemstvos the voices of those who have indulged in the *senseless dreams that the zemstvos could be called to participate in the government of the country*. I want everyone to know that I will concentrate all my strength to maintain, for the good of the whole nation, the principle of absolute autocracy, as firmly and as strongly as did my lamented father."

Onlookers have told how that, in saying these words, Nicholas II. was extremely pale and agitated, and though he began reading in a low voice, gradually it rose to an actual scream. "He howled them at us," said one witness, "and in uttering the last words he made with his hand a gesture as if uttering a threat."

The consternation caused by these words was too intense to be described. Though nearly twenty years have passed since that day those who were present on so memorable an occasion still speak of it with emotion. These words reverberated throughout Russia, thus rudely dispelling many hopes. Loyal Russians felt not only aggrieved, but ashamed that such a reproof should have been administered to them before foreigners, such as Poles and Germans, of whom there were many in the various deputations. It was felt, moreover, that none among those who had gathered in that hall of State to offer their wishes of future happiness and welfare to their Sovereign and to his young bride deserved to have such an epithet hurled at their heads; for the expression to which "senseless dreams" had been applied had only been legitimate wishes, devoid of the slightest revolutionary character. Many felt, too, that the tone adopted by the Emperor was derogatory to the memory of the Emperor Alexander II., who not only had created the zemstvos in Russia, but had considered them as his essential collaborators in the task of working for the welfare and development of the country. However, it was said that Nicholas himself was satisfied. Two days later he asked an official what the public had said and thought about his speech, to which the diplomatic reply was given, "People generally think it was a notable feat." "It is just what I wanted," replied the Tsar; "I have only expressed what are my own personal ideas."

What result these ideas were to have later on, the history of Russia during the last eighteen years has shown only too plainly.

It was not to be expected that the gauntlet thus thrown down would not be taken up. The extreme Nihilist party, who had kept quiet during the reign of Alexander III., and had seen that it could not attempt to overthrow the Government which he gripped with such firm hands, now saw its opportunity, and used it.

A week after the admonition of Nicholas II. to his people an open letter to him was published by the executive committee of Geneva, the chiefs of which returned to Russia in order to disseminate it everywhere. The police managed to seize and confiscate about thirty thousand copies, but nevertheless a few reached their destination, and it is certain that the Emperor found one of them upon his writing-table. It was impossible to find out who had put it there, and it showed that even in the shadow of the Throne the Anarchists had servants in readiness to fulfil their orders.

Here is the text of this remarkable document, never before disclosed outside Russia:—

"You have spoken, and your words are at present known everywhere in Russia; aye, in the whole of the civilised world. Until now you were unknown, but since yesterday you have become a definite factor in the situation of your country, about whom there is no room left for senseless dreams. We do not know whether you understand or realise the position which you have yourself created with your 'firm words,' but we believe that people whose position is not so high as yours, or so remote from the realities of life and on that account are able to see what is going on in Russia just now, will easily understand what is your position and what is theirs.

"First of all, you are badly informed about these tendencies against which you decided to raise your voice in your speech. There has not been heard in one single assembly of any zemstvo one single word against that autocracy which is so dear to your heart; nor has one member of a zemstvo ever put the question on the basis upon which you have placed it. The most advanced thinkers among them have only insisted upon—or, rather, humbly begged—that a closer union might be inaugurated between the Monarch and his people; for the permission for the zemstvos to have free access to the Throne without anyone standing between it and them; for the right of public debate, and for the assurance that the law should always be observed and stand above the caprices of the Administration.

"In one word, the only thing that was in question was the desire to see fall and crumble to the ground that wall of bureaucracy and courtierdom that has always parted the Sovereign from the Russian nation.

"This was the desire of these people whom you, who have only just stepped upon the Throne, inexperienced and ignorant of the national needs, have seen fit to call 'senseless dreams.'

"It is clear to all the intelligent elements of the Russian people who has advised you to take this imprudent step. You are being deceived; you are being frightened by this very gang of bureaucrats and courtiers to whose actual autocracy not one single Russian man or woman has ever been reconciled. You, too, have reproached the zemstvos for the feeble cry that has escaped their lips against the tyranny of the bureaucracy and of the police.

"You have allowed yourself to be carried so far in your ideas of protecting that autocracy—your own—against which no one thought of rising, that you have considered as a danger thereto the participation of the zemstvos in the government of the country as well as of local needs.

"Such a point of view does not correspond even to that position in which the zemstvos have found themselves confirmed by your father's wishes; a position in which they appear as an indispensable organ, and participate in the internal government of the country.

"But your unfortunate expressions are not only a mistake in the way in which you have worded them, but appear as the definition of a whole system of government; and Russian society will understand quite well that on the 17-30th January it was not at all that ideal autocracy of which you believe yourself to be the representative that spoke through your mouth, but that omnipotent and jealous guardian of its privileges, *bureaucracy*.

"This bureaucracy, which begins with the committee of Ministers and ends with the meanest policeman, is odious to all those who desire the extension of real autocracy, even the one that is maintained by the present order of things. This it is that keeps the Monarch removed from free communion with the representatives of the nation. And your speech has proved once more that every desire on the part of the nation to be other than slaves kissing the ground before the Throne and bring to its notice the needs of the country—the most urgent needs—in a submissive form, is only met with a brutal rebuff.

"Many fundamental questions concerning the welfare of the nation have yet to be placed upon a satisfactory basis. Questions of moment have arisen since the great epoch of reforms initiated by your grandfather, and these lately have come to the front more acutely owing to the great famine which has weakened the country.

"Russian public opinion has been, and is, working hard, and with painstaking efforts, towards the solution of these; and it is just at such a time that, instead of words of comfort promising a real and beneficial union between the Tsar and his people, and of an acknowledgment from the heights of the Throne that for the future public discussion and a strong upholding of the law will mark the beginning of a new era in the public life of the country—the representatives of the different classes of society, gathered before you from all the corners of Russia, and expecting from you help and consolation, only heard from you a new expression of your attachment to the old system of a worn-out autocracy, and carried away the impression of the total separation of the Tsar from his people.

"Do believe, that even for the mildest of men, such a declaration, ill-timed as it was, could only produce a crushing feeling of betrayal. The 17th January has done away with that halo with which so many Russians had crowned your young, inexperienced head. You have laid your own hand on your popularity, and have destroyed it.

"Unfortunately, the question does not touch your popularity alone. If in words and with deeds autocracy identifies itself with the all-powerful bureaucracy; if its existence is only possible when every expression of the public need is crushed, and it can live only when surrounded by an extra guard of police, then indeed it has outlived its time and lost the game. It has dug its own grave with its own hands, and sooner or later, but at all events at a none too distant period, it will fall under the weight of the real and vital forces of the nation. You have yourself by your own words and conduct put before society one clear question, which in itself alone is a terrible threat to the system of autocracy. You challenged not only the zemstvos but also the whole of Russian society to a mortal duel, and they have now nothing left them except to choose deliberately between a forward movement in the cause of civilisation or a blind obedience to autocracy. Truly, you have strengthened by your speech the detective-like proclivities of those who see the only possibility of serving their Sovereign in the crushing of every expression of public feeling and in disregard of the law. You have appealed to the enthusiasm of those who are ready to give their services to every kind of master, and who do not give one single thought to the public welfare, finding that tyranny serves their own narrow-minded views. But you have turned against you all those who want to lead the country forward in the road of progress and civilisation.

"And what will become of all those who are unable to reconcile themselves with the concessions required from them, and with a long and mostly hopeless struggle with the present order of things? After your sharp reply to the most humble and lawful demands that have been addressed to you, by what and through what means will Russian society be able to keep in quiet submission to your will those of its members who wish to proceed, further and further, on that road which leads to the amelioration of the nation's fate? Yet this is the impression created for Russian public opinion and the Russian people by your first words to it, and your first reply as a Sovereign to the humble demands of its representatives.

"Without mentioning the feelings of discouragement and helplessness of which you will very soon be convinced, your speech offended and revolted some who, however, will soon recover from their present depression, and will begin a peaceful, quiet, but none the less determined struggle to obtain the liberties which they require.

"Likewise it has strengthened in others the determination to fight to the bitter end against a hateful order of things, and to fight it with all means they may have at their disposal and in their power. You have been the first to begin the struggle, and it will not be long before you find yourself entangled by it.

"St. Petersburg, January 19th, 1895."

This letter, which sounded the first warning note of the Revolution that was to break out ten years later, is so remarkable that I thought it as well to transcribe it fully, as it explains in part the events which followed.

CHAPTER VI

THE ENTOURAGE OF THE EMPEROR AND EMPRESS

THE painful circumstances under which the nuptials of Nicholas II. and Alexandra Feodorovna were celebrated prevented them from gathering St. Petersburg Society around them, and getting to know it well enough to be able to select their friends therefrom. The deep mourning for the late Emperor obliged his successor to remain in retirement for a whole year, and that retirement was the more complete because the newly wedded Imperial couple had taken up their first abode with the Dowager Empress in the Anitchkov Palace. Consequently they were deprived of a home of their own.

It is true that in the course of the February following upon her marriage the Court was presented to the young Empress at one solemn reception. But this did not efface the feeling of being a stranger among those with whom she lived, and it weighed heavily upon Alexandra Feodorovna's mind. She felt lost, and of course was more susceptible than she would otherwise have been to the impressions that were given to her by the few people she was allowed to see.

The Empress Dowager was wrapped up in her grief, and had hardly emerged from it when her relations with her daughter-in-law became strained. Her sister, the Grand Duchess Elizabeth, lived in Moscow, and with the other Grand Duchesses the bride had nothing in common. Consequently she was left almost entirely to herself in an atmosphere which was not congenial to her tastes. She was thus thrown upon her immediate surroundings, and became more or less intimate with her Mistress of the Robes, the Princess Mary Galitzine.

This lady has played an important part in the life of the Empress.

The Princess Galitzine, who came from a family belonging to the merchant class, was a remarkable woman. She had been married when a girl of sixteen to Prince Galitzine, who was about thirty years older than herself, but rich, in a high position, and boasting of the title of Serene Highness, which so very few families possess in Russia. He was a man of an easy temperament, content with everything, and living a life of his own, in which his wife had little or even no part at all. She was not pretty, but clever, ambitious, charming when she liked to show herself so, and wonderfully attractive to men. She knew it, and did not repulse the homage offered to her. Her pursuit of pleasure was so zealous that had it not been for her husband and the influence of his family, it was freely stated she would not have been forgiven so easily her irregularities of conduct. She was ambitious, intriguing, and unsparing in her criticisms. At the same time she was a faithful friend to all who looked to her for protection and who worshipped at her shrine.

When the question of appointing the Household of the new Empress came to be discussed, people wondered who was to become Mistress of the Robes. Rumour said that it would be Madame Elizabeth Narischkine, a person of great tact, kind, generous, amiable, with no remarkable intelligence perhaps, but possessing a perfect knowledge of the world and polite in the extreme. Princess Kourakine, her mother, had been Mistress of the Robes to the Empress Marie Feodorovna when she first arrived in Russia. Madame Narischkine had been reared in the atmosphere of a Court, and also had been lady-in-waiting to the Grand Duchess Olga Feodorovna. She would have been an excellent guide for the young Empress, at the head of whose Household she is to-day, and certainly if she had been chosen from the first to occupy that position a good many of the blunders innocently committed by Alexandra Feodorovna would have been avoided.

But the Emperor determined to give the post to a lady of independent means rather than to one in the Court entourage. The name of the Princess Galitzine was put forward by one of her former admirers, wanting thus to acquit himself for past kindnesses, and Nicholas II. appointed her, being impressed by her great name and position, by the reputation for independence which she had contrived to win for herself, and a certain brusquerie in her manners and speech when she expressed her opinions.

The Princess had been a widow for some years when she was appointed Mistress of the Robes. This gave her the opportunity to obtain an apartment in the Winter Palace, and thus to be constantly at the beck and call of her Imperial mistress. She began by saying that she did not care for the brilliant position which was offered her, and that she had only accepted it because she thought it her duty not to refuse the benefit of her experience to the young wife of her Sovereign. In reality, she was delighted beyond words.

She also wanted power and money, and she got both. Her finances—which had been rather entangled when she appeared at Court—she soon set straight; not by means of the Imperial gifts showered upon her, but through the knowledge which she acquired and which she used with great intelligence and *savoir faire*. As for power, she managed to establish herself so firmly in the good graces of her Sovereign, that not only was she listened to and consulted in everything, but also she was given the highest title that can be awarded to a woman at the Russian Court, that of Head Mistress of the Robes. This title, *bien entendu*, Alexander III. had refused to confer even upon Princess Hélène Kotchoubey, because he did not care to establish a precedent in a function that can only be compared with that of *surintendante* at the Court of the French kings, the inconveniences of which were pointed out when it was granted to the Princesse de Lamballe, by the ill-fated Marie Antoinette.

The Princess Galitzine had never liked the Dowager Empress, whom she had always mercilessly criticised whenever an opportunity had occurred. She was most anxious for Alexandra Feodorovna not to fall under the influence of her mother-in-law, whose natural amiability of character would have always been exercised in favour of graciousness being shown to everybody, even the people one did not like.

Marie Michailovna, as the Mistress of the Robes was familiarly called, had but a limited knowledge of etiquette such as it was formerly in existence at the Russian Court. This led her into many blunders, for which the Empress was made responsible.

The nuances, the tact, that exquisite knowledge of the world which had distinguished Princess Kotchoubey, who was a great lady, recognised as such everywhere, were dead letters to her successor.

The dignity, the ease without familiarity, which distinguished the Russian Court disappeared, and Princess Galitzine introduced stiffness where formerly magnificence reigned. She acted as if it was beneath her to show kindness to those persons with whom she came into contact, and did what she could to accentuate the cold way in which Society was held at a distance by the Empress.

Her receptions were amusing to follow and to watch. Whenever someone unknown to her presented himself or herself, although arriving from some distant province of the Empire, the Princess Mary literally crushed them with the few dry remarks and the way in which she caused them to feel that they ought never to have come.

She hardly said "Good morning" to these personages, and never said "Good-bye"; she treated them as if they had no right to exist, and yet very often these same persons were of considerable importance in their own districts. Thus, when they returned home they naturally related that they had not even been accorded a polite welcome in the capital, whither they had travelled to pay their respects to their Sovereign.

The Princess Galitzine also wielded considerable influence in political affairs, although she never understood much about them. Nevertheless, several people were appointed to high positions by her efforts. For instance, of General Kouropatkine, who, it is said, was her special protégé, she sang the praises so long and so often to Nicholas II. that the Emperor superseded General Vannovski—who for a number of years had been at the head of the War Office, and who was an outspoken man, and decided that he could not do better than appoint General Kouropatkine to that responsible position.

She also interested herself in foreign politics. Once she had a serious altercation with Count Muravieff, just before the latter's death, concerning a dispatch which he wanted to send to London about his negotiations with Japan on the Korean question. Count Muravieff, however, though the most courteous of men, was not one to yield in important questions, and refused to satisfy the Princess Galitzine.

When the war with its disasters had come to an end, and was followed by the Revolution as an aftermath, the Princess Galitzine became even more energetic than formerly. She was a warm partisan of M. Stolypin, who owed much to her influence. They were of sympathetic temperaments, perhaps because they both had the reputation of being able to do everything that they wanted. Certainly Marie Michailovna never missed a single opportunity. She was the partisan of the rigorous system being introduced, but nevertheless welcomed the Duma when it was decided to call one together. Gossip said that she was the echo of the wishes of Nicholas II., simply because very often she had inspired those wishes.

Students of contemporary history hold the opinion that she discredited the Throne, and that she raised against her Sovereigns such a storm of hatred that it is difficult to foresee when and where it will end. She managed to make them unpopular even in the many good deeds they did, and she inculcated in the young Empress a feeling of suspicion against her people which is to be feared nothing will ever drive from her mind. The Princess Galitzine died some two or three years ago.

Madame Narischkine is a charming woman, gracious, dignified, amiable, polite, and a great philanthropist, giving up all her spare time in the cause of charity, and especially concentrating her activity upon the work of attending to the physical and moral wants of the inmates of prisons. No one knows the good she has done in that direction, and she is so busy that even if her nature was not foreign to any kind of intrigue she could not find the time, as every moment is employed in one way or another. She is a *grande dame* in manners and appearance, though quite small, and by no means good looking. But she is the right person in the right place—or, at least, she would be if the influence of her predecessor had not destroyed beforehand any effort she might feel inclined to make in order to introduce some changes in the conduct of a Court which now exists but in name, for the Empress has so entirely retired from the world that it has ceased to be considered of any importance by Society. The great mistake of allowing Court life to decline was clearly understood by the great Marie Thérèse, who, when she wrote to her daughter, Marie Antoinette, said: "I am glad to hear that you are going to take up again all the official receptions of Versailles. I know how empty and dull that kind of thing is, but, believe me, if it is not observed, the inconveniences that result from its neglect are far more important than the small annoyance that it causes."

Beyond her Mistress of the Robes, the Empress Alexandra has four ladies-in-waiting in constant attendance upon her, who live in the Palace. Her daughters have a governess who also wears the Imperial cipher in diamonds on a blue ribbon, which distinguishes the maids of honour from other ladies in Society; and then there is a German lady, a Mademoiselle Schneider, who came with the Empress to Russia from Darmstadt, and who is supposed to read to her aloud. The Empress has also a secretary who attends to her business and her official letters; but outside this limited number of persons her only other friends are Madame Vyroubiev (who stays with her day and night, and who is in possession of all her confidence), and a monk called Gregor Raspoutine, upon whose counsels she places dependence but about whom rumour has been exceedingly busy.

After the *Grande maîtresse*, or Mistress of the Robes, the greatest functionary of the Imperial Court is the Minister of the Household. This post has always been occupied by an intimate and personal friend of the Sovereign, as for instance, Count Adlerberg under Alexander II., and Count Worontzoff Dachkoff under his successor. The present holder, General Baron Freedericksz, is *the* type *par excellence* of a perfect courtier, and a gentleman in the fullest acceptation of the word.

The Baron, who began his career in the First Horse Guard regiment, is a personage very much liked, perhaps because he has always been found to be inoffensive. He has an imposing presence, and his long, drooping moustache gives him the appearance of one of those musketeers whom Dumas has immortalised in the stories of d'Artagnan. But there ends the resemblance. He has little energy, and is without independence save that derived from an enormous fortune. He would seldom oppose, still less tell a displeasing truth to, his Sovereign. He has fine manners, tact, knowledge of the world, and all the advantages of a handsome physique, clothed in a brilliant uniform. He has no desire to play a political rôle, being one of these happy-go-lucky fellows who thinks the world a nice place to live in, and has no desire to see farther than that pleasant fact.

The Master of the Imperial Household is Count Benckendorff, whom I have already had occasion to mention. He is a gentleman who has always done the right thing, even when it was not palatable to him. His brother is

Ambassador in London, where he is likely to remain for some time to come.

The Military Secretary of the Emperor is General Prince Orloff, the son of the former Ambassador in Paris and Berlin. He owes his position to his name and fortune, but it is rumoured he is liked neither by the Sovereign nor by his Consort. The Princess Orloff, his wife, by birth a Princess Belosselsky and the granddaughter of the Princess Hélène Kotchoubey, is certainly the smartest woman in St. Petersburg. She is rather spare in figure; nevertheless she looks supremely elegant when she enters a room, and the charm of her appearance is such that looking at her one entirely forgets to talk to her, which perhaps is just as well.

The Emperor has three aides-de-camp with whom he is on exceedingly familiar terms. This friendship dates from the time when, as Heir to the Throne, he was performing his military duties in the Preobrajensky Regiment of the Guards. These are M. Narischkine, the son of Madame Elizabeth Narischkine, Colonel Swetchine, and Colonel Drenteln. Nicholas II. treats them not only with kindness, but also allows them an intimacy which he does not permit to others, however exalted. In their company he often attends dinners at the messes of the different regiments of the Guards, remaining with them until the small hours of the morning, and forgetting for a few brief moments that he is a Sovereign, in the pleasure of listening to Bohemian girls singing their wild ballads, or in that of sipping slowly a glass of champagne. These dinners are almost the only recreation which Nicholas II. allows himself, and they constitute for him a distraction unspoilt by the trammels of etiquette, or the vigilance of masters of the ceremonies eager to remind the Sovereign of duties which he would fain forget.

Except the people whom I have mentioned, and the officers of the Imperial yacht, who are also more or less admitted into the intimacy of the Imperial Family, the Emperor and the Empress have no friends, no people with whom they can talk or discuss the events of the world. The solitude in which they live is complete, their isolation from mankind entire, and in view of this disastrous fact one can only wonder that the mistakes they make are not even more serious than is the case.

CHAPTER VII

THE CORONATION OF NICHOLAS II.

ABOUT a twelvemonth after her marriage the Empress gave birth to her first child, a daughter. The disappointment of the public was intense. Then the Court came to St. Petersburg for the winter months, and a few balls were given at the Winter Palace. Somehow these entertainments lacked the enjoyment which had formerly attended them. A certain stiffness prevailed, and the young Sovereigns did not succeed in winning popularity among the best Society of the capital. Their unpopularity unfortunately was only increased, as I shall show, during the Coronation festivities which took place in the following month of May.

People who had been present at the Court festivities of Alexander III. and his Consort, and remembered the gaiety which had then prevailed, notwithstanding the political anxieties that overshadowed the period, could not help remarking upon the contrast of those past days with the solemnity and stiffness of the ceremonies that accompanied the occasion of the Coronation of Nicholas II. When he entered Moscow in state, the golden carriages, the pomp, the escort of chamberlains in gold uniforms, and soldiers in their gala attire, were the same as at the Coronation of his father. Yet there was no spontaneity in the greetings of the crowd, no enthusiasm save that which is inseparable from such an affair. Indeed, the only time that the hurrahs of the crowd seemed to come from its heart was when the carriage containing the Dowager Empress appeared, whilst a dead silence greeted her daughter-in-law. Poor Marie Feodorovna herself was crying throughout her long journey from the Petrovsky Palace, on the outskirts of Moscow, to the Kremlin; but her very tears commanded the sympathy of the public—indeed, of everybody who remembered that other day when she had been one of the two principal personages in a like pageant.

The Coronation ceremony went off very well, save that when the Emperor and Empress left the Cathedral of the Assumption to go round the other churches of the Kremlin, Nicholas II., on entering the Church of the Archangels, where the old Tsars of Moscow are buried, tottered and nearly fell under the weight of his heavy mantle, and still heavier crown. The sceptre dropped from his hand, and he had to be led aside and given water to drink in order to be revived. Superstitious people quickly saw in this faintness a presage of evil for the future. That dropping of the sceptre which he should have held with the same firmness that his father had grasped it, was interpreted as a sign of weakness, not only of a physical but also of a moral character. Thus, instead of confidence prevailing, apprehension as to the future of Russia under his rule was already a frequent subject of public conversation.

The first days that followed upon the Coronation went off very well, with nothing to mar the programme approved of beforehand.

Balls were given, entertainments went on with their usual routine, and foreign princes and princesses, who had arrived from far and near to witness the ceremony of the Coronation, were entertained and taken about to see all the various sights of Moscow. The nobility of Russia gave one big ball, at which the whole Court was present, and a gala performance at the Opera was also the occasion of a gay scene. But there was no enthusiasm, no animation, and fatigue was perhaps the most prevalent feeling during the three weeks, which heartily bored everybody, and of which everybody wished to see the end. Truly the only ball that could be called a success was the one given by the Grand Duke Sergius and his consort.

At that time the Grand Duke was Governor-General of Moscow. Personally, he had not succeeded in making himself liked by its inhabitants, who regretted still the rule of old Prince Dolgorouky; but the Grand Duchess had won for herself the affection of everybody who had come into contact with her. In St. Petersburg she had seemed dull and quiet, but when thrown upon her own resources and obliged, so to say, to play the part of Vicereine, she did it to perfection, and during these Coronation festivities she showed herself the most charming of hostesses. The Grand Duke, too, was amiable in the extreme with his guests, and at this particular ball he reminded one, by the grace of his manner, of his father, the late Tsar Alexander II., whom also he resembled, physically, more than his other brothers. I remember him well on that particular evening, when representatives from the whole world crowded in his rooms. He had a pleasant word for each one, showed himself an attentive host, and had none of that proud reserve with which he had been credited whilst living in St. Petersburg.

The first unpleasant event which marred the Coronation festivities was the death of the Archduke Charles Louis, the brother of the Emperor of Austria. A ball was to have been given at the Austrian Embassy, for which immense preparations had been made by the Ambassador, Prince Liechtenstein, who had brought over to decorate the walls of the house which he had hired for the time of the festivities all the old and precious tapestries which were preserved as heirlooms in his family. Of course this ball had to be countermanded.

Before recounting the crowning disaster, I should explain that it is usual when a Russian Emperor is crowned to give a kind of popular feast to the peasants and the poorer classes in Moscow and other parts of Russia, whence peasant deputations are generally sent to be present at the ceremony. This feast takes place on an open space called the Khodinka Field, about two miles from the town. It is attended by several hundreds of thousands of people, and constitutes a unique sight. A pavilion is erected, from which the Sovereign looks on, and kiosks are all round it for other spectators. Tables are spread on the lawns with provisions for the people to eat, and various entertainments in the shape of theatres in the open air, and things of the same kind, are provided for their amusement. Presents also, in the shape of mugs for men and handkerchiefs for the women, are distributed, together with medals in commemoration of the day. Naturally, therefore, great crowds gather on this field. Before daybreak all the roads leading to the Khodinka are crowded with men, women, and children, all eager to be the first on the spot. Generally troops are there to keep order, together with strong detachments of police and every possible care is taken to prevent any panic among such an agglomeration of people, gathered in one spot, and all desirous of seeing their Tsar. Thus it can, readily be imagined that even when political complications do not happen to inspire the fear of a bomb or of some attempt to disturb the feast, those concerned with the organisation of it would be glad when it was over.

On the June morning fixed for this popular rejoicing, crowds, as usual, tried from the early hours, and even during the night, to force an entrance to the field. Mounted policemen, who had received orders not to allow access to the lawns until the arrival of the Prefect of Police—who was to inspect all the arrangements before giving the signal for admission, tried to repulse the mass of humanity that struggled to enter. The police were insufficient to restrain this crowd, but considerable enough to create a panic by forcing back upon the crowds hastening to the festivity the multitude which had already arrived. Women began to shout and children to scream, which added to the panic. Soon a terrible confusion took place which it became impossible to dissipate, the more so that by an unforgivable piece of stupidity deep ditches had been dug in order to prevent access to the field except through the official gates, which were guarded by policemen. The crowds, who did not know of the existence of these trenches, fell into them, and soon they were filled with struggling, dead, or dying human creatures, whose screams for help filled with horror those who listened; but the cries were soon stilled by the silence of death.

This awful scene did not last long. In one short hour innumerable bodies lay upon the grass, and the authorities of Moscow gathered upon the scene of the catastrophe. It was impossible to count the victims, and all that apparently could be done was to remove them hurriedly, no matter where or by what means. The feast had to take place, notwithstanding the bloody scene that had preceded it. It had to take place by Imperial order, because Nicholas II., when asked by a special messenger sent to acquaint him with what had occurred, replied that he did not see why the feast should be countermanded, or put off, because a few people had been crushed by accident.

Nevertheless, in justice, the actual truth underlying this extraordinary speech should be told. He was not advised of the extent of the catastrophe at the moment when he was asked to make a decision. The system surrounding a Russian Sovereign had prevented those who were responsible for the misfortune from acknowledging its magnitude. They attempted to make light of it, maintained that there had merely been an accident such as seems inseparable from occasions of the kind, hoping, doubtless, that it would be possible to conceal the number of dead and wounded. After all, such was the idea, they were all of the poorer class, and they would not be missed.

Consequently the trenches that had swallowed so many human lives were hastily covered with branches and earth, so as to hide their sinister contents. Carts were called, and in these bodies were thrown hurriedly, anyhow, and sent off with their ghastly burden to the different hospitals and churchyards. People driving afterwards to the feast met these carts and were horror-struck to see arms and legs hanging out of them from beneath cloths that had been thrown over the bodies to cover them. It was these late-comers who first spread in Moscow the news of the catastrophe.

But, in spite of the hurry to take them away, the number of the victims was so considerable that it was found impossible to dispose of them all at once. The Emperor was expected at any moment, and he could not be allowed to see all these bodies scattered everywhere about. Soldiers were requisitioned, and they hastily—will such fatal stupidity be believed?—thrust the corpses under the very pavilion in which the Sovereign was to alight and from the balcony of which he was to witness the feast. Thus by a terrible blunder, of which he knew nothing, but for which he was ever after bitterly reproached, Nicholas II. actually stood for more than five hours over the dead bodies of his subjects, killed in their endeavour to welcome him.

The details of this ghastly morning's work became known during the course of the same afternoon, and a feeling of intense and deep emotion shook the whole of Society—that frivolous Court Society that was gathered together in ancient Moscow to eat, drink, and be merry, without one thought as to death that was hovering near. A ball was to take place that very night at the French Embassy, and Count de Montebello, who at that time occupied the post of Ambassador at the Russian Court, wondered whether he should countermand it or not. But, in order to make quite sure as to the course which he had to pursue, he sent a special messenger to the Head Master of the Ceremonies, Count Pahlen, and asked him what he had to do. The Count took the Emperor's orders, and Nicholas II. said again that he saw no reason why the ball should be postponed, and that he would attend it.

What a ball it was! I do not remember in the whole course of my long life, ever having been at such a lugubrious entertainment. The catastrophe of the morning was the general subject of conversation, and the most harrowing details were given concerning it. The only people who appeared unmoved were the Emperor and Empress, who both, knowing nothing of the truth, seemed quite unconcerned; so that when one of the foreign princes present ventured to condole with Nicholas II. on this untoward event, he quietly replied, "Yes, it is very sad; but such accidents happen often, whenever there is a great congregation of people."

Nicholas II., indeed, remained at the house of the Ambassador until the end of the ball, taking part in all the dances, a thing he seldom did, and appearing in an excellent temper. He did not seem—how could he?—to realise the gravity of what had taken place, nor the enormity of the hecatomb with which the solemnity of his Coronation had been made memorable.

Marie Feodorovna had not waited one moment before hurrying to the bedside of the poor creatures who had nearly paid with their lives for their desire to be present at this festivity. Whilst her son and daughter-in-law, unaware of the extent of the tragedy, were dancing and smiling on the Count de Montebello and his wife, she was consoling the wounded and attending to their wants. Once again she acted the part of an angel of mercy, and once again she brought sunshine and hope to desolate hearts and bereaved homes. The incident only served further to estrange the people from the Emperor and Empress.

The details of the disaster of Khodinka were only made public little by little. At first frantic efforts had been made to hide its magnitude, but the secret could not be kept so well that it did not reach the ears of the nation. An inquest was at last ordered. It revealed such carelessness, such utter disregard of the most elementary precautions on the part of the authorities, that it was believed at one time the Grand Duke Sergius himself would have to leave his post of Governor-General of the town of Moscow. He managed, however, to clear himself. But the head of the police of the second capital of the Empire had to retire into private life, and minor officials were punished more or less severely. After which one tried to forget the sad episode, which was never more mentioned in Court circles.

Yet the country did not forget. The shadow of blood thrown over the reign of Nicholas II. by the catastrophe of Khodinka has never ceased to darken it. It has seemed to foreshadow all the other calamities that this reign was to see, and to give it that colour of misfortune which will cling to it in history.

CHAPTER VIII

THE SPRINGTIDE OF DISCONTENT

THE consequences of the Khodinka catastrophe were more tragic even than could have been conjectured. This terrible event had its effect among the lower classes—the peasants in particular. They had been content with their lot during the last years of the former reign. The event gave ample food also for the underground work of the anarchists, who had never given up their activity. On the contrary, the party silently prepared its batteries. The Coronation deputations from the rural classes returned to their homes dissatisfied with what they had seen, and discontented with the little attention that had been paid to them. Among these deputations were people who had been present at the Coronation of Alexander III., and who remembered the words he had spoken on that occasion. They had expected something of the same kind, and their disappointment was intense. Then came that horror of Khodinka Field. It was altogether to be regretted that it had been hushed up instead of being made to serve as a pretext for a closer union of the Sovereign with his subjects. His apparent indifference and icy impassiveness in presence of this unparalleled disaster had entirely alienated the affections of his subjects, who were unaware that when the tragedy first took place he was misinformed as to its gravity. Unfortunately, his absence of active sympathy with the sufferers during the days just after the accident accentuated the feeling. Among the upper classes some further dismay was felt as it became recognised that the new monarch lacked firmness of character.

One early example of this temperamental weakness created an unpleasant impression on the public. When the Siberian Railway was quite completed the question arose in regard to the Department to which the administration of this important line should be entrusted: should it be administered by the Finance or the War Ministry?

At that time Count Witte was at the head of the Treasury, whilst General Kouropatkine was in charge of the Army. Each Minister wanted to control the railway; each had numerous eloquent arguments in support of his view; and each had the opportunity to lay these arguments before Nicholas II. The Emperor at first was quite of opinion that General Kouropatkine should have the Siberian line under his control, and accordingly granted his request. When Count Witte came to him the next day, his report proved to the perplexed Sovereign that the Ministry of Finance was the proper Department to which the administration of the railway should be confided; and so his arguments prevailed, with the consequence that the decision of the day previous was changed. But on the following morning Kouropatkine returned, and again the scales were turned in his favour until Witte, with new reasons, once more secured a decision in favour of his own Department. This sort of thing, so it is said, went on seventeen times, until at last Count Witte obtained control of the railway by threatening to resign unless the administration was entrusted to the Treasury Department.

The dissatisfaction earlier alluded to not only pervaded the lower and middle classes, but also existed in Society circles, who adversely criticised the neglect of Court life which had become a characteristic of the new reign. The semi-seclusion in which Alexandra Feodorovna lived, though it was not so complete as it became later on, still was unpleasantly felt in the gay world of the Russian capital. Gradually she was no longer missed, and her presence, when she deigned to be present at an entertainment, was felt to be more a bore than an honour. And in this absence of a Court, Society became lax in its manners and morals, being certain it would never meet with praise or blame whatever it did. Nor did the effect end here, for Society, finding no subject for gossip in the doings and sayings incidental to the Imperial entertainments, which had played such an important part in the winter season of St. Petersburg, began to turn its attention elsewhere, and unfortunately politics became the vogue.

For the first two or three years following the Coronation things went on more or less as formerly; but later the position of matters in China following upon the Boxer rebellion began to engross the attention of our Foreign Office and of certain self-styled political personalities. The Yalu affair as it developed was seized upon by the press and subjected to comment of a character neither favourable to the Government nor to the Imperial Family. Subsequently Russia's relations with Japan entered upon a new phase.

No one in Russia had believed in the Yellow Peril. One person alone had foreseen it, and had he lived it is probable that things might have taken a different direction. This was the head of our Foreign Office, Count Muravieff. Unfortunately, he died suddenly at the very moment when his talents might have found the opportunity for exercise for the benefit of his country.

Count Muravieff was a curious personality, and he certainly deserves more than a passing mention. He was the last Russian diplomat of the old school, that of Nesselrode and Gortschakov, who still believed in traditions, and who had a political system.

His career, which was very rapid at the end, dragged very slowly at first. For many years he remained in Paris, merely as an attaché, although he was the great favourite and personal friend of Prince Orloff, who took him with him when he was removed to Berlin. There he soon won for himself the good graces of Prince Bismarck, who grew to appreciate and know him well when he filled the post of chargé d'affaires during the long illness of his chief.

Later on he was the right hand of Count Paul Schouvaloff, who, though a charming and clever man, a diplomat by nature, was not one by education. Muravieff, on the contrary, was expert in all the *finesses du métier*, and his consummate tact allowed him to be of the greatest use to the Ambassador, to whose success in the German capital he contributed largely. He was a very quiet man, reserved in appearance, but immensely clever, sarcastic sometimes, and always delighted when he could achieve some kind of success of which the world in general knew nothing. He liked to be the hand in the background that pulled the strings, yet vanity was as unknown to his nature as shrewdness was one of its principal characteristics. He was a keen observer, and during the years which he spent in Berlin—which at the time, owing to the immense personality of Prince Bismarck, was the centre of the politics of the world—he had carefully studied all the intricacies of international politics, and had paid special attention to the personality of the German Chancellor.

He was ambitious, and one of his great dreams was the formation of a coalition against England, whom he considered as the traditional enemy of Russia. He hated everything English, and later on, when he came to lead Russia's foreign policy, he expressed that hatred by seeking to destroy English prestige in the Near, as well as in the Far, East, where, his clear brain guessed, lurked the danger of the future. When Count Schouvaloff left Berlin, Count Muravieff also said good-bye to the German capital. He was appointed Russian Minister at the Court of Copenhagen, a very coveted post at the time, owing to the close ties that existed between the Royal Family of Denmark and the Imperial House of Russia.

Whilst there he won for himself the good graces of Queen Louise, and also the regard of the Empress Marie Feodorovna. But he was the *bête noire* of Prince Lobanoff, who had succeeded M. de Giers as Minister for Foreign Affairs in St. Petersburg, and the Prince did all he could to put him aside and to oblige him to retire into private life.

Count Muravieff pretended not to perceive this animosity, and took all possible care to avoid friction between himself and his chief. However, he was not successful; indeed, it was said that the decree recalling him from Copenhagen was ready, and about to be presented for the signature of the Emperor, when Prince Lobanoff suddenly died and, following the advice of his mother, Nicholas II. appointed as his successor Count Muravieff.

In the responsible position which became his, the Count applied all his energy to uphold Russian prestige abroad. Though he was not favourable to the French alliance, he submitted to it, and did his best under circumstances that were not of his choosing, but which he found himself called upon to justify. He sought to cultivate good relations with Germany, and one of his favourite dreams was the formation of a Russo-German alliance directed against England. He did not live to see it realised.

Count Muravieff's wife had been a Princess Gagarine, the sister of Madame Skobeleff, the consort of the "White General." Though the last-mentioned union had not been a happy one, the relations between the Count and his brother-in-law had always remained cordially affectionate. The two had the same ambitions, and though their aims might have been different, yet they sympathised with each other and relied upon each other's judgments. It was this last circumstance that was in part the cause of the animosity which divided the Minister for Foreign Affairs and General Kouropatkine, who held the portfolio of War at that time.

General Kouropatkine had been the head of the staff of the division commanded by Skobeleff during the Turkish War of 1877-78. In that capacity he had done very well. The successes of his General had, in a certain measure, influenced his career, inasmuch as they had been attributed to the wise dispositions Kouropatkine himself had made. Kouropatkine was a brave man and a good tactician, but one of those people that, while very useful in a secondary position, are less successful in actual leadership. Guided by a first-rate intelligence, such as that of Skobeleff, Kouropatkine's best abilities came to the front, and as the executive of another person's directions he was invaluable. But he lacked not only initiative, but also the ability to accurately balance the pros and cons of any given position in which he found himself. This explains, not so much his mistakes during the conduct of the Japanese War, which perhaps were unavoidable, but the wrong appreciation he had taken of the political circumstances that led up to it, and especially of the resources of Japan.

General Kouropatkine's choice as War Minister had been partly due to the personal liking of the Emperor. Kouropatkine had a certain prestige among the Army, as indeed had all those who had served under Skobeleff. As such his choice was bound to be popular, and though it was not universally approved, yet, all things considered, it was welcomed by the public.

Kouropatkine soon discovered the hidden resentment which Nicholas II. nurtured against Japan and the Japanese nation, and he at once became a firm partisan of an aggressive policy directed against the Government of the Mikado.

Count Muravieff, shrewder than his colleague, on the contrary, discouraged these tendencies, with the result that dissensions between the two Ministers on that important subject became very sharp and did not always end to the advantage of the Count.

One day a quarrel took place in presence of Nicholas II. between the two men, and Muravieff insisted upon proper preparations being made in regard to the war which he felt would be inevitable, saying that the enemy whom it was proposed to fight was by no means so despicable as was thought. Also that, especially considering the enormous distance between the two countries, no precautions ought to be neglected. To this Kouropatkine made the obvious reply that it was evident that the Count, not having been a soldier, could not judge of the situation, since with the facilities which the completion of the Siberian Railway would put at the disposal of Russia, a victory of its troops was a foregone conclusion. He added that he was so sure of what he was saying that he would not even advise the Emperor to send the best troops so far, as those already stationed in Siberia would be more than sufficient for the work that had to be done.

Muravieff controlled himself with difficulty, and when he returned home he was almost beside himself with grief and rage. He retired to his own room, giving orders not to be disturbed, and there he was found dead a few hours later.

General Kouropatkine thereafter found himself with a free field before him.

A few years, however, dragged on before the war broke out. Count Muravieff had been replaced by Count Lamsdorff, an inoffensive man, who was the victim of a situation not of his own making. In the meanwhile, General Kouropatkine started on that journey to Japan, whence he returned with more illusions than ever; and in St. Petersburg, as well as in the rest of Russia, the dissatisfaction against the existing order of things grew and grew. Everybody felt that a change of some kind ought to take place, that a corrective should be applied to the generally prevailing uneasiness. People who thought themselves wise, statesmen who believed themselves to be infallible, all combined to bring about a catastrophe such as Russia had not known before, one that was to wound the nation in its most sensitive spot—the disdain for that yellow race which already had once been its master, and whose pride and power it believed it had crushed for ever, on that far-off day when the triumphant troops of Dmitry Donskoy had driven the Tatar hordes back to the plains of Asia.

One man alone, Count Witte, had done all that was in his power to prevent the outbreak of hostilities with Japan. That shrewd Minister knew well that in the conditions in which Russia found itself at the moment, a war, even a victorious one, would have consequences which it was difficult to foresee. He, therefore, tried to persuade General Kouropatkine to give up his warlike plans. But the latter, with the war party at his back, overruled the Count. They told the Emperor that the country's honour was at stake, and that it was impossible to go back; that, besides, the victory was as certain as anything could be certain in this world; that the Army was prepared; and that at the first sight of Russian regiments the Japanese troops would fly in disorder; that the whole campaign would be a military promenade and nothing else. And when at last Witte applied to the good sense of Nicholas II. and asked him point-blank what advantages he hoped to gain by a war which might still be avoided, and which ought to be avoided, even at some sacrifice of pride, and *amour propre*, the Emperor is credited with the reply, "Why avoid it? It is time to give some amusement to the nation" ("*Il est temps donner des distractions au pays*").

It was under that impression that the Japanese campaign began. No one believed in its danger, but a good many people who shared the conviction that it would end in victory for the Russian troops, were, nevertheless, uneasy as to the consequences of a war breaking out at a time when internal affairs were not in thorough harmony. The public mind, in short, began to feel vaguely that dark clouds were appearing on the horizon, and that a storm of unusual gravity was brewing which would bring destruction along with it.

The Emperor alone remained calm and immovable, fully assured of victory, so it was said, because the spiritualistic mediums who constituted his most intimate society had all prophesied that he would win laurels such as no Russian monarch had ever won before. His immediate surroundings were jubilant also, and sculptured busts of himself were presented in great pomp to General Kouropatkine, who had begged for permission to lead personally the army at whose head he stood to victory and fame. The chauvinist press exulted; the *Novoie Vremia* even began to anticipate the day when festivities on a hitherto unknown scale would signalise the return of the troops from the plains of Manchuria laden with spoils. Some ladies who wanted to ingratiate themselves into the Imperial favour, worked at banners and flags, destined to reward the gallant heroes who were being sent to the front with such hurrahs and such enthusiasm—enthusiasm which, nevertheless, did not go beyond the small circle of people who courted the good graces of those in power. But outside those circles the war was not popular, and the soldier sent to fight so far away from hearth and home marched without any other feeling than that of dread and apprehension as to the fate that awaited him in those distant plains whither he was ordered to go. Slowly the distant clouds which I have mentioned were getting nearer, appearing darker and darker as they approached; indeed, trouble was at hand, and, unfortunately, those who knew it was coming were powerless to avert it. The Sovereign had spoken, and he had to be obeyed, even by the people who, in the dark, were preparing the day when they should attempt to destroy both his Person and his Throne.

CHAPTER IX

THE WAR WITH JAPAN

AFTER the Coronation Nicholas II. and his Consort began the usual accession visits to foreign Courts required from them by the custom in vogue among Sovereigns in such cases. They went to Berlin, or rather to Breslau, the German capital being avoided by them for some particular reason which was not disclosed, and they preferred to meet the Emperor William and the Empress in Silesia. They also paid their respects to the old Austrian monarch; they stayed for some days with Queen Victoria at Balmoral; and last, but not least, they went to Paris, where they were received with an enthusiasm such as France had not witnessed for many a day.

Their arrival on the banks of the Seine was an official recognition of the Republic such as no Sovereign had accorded to it until that day, and which in Russia had been merely tolerated, but never treated on a footing of equality by official circles. Great preparations were made in Paris to receive the Russian Imperial pair, and certainly that visit was the occasion of a great social triumph for the Empress. She was greatly admired, as was to be expected, and her beauty appealed by its perfection to the crowds, who found in her the type of what an Empress should be—polite, though not familiar; and though, perhaps, too calm and slightly disdainful, yet condescending and kind. She produced an immense sensation at the Opera, and for the first time since the long-forgotten days of the Empire, the cry of "*Vive l'Impératrice!*" was heard again in the streets of Paris. As for Nicholas II., one could see also that he was immensely pleased at the reception accorded to him. Russia at that moment was on the eve of a great industrial development which, unfortunately, was stopped by the war with Japan, at least for a while, and money was wanted in consequence.

All the Ministers of the Tsar knew this—no one better than M. Witte—and that the best means to obtain the money needed from the French Republic was to flatter its citizens by this visit. It was a purely sordid affair.

The extraordinary enthusiasm with which he was greeted in Paris gave Nicholas II. a wrong impression as to the influence which he wielded, or thought he wielded, in the European concert, and unfortunately it made him take an unjustifiable view of the probable attitude of Europe in regard to his relations with Japan; he fully believed that when the war came he could count upon the support and deep admiration of Europe.

Unfortunately, too, French people—who in their turn were dupes in this comedy of errors, just as were the Russians—had imagined that this demonstration of friendship, coming as it did from the representative of an autocracy that had never before condescended to shake hands with the rulers of a republic, meant the realisation of their dreams of a *revanche* and a defensive alliance against Germany.

When the Emperor and Empress returned to Russia they found discontent rife. Things had gone from bad to worse.

Had the war not taken place, the renewed activity of the anarchists might have required more time to develop into something tangible, but the disasters of the Japanese campaign gave them the impulse which had been wanting for them to become effective and formidable.

The war in itself was not popular, as I have already said. And the enthusiasm with which it was begun was only on the surface—an enthusiasm engineered by the numerous class of Government officials eager to please the Sovereign. These folk fondly thought that they would impress the Japanese as to the strength of Russia by the various ovations with which generals were sent off to the seat of war. No one believed the Japanese could resist; the idea was that they were miserable little beings whose efforts at serious warfare were nothing else but ridiculous. It was in vain that people who knew better reminded the public that these little fellows for years had been training themselves in the best military schools in Europe; that they had in the space of a few short years completely remodelled their customs, their habits, their system of government, and could now compare with Europeans in the realms of education and capability. All these warnings were not only disregarded but laughed at; the possibility of a defeat never entered anyone's mind.

In Russia no one was prepared for the dangers of the war which was begun with such a light heart. The troops in

Siberia with whom General Kouropatkine believed he could win the campaign were not only totally inferior in numbers, but also insufficiently equipped and clothed. Sanitary arrangements were not thought of at all, and until the first detachments of the Red Cross Brigade arrived on the field of action the wounded were but scantily attended to. Commissariat also was in a state of complete disorganisation; and as for adequate armaments, practically none existed. As the best example of this, Port Arthur may well be mentioned. Though on paper this fortress had been entirely rebuilt during the previous five years, in reality the only work done had been the digging of a few ditches and trenches, and even these were not where they were really required.

Other abuses were rife. The commissariat, though costing enormous sums, yet failed to supply soldiers as well as officers with the most necessary things. The men had warm clothes in summer and no furs in winter. Shoes were for the most part of so abominable a quality that the infantry preferred to walk barefooted. The means of transport were such as to cause the most dreadful tortures for the victims destined to travel for weeks on a railway line badly built, and in carriages devoid of the most elementary comforts. The trucks in which the army was forwarded to Manchuria were so old that one can only wonder by what miracle they did not fall to pieces on the road. Yet, according to the reports presented by the War Office, everything possible had been done to transport the troops quickly to the field of action.

The Emperor was assured that his army was ready, and that the Japanese army was in a most weak condition, quite unprepared for a struggle of any serious kind. It has even been maintained by some that this report constitutes one of those crimes which no nation can ever forgive to its author. The then War Minister had gone to Manchuria with the avowed purpose of examining for himself what chances of success there were for an aggressive policy on the part of Russia. He was given the utmost freedom for his own ideas; he had been told to study carefully the resources of Japan, its desires, and its aims. He had been well received by the Mikado and by his Ministers, and with true Slav laziness had believed all that he had been told, and only looked at what had been shown to him. Warnings had not failed him; officers whose duties lay on that distant Manchurian frontier had reported to him the enormous preparations made by Japan, and drawn his attention to the care with which all our armaments had been studied by competent Japanese officers. Their misgivings had not been entertained by Kouropatkine, who upon his return to Russia addressed a long report to the Emperor, in which, among other things, was said:

"Japan at the present moment is reorganising its army and navy, and proceeding very slowly with this task. Japanese officers, though they have studied at our academy as well as in military schools in Germany, have not mastered the various workings of European tactics. They are still savage and untrained, and their army could not very well at present engage in any conflict with us. It is true that they are ambitious, and that the annexation of Korea is their earnest desire, but they have no means of satisfying that ambition. If we want to strike at their military or naval organisation, we could not select a more favourable moment than the present one, when everything is still in a state of chaos, and when Japan, having ceased to be an Asiatic nation, is nevertheless far from resembling a European one. As regards ourselves, we are perfectly ready, and could in the space of thirteen days have four hundred thousand men on the Japanese frontier, which is three times as many as would be needed to repulse the army of our adversary. The war would be a simple military promenade, and no necessity could even arise of moving any of our troops from the German or Austrian frontier or to diminish the garrisons in Poland."

This report is one which Russia will not soon forgive. Mistakes of tactics and strategy were not of such importance that they could not be condoned, for there were terrible difficulties to be faced, and perhaps no one could have done better than the responsible Minister. Yet not to have been able to appreciate the strength of the enemy he knew he would be called upon to fight, not to notice his preparations, not to pay attention to the warnings which he received was a fault impossible to justify to posterity or history, even though dozens of books be written in the attempt. Critics consider that a Minister of War ought to have known the condition of the army of which he was the head; and as a responsible adviser of his Sovereign he ought, before telling him things which it is difficult to credit that he believed himself, to have seriously considered whether he had the right, in order to please that Sovereign, to sacrifice the dignity of his country and the prestige of its troops. The battle of Liao Yang was certainly a terrible misfortune; the retreat that followed upon it was perhaps a disgraceful incident, but it cannot be gainsaid that the initial blunder out of which all these calamities arose was the report of General Kouropatkine.

A further calamity was that the Commander-in-Chief was not liked by the troops in his charge, his personality did not inspire them with enthusiasm. He had little moral authority over his troops, who were equally indifferent to his praise or to his blame. One caustic writer said, "He was a nonentity until the moment when he became useless."

The quick way in which Japan took the offensive at the beginning of the war is still fresh in people's minds. At first this unexpected movement with which the campaign opened, and which involved the destruction of two war vessels, struck consternation throughout the whole of Russia. Then a reaction came; the press tried to quieten people's apprehensions, and to persuade the public that this meant nothing, and that the reverse was because war not having been yet officially declared, our officers were not on their guard. So everyone tried to make the best of bad circumstances, and to hope for news of a victory, a culmination in which everybody, beginning with the Emperor, firmly believed.

Alas, victory never came; and though individual acts of courage were not rare during these sad months, yet upon the whole no success of any magnitude attended Russian arms. Several incidents in that disastrous campaign struck home to the whole country, and opened its eyes to the deplorable nature of the situation. Even St. Petersburg Society, usually so impassive, became excited, and brilliant officers of the Guards, moved to indignation at the turn things were taking, asked as a favour permission to go to the front. Such permission was grudgingly granted; people of independent opinions might then see for themselves what was happening and make public the tragedy which was taking place in those far-away Manchurian plains. Circumstances, however, grew too strong for him, and finally Kouropatkine allowed these volunteers on the field of operations, to observe the disasters which his misplaced self-confidence had brought about.

When the *Petropavlosk* went down in the Pacific with its load of human beings and the brave Admiral Makaroff, together with his staff, consternation prevailed in St. Petersburg. The Emperor called a council of war to deliberate over what ought to be done in order to redeem the lost, or at least seriously impaired, prestige of the country. Someone suggested that the best course would be to conclude peace before events became too strong for the country, since the situation might become such that would cause the Japanese to demand terms which would be quite unacceptable to Russian honour and pride; but this suggestion was very quickly overruled, and it was decided to reinforce the Manchurian army, and to send the Baltic fleet over the seas to make a naval demonstration before Japanese ports.

This last suggestion was made by the Emperor himself. It was received with consternation by those who heard it, but no one dared to contradict it. One officer alone tried to expose the dangers attending such a resolution. His arguments were eloquent, and should have been convincing, but he was not listened to. Nicholas II. declared that it was his wish the fleet should start, and added that he felt convinced it would not be called upon to fight, because the very fact of its being sent would frighten the Japanese into asking for peace. He would not take into consideration the fact, in the first place, that Russians are not naturally sailors, the dangers of the voyage, the difficulty the ships would find in coaling, and the rotten state that several of the vessels sent on this adventurous excursion were in. He would not believe that the men-of-war composing this famous fleet were old and no longer seaworthy, that their armaments were singularly out of date, and that their crews were all more or less in a condition of rebellion against the Government, whom they accused of having been the principal cause of the present disasters. He simply said: "I want the fleet to start, and it must do so as quickly as possible."

It was a sad day when this decision of the Tsar became public—sad for Russia and sad for the men sent to die. None of the officers of that ill-fated squadron believed he would return alive from this senseless expedition, and the farewells exchanged with the dear ones left at home were more than mournful. All these men knew they were about to die, and that the months left to them would be one long agony at the thought of the fate to meet which they were starting. And one bleak, rainy morning, amidst tears and sobs of bereaved wives and mothers, the Baltic fleet sailed away towards distant Tsushima. Nicholas II. had come to bid it good-bye, as if in order to hear the famous words, "*Ave, Cæsar! morituri te salutant!*"

CHAPTER X

MUKDEN AND TSUSHIMA

I WILL not speak of the opening episodes of the war, nor of the early battles which one after another, in sad succession, were lost by the Russian troops. I will not even say much about the siege of Port Arthur and the sequel, which added shameful pages to the mournful ones of its defence and surrender. There, also, irreparable mistakes were made, and stupidities crowded on the top of each other. Whilst the siege lasted, people were loud in the praise of General Stössel and his bravery, notwithstanding that it was very well known he was unequal to the mission imposed on him. It was an open secret in St. Petersburg that it was owing to the efforts of General Kondratenko, the head of his staff, that the fortress had ever held out so long against the Japanese forces. It was another open secret that the most disgraceful financial jobbery and money-making were charged against the Commander of Port Arthur, and in these accusations his wife was involved. It was generally believed that they sold the milk and other provisions to the sick and wounded at extortionate prices, and that they engaged in the most shameful bargains in regard to the stores over which the General held authority. All this was common talk and common knowledge, and yet the public was full of admiration, a commanded admiration, for General Stössel and the brave defence which he made.

Perhaps this was just as well, because it would have been of no use to attempt to blame him whilst he was in charge of a responsible post from which it was not even possible to remove him. But then, why, when all was over, when the legend that had accumulated round his head had transformed him into a hero, why deny this very legend? Or, after having covered the General with honours, allowing him even to accept foreign distinctions such as the decoration *Pour le Mérite* given to him by the German Emperor, why tear from his shoulders the epaulettes that, rightly or wrongly, had been given to him? Why enlighten the world as to the shameful story of that siege, and the way the defence of the town was conducted? Why begin that counterfeit court-martial which told Europe that instead of a hero General Stössel was a coward and a traitor?

The stupidity of such a course of action is evident even to the veriest outsider. It would have been far better to have let the legend remain undisturbed, to throw a veil of oblivion over what could not be changed or mended, and not to break the hearts of those who had done their duty, and done it well, too—the officers and soldiers composing the garrison of Port Arthur, who found themselves mixed up in this deplorable affair, and upon whose innocent shoulders was thrown the burden of having been connected with a story of sordidness, cupidity, and cowardice for which they were not responsible, but the shade of which was to darken their lives for ever.

Only to rehabilitate them in the world's sight do I reopen the sad and shameful story of their betrayal and Russia's.

There is an episode of the siege of Port Arthur which is very little known and which deserves special mention. When the news of General Kondratenko's death was brought to the Commander of Port Arthur, his first words were, "Has he left any special letters or instructions, or have any reports been found among his papers?" It seems that the day before he was so tragically killed, Kondratenko had had a heated discussion with General Stössel. The latter was upholding the necessity of a prompt surrender of the town, but the former strongly opposed the suggestion, using many arguments, amongst which the principal was that some of the forts still held could hold on for about three weeks longer, and that it would be time to talk of surrender when these had fallen or been destroyed. Stössel then said that a quantity of valuable property was locked up in these forts, and that it would be useless to allow it to be wasted. Now the property about which the Commander-in-Chief was so anxious belonged almost entirely to himself and to his wife, and had been removed for better safety to the very forts which the Chief of the Staff proposed to sacrifice before surrendering to the enemy. Kondratenko was known to possess a violent temper, and he turned upon his chief, and, calling him traitor and other words of the same character, declared that he would at once send a report to St. Petersburg concerning this incident, and denouncing Stössel as failing in his duty because of personal cupidity. A few hours later Kondratenko was killed, and, as has been told, the first words of Stössel upon hearing of it were to inquire what had become of his papers, in which he evidently feared to find a confirmation of the threats the dead man had made.

Kondratenko was excessively popular among the troops. He was known to be extremely brave, and mindful of the soldiers confided to his care. His death was deeply deplored, and it completely discouraged the garrison of the besieged town, so that when General Stössel immediately thereafter formally proposed to surrender, scarcely a voice was raised in opposition, and it was felt that the sad end of this memorable siege being inevitable, the sooner it took place the better.

One officer alone proposed to try to communicate once more with the Commander-in-Chief, and to ask for his instructions. Upon that General Stössel took from his portfolio a letter from General Kouropatkine, telling him that he left him free to do what he thought best without referring to anyone. Stössel declared that this letter was sufficient to safeguard his responsibility, and that he took it upon himself to send an envoy to General Nogi.

Later on, when the General was tried, a friend both of his and of General Kouropatkine came to see him, and begged him not to produce this letter during the trial; it was promised in return to so arrange matters that even if he were condemned an Imperial pardon would follow upon the verdict. What interest was involved in the concealment of this document—which in a certain measure would have explained General Stössel's course of action, even if it would not have justified it—has never been known to this day. Some people affirm that in writing thus General Kouropatkine had for his excuse political reasons upon which it was unnecessary to enlighten the public.

When Port Arthur had fallen it was felt that the first part of the war was over, and that unless a decisive battle turned the tables upon the Japanese their success was an accomplished fact. That battle was expected with eagerness by the whole of Russia, where existed still a vague hope that when Kouropatkine should have enough troops at his disposal he would be able to attack the enemy successfully, notwithstanding the unfavourable conditions in which he as well as his army found themselves placed. Everyone urged him to attempt a supreme effort which was to avenge all the disasters of the past. But instead, Kouropatkine, who had now lost his nerve, continued slowly to withdraw his forces, retiring no one knew why or whither.

He had a friend, General Gripenberg, who was in command of one of the three army corps that were to operate simultaneously against the enemy. That officer, however, found himself differing so entirely from the Commander-in-Chief as to the tactics which ought to be pursued, that Gripenberg asked Kouropatkine point-blank what object he had in avoiding with such manifest care a battle that would at least have the advantage of clearing the air and giving some new energy to the demoralised troops. The latter replied that he thought that by drawing the Japanese army into the interior of the country he would tire it, and thus by sapping its *moral* render it the more easily to be beaten.

It is said that Gripenberg laughed outright at this plan, and the two friends at once became bitter enemies. The Commander-in-Chief tried in vain to reason with his former comrade; he implored him not to abandon him at such a critical moment, and not to give their common foe the satisfaction of witnessing the dissensions which divided them. Gripenberg remained inflexible: "Once more," he said, "I ask you, will you or will you not change your decision and attack the Japanese?" "I cannot do so," replied Kouropatkine. "Then I cannot stay here, or obey your orders, and I shall leave for St. Petersburg, and myself report to the Emperor all that is being done here, and the incapacity of which you give new proofs every day." In this way the two generals parted.

Gripenberg, as he threatened, went to St. Petersburg. He saw the Emperor, with whom he had a long talk, and was rewarded for his journey by being appointed an aide-de-camp general to the Sovereign. It was felt that by conferring this dignity upon him Nicholas II. was blaming Kouropatkine for his inaction, but nevertheless no change of Commander-in-Chief was announced as being in contemplation.

Gossip, however, became more busy than ever concerning the events that were taking place in Manchuria, and the last hopes anybody had cherished of a victory died away. It was felt that it would be best to conclude an honourable peace before a crowning disaster completely wrecked the reputation of the Russian army and of the generals in command.

Whilst the capital was busy with comments on his course of action, General Kouropatkine at last made up his mind to attack the Japanese forces, and did so without apparently taking the least precautions to ensure the safety of the retreat of his army in case of a defeat.

What induced him to make this desperate attempt no one knows. Perhaps he felt he had to justify his former inaction; perhaps, also, he thought it better to end the suspense in which his army as well as his country existed from day to day. At all events, he did attack the Japanese army, and thus initiated one of the most disastrous military events of modern times.

Everybody knows that the Russian forces were defeated; but what is not so well known, what remains unexplained to this day, was the panic that followed upon it, as well as the details of the subsequent retreat. Panic seized the troops, who rushed blindly away from the enemy without being aware whither they hastened. Their only desire was to get away from bullets and shells; to flee from a danger which often did not exist in the vicinity from which they retreated. A disordered troop of frantic men dragged itself through these vast Manchurian plains in the depth of winter, with all the horrors of cold, wind, and snow accompanying their retreat and adding to its poignancy. In that flight no one knew friend from foe; the soldiers, badly clad, tore from the dead bodies of the Japanese their winter clothes and shoes, heedless of the danger that these borrowed garments might bring to them. To understand the significance of this it is necessary to picture the situation in the darkness of the night, when it became impossible to distinguish friends from foes, and when one killed everyone that one met on one's way for dread of being killed oneself.

Horrible scenes were enacted in that cold, frozen desert through which the Russian troops, wearied, famished, and bereft of courage as well as of strength, had to drag themselves. The few people who found a piece of bread or a warm piece of clothing were sure to have it snatched from them by ravenous, half-frozen creatures in whom despair had destroyed every feeling of humanity; mercy existed no more; every man became a wild beast. No orders were listened to; indeed, there was no one to give orders. Officers as well as men had only one thought: to escape from the terrors of cold and starvation, to forget if only for a moment that nightmare of hopeless agony through which they had to grope their way towards a haven which they could neither see nor even believe in.

How many days that delirium of torment lasted no one knows, because no survivor can tell how long it took to reach a spot where could be breathed air uncontaminated with fear or with disaster. Some found shelter; others, with no strength left to go farther, fell on the road and either died through being buried in the snow or being choked by the mud of those dreadful plains, which were impassable at that time of the year; or, still living, were devoured by birds of prey, without the strength to resist. An officer relates that, whilst trying to rally some of his men, he was startled by the moans of some creature in agony, and trudging through the darkness to the spot whence these moans proceeded he found a soldier weakly struggling with a huge vulture, who had begun to snap at his arm and was tearing the flesh off in pieces. As for horses, no sooner had they fallen than eagles and other birds of prey threw themselves upon their bodies and very quickly tore every piece of flesh from the bones. These birds were so inhumanly bold and so sure of the quarry that was awaiting them, that they refused to be driven away, hovering over the heads of the miserable beings who were running for their lives. This sinister escort only added to the horror that had already seized these poor wretches. It was worse than fighting, worse than hearing the bullets whistling in one's ears; far worse even than the screaming of shell fire. It was a ghastly reminder of the inevitable end. To listen to the noise of the great wings flapping in every direction seemed as if the angel of death was mockingly and mercilessly journeying with them, ready any moment to snatch up the souls of men.

I find it utterly impossible to give an idea of all the terrible things that occurred during this retreat of Mukden. Even the Japanese, hardened as they were, were moved to pity by the sufferings of the Russian army, fighting for its life under such awful conditions. As for the victims, they became at last quite indifferent to their woes; it all seemed so endless, so hopeless, that it was better quietly to submit, and to rely on fate either to save or to kill as might be.

The Red Cross detachments, as usual, behaved heroically, but they also were left with practically no other resources than their devotion to their duty. Often it happened that the horses harnessed to the carts that carried the wounded fell on the way, and instantly these were seized by hungry soldiers and eaten with relish, even raw. Then the sisters and doctors transferred their charges to other vehicles, and often pulled these carts themselves with ropes until they could find other animals to drag them on. Brave men who had seen other battlefields, and were used to the horrors of war, became white-haired and aged during those terrible days, and, when it was all over, never cared to think of them or hear them mentioned. It was a nightmare, and worse than a nightmare.

When at last the remnants of that army, to whom so many victories had been promised, were gathered together, and rallied into something like order, General Kouropatkine made up his mind to resign the position which he held and the responsibilities which he had never been able to understand, because he never realised their moment. He wrote to the Emperor asking to be relieved from his command, saying that he had been so unlucky that he feared the army had lost confidence in him. Speaking thus, he flattered himself. The army had not lost confidence; it had never had any in his capacity or his ability to lead it. The General's resignation was accepted by his Sovereign, and he was allowed to come back to Russia to "exonerate" himself and to explain in his own way the causes of the disasters that had accumulated upon his country and upon himself.

An old officer, whose whole life had been spent on active service—General Linevitch—was given the responsible post of Commander-in-Chief. He did the best he could do under the trying and difficult circumstances in which he found himself placed, but he could not restore confidence. The troops—among whom the war in the abstract had never been popular—had only one idea, and that was to return home and to see peace concluded, no matter under what conditions.

General Linevitch at once asked for reinforcements, and during the months that followed new troops were sent every day to Manchuria. They went rebellious and exasperated at the idea of fighting in what they considered to be a forlorn cause. It has often been made a reproach to Count Witte that he concluded peace at Portsmouth at the very time when, the army having been considerably strengthened, a renewal of the campaign might have brought back victory to the Russian arms. Nevertheless, all such reproaches were unmerited. The great reason that made Count Witte sign the famous treaty was his knowledge of the dissatisfied condition of the bulk of the army, and the conviction that existed among all who were aware of what was actually going on in Manchuria, that if they were ordered to march again; the troops very probably would refuse to obey. Revolution was everywhere in the air, and by allowing the opportunity given of obtaining more or less favourable conditions of settlement with Japan to escape, was to incur the far greater risk of insubordination and revolution. In that awful disaster everything had perished, even the devotion of the soldier to his flag.

Whilst the tragedy of the Manchurian plains was going on, the Baltic fleet, under the orders of Admiral Rozhdestvensky, was sailing towards Vladivostok, and preparing itself to encounter the Japanese squadrons, which they well knew were far superior to their own, both as regards numbers and armaments. It was a sad journey; all the men who had been sent on it, against all warnings suggested by reason and a knowledge of the conditions under which they were being dispatched, were certain that they would never return to their country and to those dear ones to whom they had bade good-bye with an anguish that they dared not express. The crews also were despondent. As for the vessels themselves, they were, for the greater part, old ships, unfit to stand such a long voyage, and neither armed properly nor equipped according to modern requirements. It was a hopeless enterprise, and all concerned knew it but too well.

Nevertheless, the fleet did its duty. On that grey May morning when the Japanese men-of-war were first encountered, it desperately prepared to fight, and at least to try to avert the shame of falling into the enemy's hands. But when the first shot fell on the immensity of the sea and shook its calm, it was as a funeral knell for thousands of lives about to be destroyed.

Their agony did not last long. It was not like at Mukden, a struggle of days and weeks, leaving its victims indifferent even to death. At Tsushima a few short hours saw the end. The Russian vessels were very quickly silenced; some were taken by the enemy, others sank in the waves. One ship escaped, forced her way through the Japanese fleet, and carried to Vladivostok the news of the disaster. Soon it reached Russia, and terrible was the despair which the tidings caused. It was felt that after this unprecedented calamity no hope was left to the country, and that once more the yellow race, immense, implacable, was going to crush the empire of the Tsars. Scarcely an eye was dry on that memorable day when one heard in St. Petersburg of the new victory of the Japanese arms, and few but were not crushed by the shame and humiliation which the country was undergoing: a shame that nothing could redeem.

One person alone kept cool and calm; it was the Emperor who, when he was told of the misfortune, read quietly the dispatch describing it, and after having done so went on with the game of tennis that he had interrupted in order to peruse it. So ran the story. Here was the whole of Russia mourning her children, yet—the inference is inevitable—the event was not of sufficient importance to make Nicholas II. abandon the healthy exercise he liked to indulge in on bright summer afternoons!

CHAPTER XI

THE BIRTH OF THE TSAREVITCH

WHILST the war was running its course the Emperor, in the solitude of his palace at Tsarskoye Selo, was anxiously awaiting the day when the Empress would again become a mother. In the years that had elapsed since he had wedded Alexandra Feodorovna, four daughters had been born to the Imperial couple, and their arrival into the world had been a source of bitter disappointment to their parents. The idea that the Throne could pass to a collateral line was a cruel grief for Nicholas II. In his first manifesto issued to the nation, on the day of his accession, he had proclaimed as his heir his brother, the Grand Duke George Alexandrovitch, to whom was granted the title of "Grand Duke Tsarevitch," generally borne only by heirs apparent, and not presumptive. The manifesto added that this title was only to be borne until God "had seen fit to bless with the birth of a son" the marriage of the Sovereign, which was then about to take place. But the years went on, and the much-wished-for boy still had not arrived to fill with joy his parents' hearts. As one girl after another came to increase the Imperial Family, people at last gave up the idea that the Empress would ever become the mother of a male heir, and this did not add to her popularity.

In the meantime, the Grand Duke George, whose health had always been more or less delicate, developed acute symptoms of tuberculosis. He was at first ordered to the South of France, whither his mother, the Empress Marie Feodorovna, accompanied him, but he derived no benefit from his stay.

At last he was sent to the Caucasus to try what high mountain air would do for him. The Grand Duke liked the Caucasus, and especially the free kind of life he was able to lead in the residence which he had built for himself on the heights above Abbas Touman, in the vicinity of the Kazbek. He was of a very retiring disposition, timid in the extreme, and was never more at his ease than with his inferiors or people with whom he need not trouble himself to stand upon ceremony. He knew that, as Successor to the Throne, he was not looked upon with friendly eyes by a certain section of the Court, although he had no ambition whatsoever, and only wanted to be left alone. This made his retirement more congenial; he felt he had more independence than he could have obtained in St. Petersburg had he stayed there. His mother visited him frequently, and endeavoured to persuade him to return to the capital, if only for a few months during the summer season, but he constantly refused, declaring he was quite happy amid the rugged beauty of the wild surroundings. People said that he had found another attraction at Abbas Touman, and that he was secretly married to a lady he had met there. It is difficult to know how much truth there was in this rumour, but it is certain that some legend, full of intangible mystery, hovered about the Grand Duke George, and that, when talking about him, people supposed to be well informed gravely shook their heads and said that "it was a pity, a great pity." They would never explain, however, why they used such words.

But, as years went on, the public ceased to interest itself in the doings of the Tsarevitch, until, one fine summer day, it was startled by the news of his sudden and unexpected death.

Tragedy was not absent from it, and the end of the second son of Alexander III. had something appalling through the extraordinary circumstances that accompanied it. He had gone out alone for a ride on his bicycle, as he often did in fine weather. As he did not return in time for dinner, people began to get anxious, and his attendants started in search of him. They met on the way an old woman, who related that she was seeking help for an officer who had fallen on the road and evidently hurt himself. That officer proved to be the Tsarevitch, who was found lying on the grass, with blood oozing out of his mouth, and already lifeless. It was related later on that he had been seized with sudden hæmorrhage from the lungs, and had died before help could come; but the real circumstances attending that sad end never were known, or, if known, never told to anyone.

The attendants of the Grand Duke were severely blamed for allowing him to go out alone on such expeditions; but they tried to excuse themselves by saying that he refused to be accompanied by anyone in his frequent and much enjoyed mountain excursions, and that it was next to impossible to disobey him. True or not, the excuse was admitted, and the remains of George Alexandrovitch were brought back with great pomp to St. Petersburg and laid to rest in the fortress beside those of his father. The Empress Dowager was perhaps the only person who really mourned for him; in Court circles one felt that his death was the solution of a difficulty which would inevitably have arisen had circumstances occurred to dispossess him of the title of Tsarevitch. His brother, the Grand Duke Michael, was not, however, awarded the title, but merely recognised as heir presumptive to the Crown, without any other qualification.

This Grand Duke had been the favourite child of Alexander III., and as such enjoyed the affection of the nation. But he, too, was of a retiring disposition, and though he represented his brother with much dignity on important State occasions, such as the funeral of Queen Victoria and the Coronation of King Edward VII., it was very well known that his tastes did not lie that way, and that he preferred home life to any kind of festivity. He gave a proof of the direction in which his tastes lay when he married the lady of his heart against the wishes of the present Tsar and of the Dowager Empress. In consequence, he was deprived of his right to a possible Regency, and even of his civil rights; moreover, the management of his own private financial affairs and of his personal properties were also taken away from him.

After the birth of the fourth daughter of Nicholas II., the Grand Duchess Anastasia Nicolaievna, the Empress gave herself up entirely to practices of a narrow devotion, mixed with superstition.

It was then that rumours arose that she favoured the visits of spiritualistic mediums. Also a report was circulated that she went from convent to convent and from church to church, promising golden vestments to all the miraculous images of the Virgin, of which there are such a considerable number in Russia, if only she were granted through their intervention the son for whom her soul longed.

Following upon this, according to popular report, the Empress fell into a kind of melancholia that gave at one time considerable cause for anxiety to her medical attendants. As one misfortune after another crowded upon the country, that melancholy took an acute shape, and it is not to be wondered that when, after an interval of two years or something of the kind, there appeared again in her state of health a likelihood of her becoming a mother, the event was awaited with anxious expectation, not only by herself but also by the Emperor.

It was about this period that the revolutionary propaganda, which previously had only slumbered, began to show renewed activity. Discontent had reached its height, and it is only to be wondered that the era of political assassination under which Russia was to be terrorised for such a number of years, and which it is to be feared is not yet ended, did not begin sooner. Indeed, the anarchist party had from the very beginning of the reign of Nicholas II. evinced signs of preparation and activity, believing that it had at last some chance to push through its programme of bloody reforms, because events had given some colourable pretext for remonstrance.

Elsewhere I have given the actual text—never before published—of the letter which Nicholas II. received from the Revolutionary Committee in answer to his "senseless dreams" speech. His only feeling when he read it was indignation at the audacity of those people who thus tried to rule the actions of the Sovereign and to reprove them by sketching out to him a programme of government so different from his own. He instructed his Ministers to find out the authors of this message. Immediately were put into requisition all the numerous political spies that the police has at its disposal. The Universities especially were watched, as it was well known that among the students a great percentage of anarchists was to be found. Immediately after these measures had been adopted an extraordinary agitation could be observed in all the higher educational establishments, and one February afternoon and evening manifestations of students took place on the Nevski Prospekt, in front of the Anitchkov Palace, where the Emperor was residing with his mother and his young wife.

At that time, however, the special service of the Okhrana, or personal guard of the Sovereign, still existed. General Tchérévine took energetic, though not violent, measures to put an end to the disorder, so that it might not have time to develop itself dangerously or to disturb—outwardly at least —the established order of things.

But after the Coronation matters changed, and the revolutionary committees became more active. The catastrophe of the Khodinka Field was used to attack the person of the Sovereign, and they did not spare him. Anarchist proclamations were distributed right and left, and in reply the police made wholesale arrests without due discrimination between the people whom it suspected of favouring the active revolutionary propaganda and those who were really guilty.

Among the persons who were thus imprisoned was a young girl of extraordinary talent and beauty, who, though full of sympathy for the cause of what she considered liberty, had, nevertheless, never been in communication with the leaders of the anarchist party. Some forbidden books had been found during a police search that had taken place in the rooms which she occupied in some furnished lodgings, and this afforded quite sufficient pretext to arrest her and transfer her to the fortress.

What took place during some six months that she spent there, separated from everybody, and not even allowed to communicate at first with her own father and mother, no one knows. Certainly some cruel scenes must have been enacted, because one day, at the very time when, owing to energetic efforts on the part of her friends, Mademoiselle Vietroff was about to be released, she was found dead in her cell, burned to death under the most horrible circumstances. She had had the courage to empty over her bedclothes the oil out of a paraffin lamp that she was allowed to have, and to set fire to them, after having laid herself down on the bed, where she remained until the flames had done their work.

The scandal was enormous, and people wondered what could have induced this lovely, charming, highly gifted girl, to commit such an awful suicide. Dark things were hinted at, and terrible rumours accused the authorities of the prison of having driven her to seek release from suffering and shame through the only means left at her disposal.

Immediately after her funeral imposing manifestations by students took place in front of the Kazan Cathedral, and proclamations were freely distributed among the public relating the details of this terrible death.

The sensation caused by it was equal to that which seized upon Russian Society when, under the reign of Alexander II., Vera Zassoulitch fired upon the Prefect of St. Petersburg, General Trépoff. That attempted murder was the beginning of another phase of the revolutionary movement which ended with the assassination of the Emperor. Mademoiselle Vietroff's suicide opened the later phase out of which was to burst the Revolution which claimed so many victims in 1905.

The country did not recover its calm after that sad occurrence. Students and Universities became more active than ever in trying to sow discontent among the working classes, and especially in the factories, where anarchist ideas generally find the most support. The Government, as usual, blundered; either they did not see the danger, or saw it too late, or, again, looked for it there where it did not exist. It persecuted uselessly young boys led astray by their comrades, and utterly unable to endanger public order, and it let alone the most mischievous leaders of the movement who succeeded in removing suspicion from themselves. The police behaved atrociously in its measures of repression. Sure of the protection of the Tsar, the police proceeded in the most ruthless manner to persecute every manifestation of public opinion, when it imagined it was directed against its authority, and it had no regard as to the personality of those whom it thought fit to attack. Thus one day, a general in a very high position, who held the important post of administrator of the private fortune of the Imperial Family, Prince Viazemsky, happened to pass along the square opposite the Kazan Cathedral whilst the police were trying to disperse some groups of students who had assembled there for a funeral mass for one of their comrades. He was so indignant at the brutality displayed in securing the dispersal that he interfered in order to put an end to it. Immediately the head of the secret service of the Okhrana complained to the Emperor, who, without even listening to the explanations which Prince Viazemsky wanted to offer, deprived him of his post, and ordered him to go abroad at once, exiling him from the capital, without even allowing him to try to clear himself.

When the war with Japan broke out it was felt that whatever might be its end, the miseries that it would entail, even if victory came to the Russian arms, would serve as subjects not only of discontent, but also of encouragement to the revolutionist party. Consequently, rigorous measures became more frequent than before. The Minister of the Interior at the time was M. de Plehve, a man well known for his despotic character, who had for long been at the head of the secret political police before he became a member of the Cabinet. He was perhaps the most intensely hated personage in Russia, and in a certain measure he had deserved the dislike and the animosity of the public, whom he persecuted ruthlessly whenever he thought he could detect the least symptom of opinions not in accord with those which he advocated. During his tenure of office people without number were exiled or imprisoned; a good many were hanged in secret in the courtyards of the various prisons in which they were confined; and consciences as well as individuals were terrorised not into submission, but into silence.

But Plehve, with all his faults, at least was an honest man, a conscientious man, and not a flatterer. He knew he was destined to be murdered, but he would not have gone one step to escape the danger that he felt was continually lurking over his head. He was inexorable in the way in which he fulfilled his duties, but he would have been incapable of telling a lie to please his Sovereign or to gain some personal advantage. Yet his sarcastic temper and want of consideration for the feelings of others were bound to create enemies even among his colleagues; indeed, they did not scruple to use every means to destroy his influence.

The Emperor considered him something like a watch-dog, whose services and vigilance one could not do without, but whom one had no necessity to treat decently or to admit into one's confidence. One day, when Plehve wanted to deal with some matter not immediately connected with his department, Nicholas II. told him quite plainly that he ought not to speak to him about things which concerned other people. And yet when the offended Minister offered his resignation the Emperor refused to accept it, giving as his reason that "He had no one at the moment who could replace him so well at the head of the police." "At the moment," you will note, to the servant of his own creation!

Plehve was very fond of knowing everything that was going on, and while knowing perfectly well that he had any number of adversaries among those who surrounded the Sovereign, he wished to be kept aware of everything that was going on in the family circle of Nicholas II. Having at his disposal all the necessary means of being well informed, it was related that he had organised a police service at the Imperial Palace of Tsarskoye Selo which kept him conversant with all that was being done and said there. It was even said that he had had his telephone wires connected with those of the private telephone of the Emperor, and could thus listen to the latter's conversations. This fact, so the report continues, came to the knowledge of the Sovereign after the murder of M. Plehve, and he was so enraged that he forgot the respect due to the dead. He did not attend the funeral ceremonies, and it was only with the utmost difficulty that he was persuaded to consent to a pension being given to the widow of the deceased statesman.

Plehve was murdered under the most awful conditions. He was driving to the Warsaw railway station on his way to Tsarskoye Selo for his weekly report to the Tsar. When almost opposite the station a bomb was thrown in the front of his carriage. The effect was terrible. The carriage and its occupant were reduced to pieces, and it was with great difficulty that some remains of torn flesh and bones were found and gathered together to be brought home. To recognise them was impossible; nothing remained to tell that a mighty Minister had been blown into atoms.

The news of the event was at once telephoned to Tsarskoye Selo. The only comment which the Emperor made was that it would be necessary to send immediately a high official to put under seal the papers of M. Plehve, so that none should get lost or mislaid. He did not even send a message of condolence to the widow. It was said by way of explanation that the news of the murder must be held back from the Empress, who was on the eve of her confinement, and whose nerves might receive a shock in consequence, and that the Emperor did not want to leave her at such a time.

This explanation was not believed by the general public. The Emperor, however, did not mind what the world thought about him, or in what light it regarded his actions. He was only thinking of the child the Empress was expected to give birth to. Would it at last be a son, an heir to the dynasty of the Romanoffs, or would another daughter be born to him? That was the thought which alone engrossed him, and was the first object of his preoccupations. The war with Japan had already begun; our first ships had been sunk, several battles had been fought and lost, the *Petropavlovsk* had gone down with its load of men, brave Admiral Makaroff at their head; our soldiers were trudging in the dusty, hot plains of Manchuria, suffering from the torrid heat until they should perish from the icy cold; thousands of homes were mourning their dear ones fallen under the bullets of the enemy; revolt was brooding in the country, Ministers and people in high positions were daily falling under the knives or pistols of assassins. Yet none of these things concerned Nicholas II. so much as the yearning that God should give him a son.

At last, one August morning, it began to be rumoured in Peterhof, where the Court was spending the summer, that a happy event was impending. Courtiers and Ministers and ladies-in-waiting assembled in the halls of the Palace in expectation of the announcement of the birth of the fifth child of the Imperial pair. They did not wait very long. As the clock struck noon a doctor entered the room and told the assemblage that at last an Heir was born to the Throne of All the Russias.

Great was the joy in the Imperial Family, and great was the excitement in St. Petersburg when the guns of the fortress proclaimed by three hundred shots that the succession to the Throne of the Romanoffs was so far assured in the direct line. But through the country as a whole the event, which under different circumstances would have been hailed with joy, passed almost unperceived, so much was the public mind absorbed by the grave political events that were taking place. Russia was mourning too many of its children to welcome with anything but indifference the boy whose advent into the world had filled with such joy the hearts and the lives of Nicholas II. and Alexandra Feodorovna.

CHAPTER XII

THE DEATH OF MADEMOISELLE VIETROFF

I DID not like to interrupt the preceding chapter by reproducing in full the proclamation that was distributed among the public after the death of Mademoiselle Vietroff. I shall quote it now, believing that it constitutes an historical document worthy of remembrance in spite of the harrowing details it contains. It is remarkable because it had certainly a visible influence upon the subsequent events that led to the outbreak of the Revolution in 1905. It was very often mentioned as the first appeal of the student classes to the masses, who up to that time had not participated in the anarchist movement; and as such it may not be devoid of some interest for the reader.

This is the document. It was circulated, just as I reproduce it, by thousands of copies, without any signature:

"On the 12th of February of the present year (1897) died in the fortress of St. Peter and St. Paul, after two days of terrible sufferings, a student of the Higher School for Women, Marie Feodorovna Vietroff. According to the words of the Assistant Public Prosecutor, on the 10th of February she threw the contents of a paraffin lamp over her clothes and bedding and set fire to them afterwards. As we therefore see, awful cases of people burning themselves to death, among other terrible ways of committing suicide, as the only means of escaping a doom more horrible than death itself, are again occurring.

"The deceased lady was imprisoned not so very long ago (during the night of the 22nd of December). She had been accused merely of secreting illegal literature. The only punishment she could legally have incurred, therefore, would have been to be sent beyond the limits of the town of St. Petersburg.

"According to people who knew her well, she was a person of very strong personality, and would not shrink from even penal servitude in defence of her views. There was nothing in her disposition which could have led one to think that she would have proved herself to be such a coward as to feel frightened at the future that seemed to lie in store for her. She was not at all of a melancholy disposition. The letters which she wrote to her friends from her prison, and the diary which she kept during that time, tend to confirm that belief. It was also only latterly that the visits which her sister had been allowed to pay had been interrupted; and during these visits she was always very cheerful.

"What sorrow, therefore, and what despair could have led her to put an end to her life in such a horrible way?

"She is the only one that could have replied to this momentous question; she, or else those who were the direct cause of it. But she has already settled her accounts with this life, and, of course, neither the witnesses nor the instigators of her fearful death will give a true account of the circumstances that brought it about. It is only the few words that have escaped the lips of fellow-prisoners of her (who since her death have been transferred from the fortress to the house of preventive detention) which give a faint inkling of the truth and from which we can surmise the details of the tragedy of Marie Vietroff's death, and of the circumstances that drove this energetic girl to decide upon the step which she took. We can only make shrewd guesses that this death was but the final end to a moral tragedy of the most painful and awful kind. Our presumptions are justified, if we take into consideration the personality of the deceased on the one hand, and the habits and customs in our prisons on the other. The tactics observed by the authorities in charge of these establishments have been sufficiently demonstrated in more than one case where individuals have been driven to desperation, or tortured to within an ace of death, and then sent out of prison to end their lives, where the authorities could not be blamed for the result, thus carefully evading the consequences that might have resulted had their victims succumbed within prison walls.

"If, in the case of Mlle. Vietroff, the authorities could not follow their usual tactics, it means that they must have been directly responsible for the miserable end of the wretched creature. If this had not been the case, why, during the two long days that the unfortunate girl's dying agony lasted, were her parents, relations, and friends not informed of her fate? Why was the mere fact of her death kept secret from them for two whole weeks, and why were even books taken over for her in order to allow her people to believe her to be alive? Why was the fact of her death only revealed when the details of it began to ooze through to the public from the tales of the prisoners who, after having shared her captivity in the fortress for some time, had been released from it?

"If the people to whom we have just now been alluding had no hand in the death of Mlle. Vietroff, they would surely have advised her family of it earlier. If they had not been the direct cause of her suicide they would have allowed her to see her friends before she died, to whom she might have explained the reasons which induced her to take such a terrible resolution; and this alone would have turned suspicion away from them.

"Nothing of the kind was done, and this points clearly the part which the executioners of the Tsar have had in this tragedy. As if we did not know their way of acting! As if we are so very far away from the times when girls were beaten to death, and when they also preferred suicide to an existence which would have been otherwise spent in the shame of disgraceful remembrances! As if the tortures invented by the Tsar's janissaries were a mystery to us!

"We are convinced that only the feeling that she had been placed in some position from which there was no escape could have driven Mlle. Vietroff to the dreadful necessity of doing away with herself, and to prefer suicide to a life tainted with unbearable remembrances. We know not what was done to her by the mysterious executioners who drove her to her death; and such a death—a death the very mention of which sends a cold shudder through our bodies. Such facts cannot be kept secret; they must be made public, if only in order to avoid their recurrence; they must be proclaimed everywhere, and in writing this letter we are deeply convinced that thousands of people will be eager to assist at the funeral service for the dead victim, Marie Feodorovna Vietroff!"

Thousands of people did assist at these prayers. The vast square before the Kazan Cathedral was thronged with men and women, crying and sobbing; and in spite of the repeated warnings of the police the vast crowd would not disperse.

Such a manifestation, indeed, as followed upon the appeal that I have just now reproduced had not taken place in St. Petersburg since the troubled times which had preceded the assassination of Alexander II. It created a deep impression on all those who chanced to see it; it opened a new era in the history of modern Russia. It was the forerunner of the great storm which a few short years later nearly drove the Romanoffs from their Throne.

CHAPTER XIII

THE BEGINNING OF THE REVOLUTION

As can easily be imagined, the reverses which followed each other from the very beginning of the war, were deeply reflected in the country, and gave but too good an opportunity to all the adversaries of the Government to try to discredit it in public opinion. After the assassination of M. Plehve the anarchists grew bolder, and, encouraged by success, went on with their murderous designs. Moscow, which formerly was the centre of conservatism, had become, by a strange freak of destiny, the bulwark of revolution. The spirit of the town had always been independent, and adverse to the Central Government established in St. Petersburg; but, on the other hand, it had always remained faithful to its Tsars.

After Khodinka things altered, and distrust of the Sovereign, as well as dislike for his Ministers and advisers, replaced the former devotion for the person of the monarch. The Grand Duke Sergius was intensely disliked, in spite of the great popularity of his wife. He was made the scapegoat of the mistakes committed by others, and people often accused him of things he had been unable to prevent as well as of those of which he personally disapproved. His entourage, too, were in part responsible for the hatred which the population of Moscow professed for his person. They were for the most part composed of people absolutely devoid of political sense, who were too weak even to flatter, but who thought themselves strong, because they advocated the use of the stick or of the lash as the remedy for all kind of possible evils.

The Grand Duke himself, whose intelligence was moderate, whose education had been conducted on the principle of strict obedience to the orders of the head of his House, and who had the great defect of believing that he possessed principles, whereas he had only passions, did not realise the gravity of the crisis which his country was going through. He imagined that by hanging a few people, and exiling a good many, he would be able to subdue the revolutionary tendencies which he was forced to recognise were little by little taking hold, not only of the lower orders, but also of the higher classes of Society in Moscow.

He was courageous by nature, more so than his nephew and brother-in-law, the Emperor, and he disdained the threats which he heard every day levelled at his person. However, at the end of the year 1904, these threats assumed such proportions that it was deemed advisable for the Grand Duke and his wife to remove from the palace of the Governor-General, where they resided, to the Kremlin, and the Grand Duchess, alarmed by all she heard, and having been told that her presence at his side would preserve her husband from any attempt to murder him, made a point of accompanying him wherever he went. However, one morning she was prevented from doing so, and as if to prove that she had been his guardian angel, it was on that very morning that Sergius Alexandrovitch was killed.

A cross is now erected on the spot where he was blown to pieces, and reminds the world of this dastardly crime. It is useless to repeat its harrowing details, or to relate how his mangled remains were picked up during three whole days (one of his fingers was found on the roof of the Arsenal). The people who first reached the spot where the catastrophe had occurred cannot to this day speak without a shudder of what they saw. A stretcher was brought hurriedly, no one knows from where, and upon it were deposited what remains it had been possible to pick up; and whilst this was being done one saw a woman, bareheaded, with a blue cloak thrown upon her shoulders, hurry up to the spot where the catastrophe had taken place and throw herself upon her knees beside the stretcher. It was the Grand Duchess Elizabeth Feodorovna, who, hearing the noise of the explosion, had rushed to see what had happened.

Bravely she followed the soldiers, who slowly brought back the remains of the Grand Duke to the Kremlin, and her composure in that trying moment of her life was the admiration of all who saw it. She found the courage to dispatch at once a telegram to the Emperor, in which she begged him, among other things, to allow her husband to be buried in Moscow, the town he loved so well, as she expressed herself; and she further begged Nicholas II. not to endanger his own person by coming to the funeral, and to grant her permission to spend the rest of her life beside the murdered Grand Duke's grave.

Her message relieved Nicholas II. from a great anxiety and difficulty. He knew very well that his duty would have required him to be present at his uncle's obsequies, but he did not care to do so at all, and thus expose himself to the possibility of a like fate. The request of the Grand Duchess gave him the opportunity for which he longed, and so he dispatched his other uncle, the Grand Duke Alexis, to Moscow, to represent him at the funeral, and he replied to his aunt and sister-in-law that he would follow her wishes in everything, and that she had only to order what she wanted.

Elizabeth Feodorovna then did one thing which was bitterly criticised afterwards, and not without reason. She insisted upon going to the prison where her husband's murderer was confined, to hold conversation with him. It was said that she wanted to assure him of her forgiveness;

but, as some people remarked, taking into account that she could not save him from the gallows, her step in visiting him seemed entirely out of place.

There was in all her actions at that sad time an exaggeration which did her more harm than good, and which destroyed many sympathies. However, Moscow loved her, and perhaps felt grateful to her for her willingness to remain in the town where her married life had been wrecked. When, later on, she developed considerable activity, not only in the domain of charity, but also in politics, she still kept the affection of the inhabitants of the old capital—so much so that it is at least certain that if ever another revolution breaks out in Moscow, the Grand Duchess will be respected by everybody, equally with the nuns of the community of Martha and Mary, which she has founded for the relief of the poor and sick inhabitants of the city.

The Grand Duke Sergius Alexandrovitch was murdered in January of 1905, and the year which began with this catastrophe was to see many more bloody days before it came to an end. About the same time that the fifth son of the Emperor Alexander II. met with the same fate as his father, Port Arthur fell into the hands of the Japanese, and this loss of the fortress on which the attention of the whole of Russia had been concentrated for long months, put the crowning touch to the general indignation of the public against the Government. In St. Petersburg, especially, where factories abound, and where the workmen felt bitterly the economical crisis, which, as a consequence of the war, was ruining the country, the agitation assumed quite gigantic proportions. It was felt that a revolt, if not a revolution, was imminent, and that something had to be done to arrest its progress. The misfortune was that no one seemed to know what was to be done.

At that time Count Witte was Minister of the Interior. Unscrupulous as ever, clever as usual, he thought that the first step to be taken would be to ascertain what really were the intentions of the leaders of the anarchist movement, which lately had assumed considerable proportions among the working classes.

The leaders of this movement had hitherto escaped the vigilance of the police, and could not be discovered. On the other hand, it was evident that unless the Government discovered the intentions of these leaders, fight was impossible and no measures could be taken to check the evil. It was then that he bethought himself of resorting to the old method of *agents provocateurs*, through the help of whom he hoped to get at last to the bottom of the vast conspiracy, the existence of which no one denied.

Whilst he was looking around him for a man willing to take upon himself such a part, one of his old friends in Odessa indicated to him a parish priest, called Gapon, who, he told him, wielded a considerable influence among the working classes of St. Petersburg, and who might be useful to him in that respect. After some hesitation Count Witte decided to see the priest in question, and one dark winter evening Gapon was introduced into the presence of the Minister.

The two men understood each other at once. Few people, indeed, possess the clear insight into human nature that has been granted to Count Witte. As soon as he saw Gapon he judged that he was false by nature, desirous of enjoying the luxuries of life, in the attainment of which he would have no scruples. He was aware that Gapon had the advantage of knowing how to talk to the masses, how to inspire them with confidence in his person and with belief in his expressed principles. Gapon, on the other hand, was delighted to find in Count Witte the opportunity to win for himself the means whereby, at a later date, he could lead an easy, pleasant, indolent life, with all the pleasures that money can afford.

The Government, headed by Witte, felt that some pretext had to be found for measures of repression, which nothing justified so long as the revolutionary agitation was simply increasing. They hesitated to resort to measures of violence, which might be difficult to justify in the eyes of Europe. The Emperor, too, was constantly urging his Ministers to put an end to the discussions which he felt, rather than knew, were going on everywhere in St. Petersburg and in Moscow. Witte himself felt that if things were allowed to go on as they were the moment might easily arrive when the agitation would reach the troops, already exasperated at the disasters of the war, and throw them also on the side of the enemies of the Government.

At this moment Gapon proposed to persuade the workmen of the different factories around St. Petersburg to present a petition to the Emperor. This petition would furnish the pretext to actively crush the smouldering rebellion.

The news that this petition was about to be presented circulated everywhere for days before the workmen made up their minds to go with it to the Winter Palace. It is said that the police took care to spread a report, in the hope of producing a general panic, that the masses were about to rise, and to attack the Sovereign in his Palace; and following the precedent of the Parisians during the October days which saw the beginning of the end of the old French monarchy, to compel him to accede to their wishes. What the masses wanted no one knew, and the wildest rumours were afloat. Some said that the nation wanted peace to be concluded at once, no matter under what conditions; others that it would beg for permission to raise a popular militia to fight the Japanese; whilst people eager to appear well informed assured their friends that what the workmen wanted was the abdication of the Emperor and the establishment of a Republic. Rumours without end filled the town, and everybody belonging to the upper classes of Society trembled with panic, and scarcely dared to come out of their houses. This universal anxiety was carefully nursed by the agents of the Government in order to justify the measures it meant to take to restore an order that had not yet been disturbed.

The Empress Dowager, on the other hand, was the only person who kept cool, and who would not give way to the terror that seemed to have taken hold of everyone. She refused to leave the capital, and showed herself publicly as if nothing was the matter. It was only when the Emperor sent her a positive command to retire that she consented to leave the Anitchkov Palace and went to her own castle of Gatschina.

Nicholas II. completely misunderstood when told about the intention of the workmen to seek to see himself in person, and to lay before him their wrongs and their wants. When he was informed that all the efforts to disperse the masses about to march towards the Winter Palace had failed, he conceived the idea that the Revolution had come, and had only one thought: to fly from danger; and in the dead of the night a train was hurriedly made ready, and he escaped to Tsarskoe Selo, with the Empress and his children, without taking even the time to gather together any of his papers, Alexandra Feodorovna, indeed, leaving everything behind her, even to her clothes and linen.

It is certain that had anyone been found to tell the Emperor to decide to face the crowd he would have subdued them, only by his appearance before them. The Russian peasant has still in his heart a respect for the person of the Tsar, and until the present reign he has considered him like a father to whom one could always apply in case of need. Indeed, on that January day, when the workmen and populace of the capital marched towards the Winter Palace, not one man among this multitude but thought he would be able to tell his Sovereign that he was ready to give his life for him and for his dynasty. Not one of them had any thought of rebellion, and if that thought came later on it was after the pavement of the square in front of the Winter Palace had been dyed red.

In the darkness of the night, before leaving his capital, Nicholas II. called to him his uncles, the Grand Dukes Vladimir and Nicholas, the two energetic men of the family, and asked them what they thought ought to be done. Vladimir Alexandrovitch was for calling the troops to repulse the turbulent masses. A person who was present at this council of war then asked: "But if they are not turbulent, then what must one do?" The Tsar threw a terrible glance towards the unlucky speaker and, so it is said, replied: "If they are not turbulent, then one must treat them as if they were so." The two Grand Dukes bowed their heads in silence, and at that moment the Empress ran into the room crying that the mutineers were coming, and that they must go at once. She was holding her son in her arms, and crying violently. Her husband threw a cloak over her shoulders, and hurried, together with her, to the door, where their carriage was waiting to take them to the station, saying to his uncles as he went: "Don't spare them; kill as many as is necessary."

Whilst the Tsar of All the Russias was thus escaping from his capital with his family, the workmen who were causing this panic had also spent a sleepless night. By the representations of Gapon they had been induced to direct their steps towards the Palace. He had explained to them that the best person before whom they could lay their grievances was the Emperor, their "little father," who loved his people, and who would surely listen to them, and do all that he could for them. They had started on that road which for so many was to be the road of death, singing the National Anthem, and with a large picture of the Tsar, which they were carrying before them as a shield. Not a single obstacle met them on the march; no police were there to prevent their advance. It seemed as if it was agreed to let them pass, and, encouraged by the facilities they found everywhere, they believed more than ever in the assurances given to them by Gapon, who was marching at their head, that they would be received by the Emperor. When the procession reached the square before the Winter Palace, they suddenly found it to be occupied by two regiments of Cossacks.

It is said that an officer who had followed the procession managed to enter the Palace, where the Grand Duke Vladimir was holding his council of war, and tried to persuade him that the best thing to do would be to tell the multitude that the Emperor was not in town, and induce the people to disperse. The Grand Duke would not hear of it. "Punished they must be," he said, and thereupon gave the order to fire.

Meanwhile the workmen, not knowing what was going on, began shouting their desire to see the Tsar, their "little father." No reply was given to these appeals, no word of warning was spoken, and suddenly, before these masses had been able to realise what was happening, the troops took to their rifles, and laid low as many of the now frightened creatures as they could.

It is useless to describe the panic that followed. After a few moments, when the smoke had dissipated, the square was found to be covered with dead bodies and wounded men, women, and children. The soldiers fired again and again, and when the crowds, struck with terror, fled in every direction, they were followed by mounted Cossacks, who pursued them all along the Nevski Prospekt, killing whom they could, either with their rifles or with their whips; and when all seemed to be over, a cannon was fired, sweeping the whole length of the long avenue, and laying low all who had succeeded in escaping the first charge of the cavalry.

Gapon had escaped. As the first volley was heard he managed to disappear, hidden from friends and foes, by the care of the police for whom he had worked so well. He escaped to Paris, where he tried to pass as a martyr of the cause which he had betrayed. When he returned to Russia, as everybody now knows, he was murdered; not by the order of the Revolutionary Executive Committee, but by agents of the Government. It was too dangerous to allow such a compromising accomplice to live.

On the evening of the day that had seen such bloody scenes enacted within the walls of St. Petersburg, the Grand Duke Vladimir went to Tsarskoe Selo, to report to his nephew the events that had taken place. Nicholas II. listened in silence to the details given to him by his uncle. When the latter had finished he is reported to have asked: "Are you sure that you have killed enough people?"

CHAPTER XIV

PEACE WITH JAPAN; WAR AT HOME

THE butchery which took place on that sad day of January, 1905, marked the beginning of a period of unrest that is not yet at an end. It gave the signal for a manifestation of discontent such as Russia had not witnessed before, even during the last days of the reign of Alexander II.; and, what is more, afforded the excuse for it, because even the stanchest supporters of the Government were indignant at the recklessness with which it had tried to suppress what, after all, had not been a rebellion, but only a desire on the part of some workmen to see their Sovereign and lay before him their real or imaginary wrongs. It is probable that if Nicholas II. had only received these poor people there would have been no later Revolution, and the *agents provocateurs*, scattered everywhere by the police, would have failed to arouse the masses and persuade them to a rebellion which no one wanted, though everybody felt that a change in the methods of government must come. But that change, it had been hoped, would be brought about peacefully through the mutual efforts of the Tsar and his people. As it was, the events which took place on the 22nd of January proved to the masses that nothing could be expected voluntarily from the Sovereign; they had to shift for themselves if they wanted any amelioration of the system of government. The mistake which was committed on that day nearly overthrew the Romanoff Dynasty, and it shook their Throne perhaps more than the reverses of the war with Japan.

Gapon, nevertheless, did not lose his influence after the butchery in front of the Winter Palace. His mysterious disappearance from among the workmen, whose deputations he had headed when they started on their sadly momentous journey, had been attributed to the watchfulness of his friends, who had wanted to preserve him from the reprisals of the police. As a consequence, when he reappeared and tried to reorganise secret committees, and to devise new means of disseminating among the working classes the liberal opinions he was supposed to profess, he was received by them with great enthusiasm. He was a consummate actor, and possessed to perfection the art of advertising himself. He contrived to impress his victims with the idea that he was considered by the Government to be one of its most serious and dangerous adversaries.

Whilst he was doing his best to excite the masses, and urge them to violent measures, he was also in constant communication with M. Witte, whom he kept informed of all that was going on among the revolutionary secret societies, who were energetically preparing themselves for a struggle which, it was felt everywhere, could not be delayed for any length of time.

However, there were those among the enthusiasts who began to get suspicious as to the facility with which Gapon eluded the vigilance of the police. He constantly said that he was being shadowed, and so never could afford to spend two nights under the same roof. Yet, somehow, he contrived in a marvellous way to avoid the spies who followed him. Of course, it might have been his luck, but then it is not often that luck is so faithful to one person, and several leaders of the revolutionary movement which Gapon was supposed to favour began to watch him and follow his movements. They tried to find out what he was really doing, and who were the people he most frequently saw. But the police, who were shadowing Gapon the whole time, quickly noticed that he was no longer in possession of the same degree of confidence which he had previously enjoyed, and that the party to which he was supposed to belong began to take important decisions without consulting him, without even his being aware of them. M. Witte, who very soon was advised of this change in the feelings of the anarchists in regard to Gapon, determined then to send him abroad for some time. His mission was to find out from the leaders of the movement in London and Paris the information he had not succeeded in ascertaining in St. Petersburg.

Gapon was not sorry to leave Russia, as he felt that the part he had been playing was becoming more and more difficult every day. Before starting he contrived, nevertheless, to furnish M. Witte with some valuable information as to the impression produced in the country by the sad events that had made the 22nd of January such a memorable day in the annals of Russian history; also to draw his attention to the unpopularity of the war with Japan, as well as the widespread desire, especially among the rural classes, to see it ended.

Count Witte was too clever not to realise the danger which threatened the dynasty itself through the continuation of a struggle that was so unpopular everywhere and with everybody. He had been aware—more than any other statesman in Russia, perhaps—of the approaching peril of revolution, and that it had been ripe for many years, only waiting an opportunity to break out. He had had great dreams of social reforms at one time, and these dreams he had not relinquished, though he could very well feel that the moment had not arrived when he might attempt to realise them. He hoped, nevertheless, that his name would be associated in some way with a change in the system of government. Unfortunately, he was so disliked throughout the country, and had contrived to make so many enemies, that it was doubtful whether his best intentions would be received with anything but mistrust and suspicion. He knew this very well, and it was perhaps with the vague idea that it would help him to overcome these difficulties that he consented to go to Portsmouth, U.S.A., to represent Russia at the conferences upon which so much depended.

When he left for America, M. Witte expected he would be able to obtain much better conditions of peace than those to which he eventually subscribed. He was aware that the Japanese were more or less exhausted, and that their financial position was considerably shattered by the enormous expenses the war occasioned. He knew also that considerable reinforcements had been sent by Russia to Manchuria, and that the army therefore was no longer in the inferior position in which it had found itself under General Kouropatkine. General Linevitch, who had succeeded him in the supreme command, was not a military genius, but was liked by the troops, and if not able to attack the enemy, he could at least to hold his own, and not allow his army to be dislodged from the positions it occupied. Russia had now some chances in her favour, and this had not been the case before.

A continuance of the struggle might, therefore, be of advantage to her, and certainly from a military point of view it could be recommended. But M. Witte, who was a statesman and not a soldier, looked at things with that clear foresight which was one of his predominant qualities; and, besides, he had at his disposal sources of information such as no one else possessed. He knew that the army was not enthusiastic about the war; that, on the contrary, it hoped for peace, and, if the struggle were carried on much longer, might, indeed, refuse to march against the Japanese. That consideration decided M. Witte to consent to conditions which, under different circumstances, he would have refused with indignation. He hesitated very much before he accepted the articles of the Treaty of Portsmouth, and at the last moment nearly broke off the negotiations. Just then, however, he received certain information from Russia that did away with his last scruples, whereupon he concluded peace with Japan.

The Emperor was not pleased with him, though he felt constrained to acknowledge his services. Accordingly, on his return to Russia, M. Witte was received with pomp, and many honours were awarded to him. The title of Count was conferred upon him, and his wife was at last presented to the Empress, thus realising her secret ambition ever since the day when she married Sergius Ioulievitch. But through it all he was conscious of the Emperor's personal dislike. He knew that Nicholas had sent him to combat the astuteness of the Japanese diplomatists, simply because, in the terrible dearth of capable men from which Russia suffered, he was the only strong man, and Nicholas II. felt obliged to acknowledge this fact.

But even Count Witte would have failed in the difficult mission that had been imposed upon him had the Japanese been aware of the spirit of rebellion and dissatisfaction that undermined the feelings of loyalty of the army. His great art lay in the amount of bluff which he displayed during these important peace negotiations. Very often, when almost breaking down under the weight of responsibility, he appeared to be quite firm and perfectly decided not to yield one inch of his pretensions; whilst in reality he was trembling at the thought of what would occur were his words taken seriously and the Japanese proved as obdurate as he pretended to be. He feared still more that the latter might receive from Manchuria reports that would at once put them *au fait* with what was going on in the ranks of the Russian army, about whose real feelings he was but too well informed.

In a conversation which he had with the Emperor when he was received by him in Tsarskoye Selo, after his return from America, Count Witte spoke quite openly and frankly with the Sovereign, and did not hide from him the necessity that existed for making concessions to the public mind, and for granting certain liberties before they were imposed upon the Crown by the will of the multitude. He drew the attention of the monarch to the great progress which revolutionary ideas had made among the army, and of the dissatisfaction which was fast shaking its loyalty and its submissiveness, not only to its chiefs, but also to the person of the Tsar himself.

Nor did he hide the danger that was lurking everywhere, ready to break out at the first opportunity. At last he begged Nicholas II. to allow him to draw out a programme of reforms that would meet the requirements of the country, the granting of which would pacify public opinion, and at least deflect its attention from the prevalent and continued attitude of criticism it adopted, not only in regard to the Government, but also as to the actions of the Sovereign.

The Emperor listened to Witte, consented to all his propositions, and appeared convinced. Then, as usual, he consulted others, and was equally convinced by them in their turn, when they told him that he ought not to think of reforms of any kind; that concessions were fatal to the monarch who consented to make any, and that Russia was not ripe for a constitutional system of government.

This duel of opinion lasted some days, during which no one knew what was going to happen. Meanwhile the excitement in the country was fast assuming formidable proportions, and from distant Manchuria deplorable reports continued to arrive concerning the spirit of discontent among the troops. It was growing every day more dangerous, and foreshadowed the peril which their return might cause to law and order throughout the country.

The working classes, who had suffered so much from the war—which had arrested the whole industrial system by depriving it of so many hands, and had, furthermore, caused such misery and poverty among the families of those who had been called upon to fight—were getting very bitter against those in authority. Every day brought the Emperor face to face with new and more complicated difficulties, and yet he would not make up his mind to do anything, or to accept any of the propositions that were laid before him. The natural hesitation and want of resolution which were the characteristics of his temperament prevented him from coming to a decision. On the one hand, he could not resign himself to share with a responsible Ministry the least portion of his authority; nor, on the other, make up his mind to appeal to the country to help him to rule it according to the requirements of modern times. The situation grew daily more pressing. It was impossible to keep the army away much longer in Manchuria, now that peace had been concluded, and to bring it back dissatisfied, among a dissatisfied populace, might be the signal for a general rising that it might be found impossible to subdue, especially if any number of the troops joined it.

One cannot help pitying Nicholas II. at this particular period of his existence. He had neither enough insight to judge for himself the perils of the situation in which circumstances had thrown him, nor sufficient energy to make up his mind to one or other course of action. Good intentions he certainly possessed. He had seen his father keep aloft the flag of autocracy, and he wondered why he had not been able to do the same, attributing his failure to the fault of his advisers, and never suspecting that it was due to his own mistakes.

He must have suffered unspeakably during the weeks that preceded the famous 17th of October which saw the promulgation of the manifesto granting to Russia the shadow of a Constitution. I use the word "shadow," because it was never for a moment intended by the Emperor really to fulfil that which he promised. He still retained a faint hope that he would be able to elude the accomplishment of the reforms which had been wrung from him by the force of circumstances. He thought that the various local rebellions which had already broken out in various parts of the Empire would cease as soon as the news of the concessions which he had been obliged to promise had been duly published.

Unfortunately, events did not take the direction he had expected. Whilst waiting for the election of that Duma which was to represent the constitutional element in the government of the country, Russia was passing through one of the most terrible crises in its history. Never before had the lower orders raised their heads with such audacity and such energy. Never before had a reign of terror, such as then shook the vast dominions of the Romanoffs, carried such fear among all those who belonged to the higher ranks of society. The rising was general, and Europe does not know to this day the scenes of butchery which took place in the provinces, where the peasants not only destroyed the houses and the property belonging to the landlords, but also murdered those among them who had the misfortune to fall into their hands.

Moscow, which had always been considered as the bulwark of conservatism, was the first town to embrace the cause of revolution and to take arms against the Government. What happened there passes the limits of imagination. Troops were sent from St. Petersburg, among others the Semenoffsky regiment of the Guards, to subdue the rebellion. When these troops arrived they found barricades erected everywhere in the town, and they had practically to storm every house separately. Deeds of horror took place, and neither women nor children were spared on either side during the several days that the struggle lasted. Blood flowed freely once more, and those who remembered the catastrophe of Khodinka said that the events that occurred in Moscow were a consequence of what had happened on that distant June day, when the Coronation of Nicholas II. had been celebrated by such a terrible hecatomb of his most faithful subjects.

But though the Moscow rebellion had been crushed; though repression, and cruel repression, had, outwardly, at least, put an end to the Revolution which had in that eventful year 1905 shaken the whole of Russia and left everywhere its bloody traces, the spirit of agitation that lurked in every corner of the country had not been subdued, and Count Witte—who was well aware of this fact —kept pressing the Emperor to fix a date for calling together the Duma, and for the election of its members. Nicholas II. hesitated for a long time; but at last, bending before the necessities of the hour, he yielded, and on one fine May morning he opened, with much pomp and solemnity in the White Hall of the Winter Palace, the first Parliament of its kind in Russia.

THE WINTER PALACE, ST. PETERSBURG
As seen through the Nevski Prospekt Archway
Photo: Topical

CHAPTER XV

THE FIRST TWO DUMAS

IT was on a fine May morning that Louis XVI. opened the session of the States General at Versailles. It was also on a May day that the first Russian Duma met in St. Petersburg. More than one person noticed this strange coincidence, and wondered whether the tragedy that had ended with the murder of the French king was going to be enacted over again. As at Versailles, too, in 1789, the ceremony took place with much solemnity, and all the pomp of the Russian Court was displayed. The Winter Palace opened its doors, and the aristocracy of St. Petersburg assembled to witness the inauguration of an Assembly from which so much was hoped by many people and so much was feared by others.

I shall never forget that day. I was one of the first to arrive at the Palace, and had plenty of opportunities to watch the Assembly, and to observe the spectators, as well as the Deputies, as they arrived one by one and proceeded to the places assigned to them. It was the first time that the whole of Russia, as here represented by all classes of the nation, had assembled together in one room, and the spectacle was curious in the extreme. One saw on one side all the great dignitaries of the State, Ministers, and advisers of the Crown, military and civil functionaries, Court chamberlains, and gentlemen-in-waiting, maids of honour, high-born dames, fair women, and lovely girls—all the flower of St. Petersburg Society, with their diamonds and their long Court trains trailing behind them. On the other side were gathered the newly chosen representatives of the country: landlords, advocates, merchants, noblemen, and peasants, realising for the first time their importance from the social as well as from the legislative point of view; men full of illusions, others full of hatred; some believing honestly in the possibility of doing good to their fatherland; others only dreaming of destroying the authority under which they had lived with such impatience. Ambitions, greed, thirst for power, desire for revenge—everything was there, and the sight appeared portentous to the onlooker, perhaps because all these people kept so silent and unmoved, merely gazing before them, with eyes that looked into the future more than at what was going on around them. It was the great hour of a nation's life, that which decides its ultimate fate, and though everybody felt that it was so, yet none seemed to realise it, perhaps because we can never understand the importance of the events in which we are actors.

The Deputies assembled slowly, and did not seem to know very well what they ought to do. In one corner the Clerical faction clustered in one compact group, their long hair and flowing beards, their different coloured cassocks, making them picturesque figures, which commanded attention. Near by, the Peasant members, in their long caftans, some of which were not even new, as the Emperor remarked to one of his attendants after the ceremony was over, stared with interest at all that they saw, and appeared as if they did not know why they were there. Then, again, the Socialist Deputies kept whispering to each other, and glanced with scorn at the part of the room where the ladies invited to be present at the opening ceremony were chatting without appearing to notice the Deputies, as they slowly filed before them. The disdain in which these representatives of the nation were held among Court circles was very apparent, and made one feel that the comedy which was being enacted would very soon turn to drama and end with tragedy.

At last the stick of the Masters of Ceremonies made itself heard, and the Emperor, with his wife and mother, followed by the Imperial Family, entered the room. The procession which heralded his appearance reminded one, by its splendour, of that far-distant day when he had entered Moscow before his Coronation, also preceded and accompanied by all the pomp of his splendid Court. But the atmosphere was different. Then the nation had acclaimed him, now it cheered him; the cries were the same, but the accent was different.

Nicholas II. appeared nervous; he was paler than was his wont, and he kept twisting his white military glove. But there was no kindness in his blue eyes. The Empress appeared as cold and disdainful as usual; she seemed bored more than anything else, and scarcely noticed the low salutations with which the Imperial party were greeted when they came into the room. The Empress Dowager, on the contrary, was extremely moved and agitated. Her eyes were red, and she kept putting up her handkerchief as if to wipe away tears. She remained slightly behind her son and daughter-in-law, but keenly observed the Assembly, as if trying to read their countenances and to guess what lay behind them. From time to time she turned towards her chamberlain-in-waiting, and asked him some questions evidently relating to the identity of the various Deputies. The Socialist group attracted her attention quite particularly, and she watched it the whole time the ceremony lasted with something akin to anxiety in her lovely dark eyes, which then wandered towards her son, resting on him with passionate yearning and sadness. Her countenance was perfectly dignified, and yet a whole tragedy lurked in her figure as it bent under the blessing of the Metropolitan, who celebrated the Divine Service with which the pageant began. When it was over, Nicholas II. took from the hands of the Minister of the Household the paper upon which was written the first Speech from the Throne addressed to a Russian legislative assembly. He read it slowly at first, a little more hurriedly towards the end, but in a determined voice that hardly wavered as he proceeded with its contents. Whether he felt or not the solemnity of the hour, it is impossible to tell; still less to guess whether he was sincere in the solemn promises which he made to his people.

Hurrahs replied to his message, and from the monarchist side of the Assembly these cheers were the sincere expression of a real and frank loyalty. But it was observed that the Peasant group was very moderate in the manifestation of its feelings, and as for the Socialists, they remained silent, though observing a respectful attitude.

The Sovereign bowed to the Assembly and retired, together with the members of his family, proceeding to lunch in his private apartments before returning to Tsarskoye Selo. The meal was not very cheerful, although everybody agreed that the ceremony had gone off very well; but Nicholas II. seemed angry at some apparent want of respect that had struck him in the attitude of the group of Deputies belonging to the rural classes; and he had not been impressed by the hostile aspect of the Socialist Deputies. He expressed his regret that so many advocates had been elected, and the hope that the choice of the President of the Duma would be a wise one, and would fall upon a man chosen from among the Conservative or Governmental party.

This was not to be. From the very first day it became evident that the Duma was distinctly hostile to the Ministry as it was composed at the time, and that it meant seriously to perform its task of participating in the government of the country.

The President, who was elected by a large majority, was a man enjoying a blameless reputation, and one of the most eminent of the Moscow bar, M. Muromtsev. He had distinctly Liberal opinions, and was a personage whom even his adversaries respected. A strong supporter of a constitutional system of government, he meant to do his best to help its establishment in Russia and to strengthen the authority of the Sovereign by persuading him to share it with a responsible Ministry. He was an idealist by temperament as well as by conviction, and he had hailed with enthusiasm the promises of Nicholas II., whose sincerity he had never doubted for a single moment. In a certain sense, he belonged to the party that named itself the Octobrists, as having been called into existence by the manifesto of October 17th, though officially he was considered to be an advanced Liberal. He was essentially an honest man, and possessed, among his other gifts, that of a rare eloquence, which had made him a great power at the Bar, the more so that he had never consented to defend a wrong cause.

Had the Emperor recognised the rare qualities of M. Muromtsev, and had he consented to employ his great talents, it is probable that the agitation which shook the country during the few short weeks that the first Duma was allowed to work would have taken a different direction.

As is usual in Russia, where every new venture is welcomed with enthusiasm until the Government has seen fit to quench it, the first Legislative Assembly, or, at least, the members of it who belonged to the moderate side, although Liberal in their opinions, started to work with the best intentions. They seriously believed that their Sovereign was frank and sincere with them, that he really meant to see to the needs of Russia and to lead the nation in the path of order and prosperity, with the help of its representatives, who would be better able than his Ministers to bring to his notice all the evils which it was essential to remove, and all the abuses that wanted remedying. It was under such an illusion that they started their labours. Little did they guess or think that neither the Tsar, nor those among his advisers who enjoyed his confidence, ever intended to allow them any other liberty or privileges beyond those of talking about things; there was certainly no intention to allow change or modification.

The first conflict arose when the reply to the Speech from the Throne was being discussed. It was then that the Radical elements which the Duma contained began to make themselves heard, and to throw themselves into the fray with all the vehemence of beginners. It must not be forgotten that this Assembly, gathered together in such an unexpected manner was composed mainly of men who had absolutely no experience as to the way in which parliamentary debates ought to be conducted. Yet, eager though they were to show what they could do, they possessed no controlling power, nor were they able to keep their discussions within reasonable limits. The authority which statesmen of long standing alone can wield was entirely absent. It was natural, therefore, that confusion should ensue. Political parties, in the sense in which they are understood in Europe, did not exist then, and do not exist even now in Russia, where there are only political opinions. How, therefore, could one expect unimpassioned, or even reasonable, discussions of the innumerable subjects which required attention from such an assemblage? Each was desirous of making his own opinions and his own judgments triumph over those of his neighbour.

The great pity lay in the fact that neither the Duma, the Government, nor the Emperor would make up their minds to the fact that this first legislative session could not be anything more than a trial of constitutional government, such as it is understood in Europe; that before framing laws or attempting reforms, one ought to learn how to work. Instead of realising this truth, they all started with the idea that a great deal could be accomplished at once, and that a Russian Parliament ought immediately to take its place with those of other countries, where initial blunders were already a thing of the past, and where experience had taught that neither reforms nor laws could be framed in a few days.

The root-error was that the Duma believed it could at once impose itself and its decisions upon the Sovereign, whilst the latter simply wanted to find in it an obedient executor of his own will.

This misunderstanding caused the conflict which very shortly led to irremediable disaster.

The culmination was reached when the important question of a responsible Ministry came to be discussed. The Duma required it; the Tsar refused to make up his mind to it otherwise than as a mere matter of form. To reconcile these two points of view was impossible, and it became evident that a struggle was inevitable, which could only end in the dissolution of the Assembly or in a *coup d'état*.

Strange though it may seem, yet it is certain that, had the first Duma not been composed of such clever men, it would have fared better. As it was, all the best elements that Russia possessed had been elected, and these would not consent to become mere puppets in the hands of the Government. They thought themselves able to share with it the task of ruling the country, and they wanted at once to prove their capacities in that respect. Had the deputies elected been more timid and less intelligent, they would have settled quietly to learn how they ought to work, and paved the way for their successors, who would have found the road clear before them. Unfortunately, all the leading people, either in the capital or in the provinces, had been selected as members either of the Duma or of the Council of State, and these had studied social questions too long to believe themselves unqualified to settle them.

Nicholas II. kept himself well informed as to the way in which the debates were carried on, and instead of looking with indulgence at certain intemperances of language, proceeding more from headstrong, though well-meaning, ignorance than from anything else, took as personal offences words which meant nothing but a desire on the part of these impatient reformers to make themselves heard. He wanted the Duma to work as if it occupied the same position as a local zemstvo, never for one moment imagining that the Assembly could look upon itself as upon a power in the State. This misunderstanding as to the position in which they stood, in regard to each other, led to the conflict between the Sovereign and the Duma, which ended in the unexpected and violent dissolution of the latter.

That dissolution was the personal work of Nicholas II. None of his Ministers had the courage to assume the responsibility of such a violent measure, and Count Witte absolutely declined to have a hand in it. Even M. Dournovo, the representative of the extreme Conservative party, and the strong upholder of autocracy in the strictest sense of the word, hesitated before the consequences of this decision. But the Emperor decided upon it, and with one stroke of his pen the Duma was dissolved.

The Liberal Deputies, indignant at the measure, resolved to express their indignation upon paper, and to publish it to the whole country. The greater portion of the members of the Assembly then went to Viborg, and there signed the famous manifesto which exposed their wrongs before the world. That act was certainly an appeal to rebellion. The mistake of this step was most serious. It gave to the Government a reason for action, and enabled them to prevent the members of the late Duma from proving a future hindrance to its plans. Had the Liberal members of the Duma quietly gone home, it is more than certain that they would have been re-elected, and could have gone on with their requests for reforms, which would have had more chance to succeed as time went by. The unfortunate journey to Viborg which caused the criminal proceedings should never have been undertaken. By it they gave the Government the opportunity they wanted. The condemnation of the Deputies to several months of prison would not have been such a misfortune had it not had the consequence of making them for ever ineligible as Deputies. It was that which the Government wanted, and the Liberal party played into its hands.

Months passed, and then a second Duma was called into existence. It proved almost as rebellious as the first, with one great difference: it contained neither clever men, nor men able to do serious work. The second Duma also had a brief life, and then the Government—which in the meantime had achieved its aim: of silencing, though not exterminating, the elements of opposition in the nation—proceeded to the third elections, which satisfied it so well that the third Duma lived to die a natural death. About the fourth Duma, whose work has just begun, I shall speak later on.

Whilst Nicholas II. was getting rid of the shadow of Parliament with which he had endowed Russia, his Ministers were forsaking him one after the other. The Cabinet of Count Witte had not survived the first Duma; that of M. Gorémykin, and the one over which M. Dournovo had presided, had also not enjoyed a very long existence. A new star had arisen on the horizon, a new "*Vrementchik*," to use the traditional word applied in Russia to the favourite of a Sovereign, had appeared upon the political scene. M. Stolypin was appointed Prime Minister, and he contrived to keep that post until he was forcibly removed from it by the bullet of an anarchist conspirator.

CHAPTER XVI

THE CAREER OF M. STOLYPIN

Peter Arkadievitch Stolypin was the son of an aide-de-camp general of Alexander II. His father had been at one time very popular in St. Petersburg society, and through his numerous family connections had made a brilliant career. He was a pleasant man, a perfect gentleman in manners, but by no means clever or bright. His most salient quality was the perfection with which he could indulge for hours in small talk, and it was this capacity that had made him such a welcome guest at a dinner table or at a party.

His son, the future Prime Minister of Nicholas II., was not very well known among the select circle of Court Society in the capital. He had entered the public service when quite young, and had been at once sent to the interior of the Empire, to work out his advancement step by step. After having done so to the best of his capacity, he was appointed Governor of the province of Samara, and whilst there had attracted the notice of the public and of his superiors by the energetic manner in which he had suppressed local riots. Count Witte was the first man to whom it occurred to appoint him to a more important post. M. Stolypin, who had only waited for a favourable opportunity to approach his Sovereign, was delighted to be called to St. Petersburg, and when he arrived there it was with the firm intention to do everything to win for himself Imperial protection and Imperial favour; to show himself an able courtier and a faithful executor of the wishes and intentions of the master upon whom his future career depended.

He was a man of strong character, but of immense ambitions, very personal in all his actions, and secretive in his designs.

In his provincial life he had had no hopes of ever making anything else than an administrative career, such as Government officials generally do, and the thought that he might be called upon to occupy an important post in the capital had never entered his mind. When he was summoned to St. Petersburg he was at first stunned by this unexpected piece of luck, but very quickly recovered himself, and, being a keen observer of human nature, no sooner had he been presented to Nicholas II. than he had taken an estimate of that monarch's character, and the right way to influence it, so as to obtain for himself a leading part in his counsels. The two men had much in common, though little real sympathy existed between them. Stolypin was certainly more cultivated than the Tsar; also he had more determination, and more firmness in character, but there was lurking in the corners of his nature the same hardness, the same tyrannical tendencies, the same want of heart. Both were egotistical, with the difference that one thought it was his right to be so, whilst the other only imagined that he could win this right for himself.

Stolypin was brave, but of fatalistic temperament. He firmly believed that he would not die before the day appointed for him to do so by fate, and that conviction made him often appear to be reckless, whilst in reality he was only indifferent as to a fate which he thought was already settled by a power higher than his own. He had been told one day in his youth by a fortune-teller that he would reach a high position, which he would keep until his death, and, sceptical though he was on other points, he had faith in that prediction, which was to come true in so singular a fashion. Authoritative, selfish, merciless whenever he feared his personal interests were threatened, he succeeded during the years he was in power in making himself hated alike by the anarchists he was supposed to fight and the Conservatives he was believed to protect.

The ability with which he managed to get all his opinions and all his plans approved by the Sovereign would have been sure to win him many enemies, even if he had not made himself so offensive everywhere. Disdainful by nature, he had not the least regard for the feelings of anyone, and did not respect either those of his friends or of his foes. His high position, and the unlimited power conferred upon him by the force of circumstances more than by anything else, had imbued him with the conviction that he was indispensable, and that everything would be allowed to him because there was no one to take his place.

Another man before him had enjoyed as much, and even more of the confidence of the Tsar. It was General Trepoff, and death soon removed that rival, who was not even a dangerous one, because he had neither the intelligence nor the cunning that could have made him an opponent worthy of notice by Stolypin.

Since I am mentioning General Trepoff, perhaps a few words concerning that personage will not be out of place. Trepoff was one of the many children of the famous General Trepoff, who had for such a long time held the important post of Prefect of the town of St. Petersburg, under the reign of Alexander II., and whose attempted assassination by Vera Zassoulitch had been the first open act of warfare of the Nihilist party. His son began his career in the first regiment of Horse Guards, and at one time was considered one of the crack officers in the Society of the capital. He was invited everywhere, and at last succeeded in ingratiating himself into the good graces of the Grand Duke Paul, who was in command of the regiment. It was the latter who had him appointed head of the police in Moscow under his brother, the Grand Duke Sergius. Once in Moscow young Trepoff made himself pleasant to the

Grand Duchess Elizabeth Feodorovna, and at one time public gossip was very busy with their names. What amount of truth there lay at the bottom of all these rumours it is impossible to say, but the fact is that it was on the recommendation of the Grand Duchess that Colonel Trepoff, as he was at the time, was called to the head of the Okhrana, or personal guard of the Sovereign.

For some time his influence was very powerful, but it did not last long. Trepoff was of an imperious disposition, but perfectly loyal to his master. He might have been an excellent watch-dog, and, indeed, performed the duties of one to perfection; but he was a man with limited education, who held no opinions except those he was ordered to have. His reign was very brief, and he did not deserve all the hatred expended upon him, because his influence would never have been lasting. He did not possess the qualities of an administrator, and, short-sighted as Nicholas II. was, he still had noticed this, and would certainly have sacrificed Trepoff to Stolypin had he been called upon to choose between the two. Fate intervened and saved him the necessity. Trepoff died, worn out with too much work, and perhaps also with the anxiety of his responsible post, for which he felt himself to be unequal; and Stolypin remained the only personage capable of leading the Government of Russia under the weak and tottering rule of the Emperor Nicholas.

He very soon assumed the attitude of a dictator, and in doing so bluffed a good many people into really believing that he possessed the necessary qualities of a leader. This was not the case. Stolypin pretended to have more determination than he really possessed.

After the dissolution of the first Duma, a measure he was the only one to approve, and the only one gifted with sufficient courage to execute, he became the object of the execration of all the Liberal parties in Russia. An era of revolution began in the whole country. Even in St. Petersburg rebellion raged, assassinations were frequent, and no one felt himself to be in safety. The Nihilists, who once more came to the front in the struggle which waged between Stolypin and the whole nation, at last proceeded to extremes, and the first attempt to assassinate the too powerful Minister took place when his summer villa on the Islands of the Apothecaries, near St. Petersburg, was nearly destroyed, his children wounded, and about forty-five persons killed, whilst he alone remained untouched.

It was on that awful day that M. Stolypin showed the fatalism which was one of the dominant traits of his character. Another man would have lost his head, or at least given way to discouragement under the blow that had struck his daughter and his son. Peter Arkadievitch remained perfectly calm, outwardly at least, and he never for a single minute thought of resigning the responsible position which he occupied. On the contrary, he seemed to find a compensation for his private sorrows in the authority which the dastardly attempt against his person and his family had added to those which he already possessed. He could now represent to the Emperor, with more force than ever, how indispensable it was to show no mercy to all those who tried to shatter his Throne and his power, and could obtain the assent of the Sovereign to all the measures which he thought imperative for assuring the latter, and for the welfare of the country.

That country was about the last subject to which Stolypin turned his attention. Russia meant nothing to him, except in the sense that through her he could gain honours and dignities, and advance his own welfare. He had, it is true, Nationalist tendencies, and worked towards the development of Nationalism in the country, which perhaps was another of his many mistakes, and brought about the conflict that shortly before his death arose between him and the Council of State. In this dispute the Council refused to agree to Stolypin's bill for the introduction of zemstvos, or local councils, in the Polish provinces, where they had not yet been installed. When that conflict took an acute shape, and he had been defeated in the Upper House, Peter Arkadievitch offered his resignation to the Emperor. This was merely a move, for he had some secret influence with certain personages near the Throne, amongst them the Dowager Empress, so it was said, who advised Nicholas II. to ask him to keep office, to which he at last assented, but not without securing conditions which strengthened his authority and made him more powerful than ever.

The country did not approve, and even in St. Petersburg, where individuals were rather chary of expressing their opinions, people began openly to attack him. The fact was, that everybody was getting wearied of this kind of Major-domo of the Palace, which Stolypin had succeeded in becoming, and which reminded one of the old Merovingian kings and of the dictators who had ruled under them. The personality of the Emperor was becoming submerged in comparison with the importance that the influence of his Prime Minister was assuming. Conservatives disliked this effacement of the Sovereign; Liberals thought that if one had to be ruled by an autocrat, it would be better to have a Romanoff than one of his subjects.

Nicholas II. himself became, not perhaps jealous, but certainly impatient, at the independence that Stolypin displayed, now that he felt his position more secure. Once or twice he had found some orders that he had given counteracted by dispositions made by Stolypin without consulting his Emperor. Nicholas was not a man capable of forgiving encroachments made upon his authority, and certainly not one to forget them. Vindictive as he was by nature, the Emperor found the yoke that his Prime Minister had forced him to assume heavy to bear, and though he felt that the time had not come when he could get rid of him, yet one can well suppose that he would have seized with pleasure an opportunity to cover Stolypin with honours and at the same time retire him into private life, had he only asked a second time the permission to do so.

The Minister was too observant not to notice that, though his influence had not begun to get weakened, his person was no longer sympathetic to the Emperor. He was, however, determined to keep his post, and to have more distinctions showered upon him. He then tried to invent some conspiracies against the life of the monarch, in order to prove that he was indispensable, and that his vigilance was the best safeguard that Nicholas II. could find against the many dangers which threatened him. Provocative agents began once more to be sent all over the country, and the police received energetic orders to find conspirators, no matter at what cost. He thought that fear was the best means left at his disposal to make his position unassailable on the part of those who tried to shatter it. St. Petersburg Society did not take to Peter Arkadievitch. It considered him a little in the light of an intruder, a parvenu, who had imposed himself upon it, and forced an entrance into its rooms. Madame Stolypin, too, was little liked, and thought lacking in refinement. She came from a worthy family of German origin, who had served without distinction, but with much zeal, its Sovereign, and which belonged essentially to the middle class. Neither her manners nor her tact made her a fit wife for a Prime Minister, and a certain spirit of intrigue and of gossip, caused her to be disliked, rather than anything else. She never made herself at home, or popular, among the smart circles of the capital, where she was received, but seldom welcomed.

Nevertheless, though the Emperor began to get just a little tired of the state of dependence in which M. Stolypin kept him, nothing of this impatience appeared in public. He was still a favourite, and the man to whom everybody turned whenever one was in want of a favour or of a protection of some kind. When the Imperial Family left for the Crimea in the autumn of the year 1911, with the intention to stop on its way in Kieff and in order to allow the Emperor to be present at some manœuvres in the south of Russia, M. Stolypin accompanied them, and was the principal personage in their numerous suite. That journey was to see the end of his ambitions and of his career, for it was during its course that he was killed.

The murder took place at Kieff during a performance at the theatre. The Prime Minister fell under the bullet of one of his own agents, a Jew called Bagrov, who had been employed by the political police as a spy for a number of years. It was with a ticket signed by Stolypin himself that he had obtained an entrance into the theatre, and he fired at his chief with a revolver which belonged to the Government, and which had been given to him by one of the heads of the Okhrana or private guard of the Emperor. Stolypin fell, or rather dropped in his chair, with just one exclamation, "I am done for!" Nicholas II. was sitting with his daughters in the State box, but he never made the slightest movement to show that he was impressed by the tragical event. The crowd that filled the theatre began to cheer him with unusual enthusiasm, which he accepted with a slight bow in the direction of the audience, but he did not seem to evince particular interest as to the fate of his wounded Minister. He returned to the Palace without visiting the wounded man, or making personal inquiry as to his condition.

At first there was some hope of saving Stolypin, though a renowned physician, who held the post of professor at the University of Kieff, at once told his friends that the situation was desperate, because the liver had been perforated by the bullet. The wounded man himself had no illusions as to his fate, and he bore the terrible sufferings which he had to endure with great courage and fortitude, asking only from his doctors to keep him alive until his wife and family had arrived. A great surgeon was summoned from St. Petersburg, and everything possible was done to ease his last days, but it was felt from the very first that a recovery was impossible, and those who had expressed some hope had only done so in order to spare the feelings of the dying man and of those near to him.

The whole of Russia was aghast at the assassination of Stolypin; even his enemies were dumb with the horror of it. Assurances and expressions of sympathy came from every side; the person who appeared the most unmoved was the Emperor. It was only on the third day after the attack that he visited the dying statesman. He expressed no sympathy to the dying man beyond some conventional inquiries and official words of regret. It may be assumed that at heart he was neither sorry nor perplexed as to the consequences which the event could have, and that, if anything, he felt relieved at the solution of the problem which the dismissal of M. Stolypin would have proved. It was certain that such an eventuality would have arisen very soon, because the Tsar could not have borne much longer with a man in whom he saw a rival in authority rather than a helpmate or a faithful servant.

Stolypin lingered but a few short days after the one upon which he had been struck. The Emperor came to his bedside just before the end, and was received by Madame Stolypin, who used this opportunity to address a few tactless words to the Sovereign, which he resented afterwards. Nicholas II. only remained a few minutes with the dying man, and after some formal expressions of grief he retired.

Stolypin died two days after this visit. His funeral was made the occasion of great manifestations of sorrow on the part of the Conservative, or Old Russian party, who transformed him into a martyr, fallen for the defence of his country and of his Sovereign.

Nicholas did not consider it to be his duty to attend the funeral of his murdered servant. He was to leave Kieff for the Crimea on the very day upon which it took place, and it would have been easy enough to put off this departure for a few hours. But there was no one to suggest it to Nicholas II., who himself never thought of the opportunity which he would have had to make himself popular had he walked behind the coffin of his murdered Minister, and thus showed publicly that he knew how to value the services rendered to him and how to recognise them.

This indifference contributed considerably to lessen the already very small popularity which the Tsar enjoyed. M. Stolypin had not been liked; many people rather rejoiced at his death, and for others it came as a great relief; but even his many enemies felt that it ought to have produced a terrible impression on the Emperor, before whose eyes he had been struck. All wondered at the impassiveness the monarch displayed in those tragical circumstances, and some asked themselves whether he had realised their importance. It seemed strange that, after having worked for years with the murdered man, after having made him a powerful Minister and a personal friend, after having shared with him political anxieties and apprehensions of all kinds, after having confided to him the welfare of the whole vast Russian Empire, after having trusted him above all other people and listened to him rather than to anyone else, the greatest proof of sorrow that his assassination provoked in Nicholas II. took the form of a considerable pension accorded to Madame Stolypin. He gave her money, but did not think it worth while to offer her the one supreme sign of sympathy he could have accorded—that of praying beside the coffin of her husband. The whole of Russia was represented at the funeral service held over the remains of Peter Arkadievitch Stolypin; the Emperor alone was missing.

CHAPTER XVII

A CHARACTER SKETCH OF M. KOKOVTSOV

M. STOLYPIN was not yet dead when people began to make speculations as to his successor. He had occupied both the office of Minister of the Interior and that of Head of the Government. There were, therefore, two most important Departments to provide for, and though candidates were many, eligible people were but few. The Emperor did not like to see new faces about him, and this added to the difficulty. Of course intrigues went on, and ambition as well as eagerness had a considerable part in them, because, though everybody knew the great danger that attended the position of Prime Minister, it was nevertheless the most coveted post in the whole of the Empire. All the colleagues of the murdered statesman thought themselves entitled to become his successor, and each of them had his particular circle of friends who went about declaring that their candidate had the most chances. However, people in the know never doubted for a single moment that Vladimir Nicolaievitch Kokovtsov was the only man in Russia strong enough to replace M. Stolypin, and to take upon himself the onerous duties of Premier. But whether he would consent to leave the Treasury, at the head of which he had been for some years, was a matter of much speculation, and this uncertainty alone prevented the majority of St. Petersburg Society from congratulating him on his promotion.

Doubts were very soon at an end, and when M. Kokovtsov

FAMOUS RUSSIAN MINISTERS

Prince Gortschakov   Count Ignatieff
M. de Giers   M. Stolypin

M. Kokovtsov

was summoned to Livadia his nomination was a foregone
conclusion. Nevertheless, he had a surprise in store for the
public, because he only accepted the Premiership, and
refused to give up the Department over which he already
presided, saying that he knew nothing about civil
administration, and would only make blunders if he took
the burden of it upon his shoulders. He recommended,
therefore, to the Emperor one of his personal friends, M.
Makarov, as the man most able to fulfil the duties
connected with the direction of Home affairs.

M. Kokovtsov was a small man, with a short beard very neatly trimmed, and a general look of tidiness in every detail of his person as well as of his clothes. He had a pleasant face and was very affable in his ways, but he never looked one straight in the eyes, always seeming as if he was too much occupied with his personal appearance to think of watching that of others. Somehow or other he gave one the impression that when he conversed with you he was preoccupied with something he had forgotten, and the way in which he kept his glance riveted on his coat or on his trousers suggested the idea that these garments were dusty, and that he was angry at his valet's carelessness in brushing them. In a word, one felt that he was too neat, too well groomed, too polite, too civil, and too anxious not to forget what he ought to say or what he ought to do. His manners seemed to have been learned only recently, and somehow one always expected to find near him, ready to be consulted, some manual of etiquette for beginners, with indications as to what one must do in good society, and the errors in which one must not fall if one wants to frequent the company of cultured people. One would have preferred to find some hesitation or some impatience in his way of talking or discussing, but the clear manner in which he expressed himself always reminded one of fables, recited by children, and learned by them at school. This is the impression created. In reality, M. Kokovtsov is certainly a clever, intellectual, and intelligent man, cultivated, and extremely well read. He speaks several foreign languages, of which fact he is inordinately proud, and can hold his own everywhere, even with gentlemen born and bred. His own origin is neither low nor high, but essentially middle class, and he bears the stamp of having lived for a long time with middle-class people. His early career in every respect was a normal one; he rose step by step as years went on, and whatever duties were imposed upon him he fulfilled exactly and thoroughly. In a country where political men are many, he would not have been employed otherwise than as an excellent *sous ordre*. In Russia, where there is such a poverty of statesmen, he undoubtedly fills the position of one.

Vladimir Nicolaievitch is subtle by temperament, and very secretive in all he does. He is excessively alive as to his own interests, and it is said that he does not disdain to use his official position in order to improve his private one. For instance, his brother was chairman of the Kieff

Voronege Railway, in which he himself possessed a considerable number of shares. Certain financiers believe that the shares in question would never have climbed to the high price at which they are now quoted were it not for this combination of circumstances. Other examples of the history of commercial concerns in which he was interested have formed topics for gossip, to the effect that it is very much to be regretted that he had allowed people connected with him to be suspected of using the information he could have given to them, or the protection which it was possible for him to afford to them, in order to enrich themselves or to improve their positions. Cæsar's wife enjoyed certainly a better reputation than certain persons standing in close relationship with our Prime Minister.

The great defect of M. Kokovtsov is that he is above everything a financier, and this is not exactly what is required from the Head of a Government, who ought to look at things and at facts from a higher point of view than that of pounds, shillings, and pence, though these play such an important part in the world.

He has had very great successes in his administration of the Russian Exchequer, and certainly he has made for himself among European financial and commercial circles an excellent position and reputation, which he undoubtedly deserves. But his mind has remained for such a long time concentrated upon purely material questions that it is not to be wondered if other matters interest him less. Social matters have very little attraction for him, except perhaps in the sense that the condition of the working classes being connected with the financial one of the country could not be neglected. But it is to be doubted whether he has quite realised the danger that threatens not only Russia, but the whole world, from the army of artisans and factory workmen who now know what force they represent, and who want to take the upper hand in everything. In giving this character sketch I do not wish to detract from the solid qualities of the Prime Minister, nor to accuse him of lack of political foresight. On the contrary, I am convinced that he has made higher politics the subject of his studies, and that he has even mastered them in a certain sense, as well as a man who has taken to them late in life can do. His intelligence is extremely perceptive, and he is not wanting in *finesse* nor in diplomatic aptitude. His suave manners ensure him success with those with whom he has to deal, and certainly these qualities have impressed the Emperor favourably, and won him the confidence of his Imperial master; but nevertheless he has not proved himself so far able to take a leading position among Russian statesmen—I am not even thinking of foreign ones. The energy that distinguished M. Stolypin is not one of the characteristics of his successor, who is only firm where he can do so with impunity, and who is not gifted with the courage or the fatalism that made Stolypin view with such impassiveness the bullet or the knife which he was but too well aware would strike him one day. His ambitions also lead him in quite a different direction than that in which his predecessor travelled. M. Kokovtsov is not of a fighting temperament or disposition. He entertains for blood and sanguinary deeds the aversion that every clean man feels for dirty things, and he is a great lover of his own comfort and his own welfare. His placid temper makes him avoid every subject of dispute, and he is more insensible, than is the case with Russians in general, to the honours and dignities that have been showered upon him lately. Too wise to take upon himself a risk that might endanger the reputation for cleverness which he has succeeded in acquiring, he has managed to steer clear of difficulties and to make others responsible for his mistakes. His refusal to take upon himself the difficult duties of Minister of the Interior proceeded from the clear perception he had that this post was the one where responsibilities are the heavier and where one can the least escape them.

No one knows whether M. Kokovtsov's opinions are Liberal or Conservative, so carefully has he always avoided parading his views before the public. Some people who know him well affirm that he is an opportunist. The fact is that he has seldom been cajoled into saying in private anything else than what he has uttered in public.

His last speech at the opening of the present session of the Duma was certainly a clever production, but it hardly bears analysis, because when examined carefully its emptiness becomes immediately apparent, and one realises that its contents are nothing but vague promises for which neither the Government represented by him nor the Emperor can be made responsible, so carefully have they been worded.

The Duma does not care for M. Kokovtsov, and does not appreciate the adroitness of his mind. At the same time it does not entertain for him the respect which, in spite of the hatred which he had inspired, it felt for the character of M. Stolypin. And if the present Legislative Assembly contained more independent elements, it is probable that the opposition to the person of the Prime Minister would take a more acute form. But the last elections have been conducted so entirely under the influence of the Government that with the exception of the most prominent members of the Opposition, such as M. Maklakov, M. Milioukov, and others of the same importance, scarcely any of the Deputies whose opinions made them the antagonists of the Cabinet were re-elected, and the official candidates stepped into their places. This last fact was entirely due to the clever manner in which M. Kokovtsov conducted the election campaign, and the instructions which he gave to the Governors of the different provinces of the Empire, as to the best way to ensure the success of the men in whom he had confidence, and whom he hoped to find submissive machines ready to vote according to his direction. Nevertheless, even this Assembly, composed almost entirely of his creatures and sycophants, became disgusted at some decisions of the Government and voted against it upon several occasions. In Russia, however, a Cabinet does not resign if it is in the good graces of the Sovereign, and M. Kokovtsov never dreamed of retiring on account of the censure of the Duma.

This does not mean that he will remain long in power. Very likely he had hoped to be able to resign the responsible post after the tricentennial celebrations of the Romanoff Dynasty, and as he did not then receive the title of Count, nor the blue ribbon of St. Andrew, he is doubtless waiting for another opportunity to arise, after which he will not be sorry to retire into private life.

His private fortune is considerable, and he has judiciously enlarged it during the years that he has been in office; he is clever enough to feel that his personal influence on the Emperor is not quite the same as it was earlier, and very likely he would prefer to retire into private life before this fact became generally suspected. I should not therefore be very much surprised if he left the field free to more enterprising spirits. He will be glad to retire with the knowledge that during his tenure of the Premiership no political crime darkened it, and that it was not disturbed by revolution.

The fact seems clear that the Anarchist party is once more coming to the front, and that very likely we shall soon see a new rebellion break out, better organised than the last one, with more partisans, and with more chances of success. The Universities, where, as usual, riots occurred earlier than in any other centre, have lately been the scene of tumultuous meetings, during which the students discussed the measures adopted by the Government in regard to them and in regard to the administration of the country. Censure votes were passed, and the agitation was so strong that at last the police interfered, with its usual brutality, which only aggravated the discontent of all these young people, among whom generally are found the first elements of a rebellion against the organised order of things.

On the other hand, in the different factories, of which so many exist in St. Petersburg, the anarchist propaganda has also made enormous progress; the recent strikes that have taken place prove it but too well. Though the country is certainly more prosperous than it has ever been, yet the growing cost of living has prevented many people from feeling this prosperity, and discontent is more apparent than a year or two ago.

M. Kokovtsov must be aware of this state of things, and very likely he is just a little tired of the perpetual anxiety under which he is obliged to work and to live. He is also not quite in accord with his colleagues, and not able, like M. Stolypin, to impose his own will against their intentions. His relations with M. Makarov, whom he had recommended for the post of Minister of the Interior, did not for long keep on an amicable footing, and the latter had to retire owing to some differences which arose between him and the Premier. M. Kokovtsov thought that the choice of the new Minister would be left to him, but there a surprise awaited him. The Emperor for once wanted to appoint a man whom he personally liked, and who had pleased him by the manner in which he had seemed to enter into the spirit of the orders which he had given to him. And without taking the advice of Vladimir Nicolaievitch, he appointed in the place of M. Makarov, M. Maklakov, Governor of the province of Tchernigov, a comparatively young man, under forty-five years—an age at which Ministers had never before been chosen—who had attracted his attention during his journey in the south at the time of M. Stolypin's assassination. M. Maklakov, whose brother is the leader of the Opposition in the Duma, is just as Conservative in his opinions as the latter is Liberal. Like all the members of his family, he is clever, and some people see in him a second Stolypin. Whether this will be so remains to be seen, and it is too early to prophesy. The man is unknown, and of course surrounded by flatterers and jealous people. Those who see in him the favourite of the Sovereign cringe before him, and try to make themselves useful to him; those, on the contrary, who doubt his ability to replace M. Kokovtsov, which rumour says will soon be necessary, do not find words hard enough to condemn the choice that has placed him at the head of the most important Department in the Empire.

It seems that what drew the attention of the Emperor to M. Maklakov was the following occurrence. When Nicholas II. visited Tchernigov—it was immediately after Mr. Stolypin had been assassinated by the Jew Bagrov—everybody around the Sovereign was lamenting the death of the Prime Minister, and one thought that by doing so one was pleasing the monarch, and that by saying the loss which the country had suffered in the person of Stolypin was irreparable, one was only giving expression to the feelings which animated him. M. Maklakov alone remarked that though it was terrible and sad that such a dastardly crime had put an end to such a useful life as had been that of the late Minister's, yet one had no reason to fear the future, because with such a wise Sovereign as Nicholas II., one was sure that the interests of Russia would not be neglected, and that he would know where to look for a worthy successor to Stolypin and where to find him. The words pleased the Tsar, and when the retirement of M. Makarov became an accomplished fact, he called M. Maklakov to St. Petersburg, and appointed him in his place.

M. Kokovtsov did not like this, and resented the way in which he had been ignored. Friction between the two men has already occurred, and may in time result in strengthening Vladimir Nicolaievitch in his decision to retire, not from public life, but from the Premiership, in the full glory of his success.

In such a position he would always be consulted in important matters and questions, and could enjoy the liberty of doing what he liked. One of the amiable weaknesses of the present Prime Minister consists in his admiration of the fair sex. This has often occasioned severe criticism, as it was generally felt that when one has assumed the task of ruling an Empire like Russia, one ought to be more reserved in one's actions, and not allow the world to say that one is ready to forget the interests of the country whenever a fair siren has consented to smile upon one. The rumour has been current in St. Petersburg that one could obtain what was wanted from M. Kokovtsov through the intervention of a lady friend.

But, with all his defects, Vladimir Nicolaievitch has done a great service to the Empire, and that was to place his veto upon the ridiculous enthusiasm that was engineered quite artificially in the country for the cause of the Slav kingdoms. At one time it was feared that these madmen would entangle Russia in a war with Turkey or with Austria, which it is doubtful would prove to the advantage of Russia. M. Kokovtsov alone had enough common sense to oppose his influence to that folly, and to prevent the continuance of this senseless agitation. He exposed to the Emperor the situation in which Russia found herself, and the disaster that a war would entail upon her. He spoke of the state of the finances, and of the ruin which a campaign would bring. He opened the eyes of Nicholas II. to the condition of the country, and to the peril that threatened the whole world were a general war of the different States of Europe to break out. He had the tact to impose silence on the Chauvinistic newspapers that excited the public mind not only against the Turks, but also against the Government, which would not allow itself to be drawn into the quarrel of the Balkan States with the Sultan, and he contrived, together with M. Sazonov, to avoid difficulties with Austria, and to ignore the provocations of the Austrian press.

Of course, it is impossible to tell what the future holds in reserve, but if only for the ability with which during the course of last winter, amidst innumerable difficulties, M. Kokovtsov has displayed, for the dignity with which he has repulsed the advice that was given to him by people who spoke of the honour of the country engaged in defending the Slavs, and by the firmness which he preserved the whole time that the crisis lasted, he deserves the gratitude of Russia and of every sane and well-intentioned person not only in Russia, but in the rest of Europe also.

CHAPTER XVIII

THE FOREIGN OFFICE UNDER NICHOLAS II.

THE present head of the Foreign Office is M. Sazonov. In the chair occupied in former years by powerful personalities, such as were Count Nesselrode and Prince Gortschakov, sits a small, meek, little creature, with a figure and nose that remind one of Don Quixote as he is represented in the drawings of Gustave Doré. His whole appearance is insignificant, and suggests embarrassment, nervousness, insecurity as regards his position, and uncertainty as to what he is to do or to say. He always seems as if he wanted to ask everybody's forgiveness for wrongs done and duties neglected. In a word, he lends himself to ridicule, and certainly does not suggest the idea of a Minister who gives himself a true account of the importance or strength of the position which he occupies.

M. Sazonov has been often laughed at, and rarely been taken seriously, until quite recently, when his conduct has come out in a most unexpected light, and he has shown, in the way in which he has handled the Near Eastern question, true political and diplomatic genius. His anxiety as to future complications in which Russia might get entangled has made him show a quiet firmness which no one ever expected from him. It was said once in St. Petersburg that our Foreign Minister feared the east wind, because it might blow away his frail person. The words were cruel, and of course were repeated everywhere, but they were not deserved. M. Sazonov proved himself to be a very energetic little man, sure of himself, and determined to enforce the policy to which he had made up his mind. His nervousness served him well on this occasion, and his fear of responsibility made him avoid all the opportunities, of which he had but too many, of assuming any. He had a horror of war, and, considering the many partisans that an aggressive policy has had in Russia lately, it was a piece of good luck for the country that it did not find an echo in the Foreign Office. Had M. Izvolsky been in possession of the chair, it is more than likely that we would have been engaged already in a conflict with Austria; under our actual Foreign Minister such an eventuality is not to be dreaded. But he has common sense, and sees clearly the situation in which Russia finds herself at the present day, and the impossibility of being able to pursue an aggressive policy for some time. As such he is the right man in the right place at the right time.

M. Sazonov was appointed to his present post through the influence of M. Stolypin, whose wife was his sister-in-law. Whilst Peter Arkadievitch was alive his position was stronger than it is at present, when his policy does not find itself in accord with the views of M. Kokovtsov. But upon one point the two men are agreed, and that is on the necessity of not giving way to the clamours of the press and of the enthusiastic idiots who think it is Russia's duty to waste her money and the blood of her children in order to further the ambitions of King Ferdinand and the other small potentates who rule in the Balkan Peninsula.

M. Sazonov has always been on good terms with the foreign diplomats accredited to the Court of St. Petersburg. He does not believe in quarrelling with anybody, and he always finds pleasant words to say even to those with whom he does not agree. He nervously shakes hands with all those whom he meets, and always accepts their invitations, and asks them in return to sit at his hospitable board. He could not be unpleasant, and he could not say a harsh word, even where deserved. He rules the Foreign Office, not with an iron hand, but with a very soft velvet glove, and is sometimes afraid of his own subordinates; does not dare to contradict them if they show themselves arrogant, and rebukes them only with apologetic expressions. He cannot scold, and he does not know how to punish. But at the same time he has got passive firmness, with which so many timid people are gifted, which makes them stick to their decisions with a persistence that people with a firmer temperament often do not succeed in displaying. When M. Sazonov last autumn went to Paris and to Balmoral, people did not spare him their railleries upon his return home. He was accused of having, like a meek lamb, acquiesced in all the propositions which foreign Cabinets had made to him, and was laughed at for the result of his journey, which he had pompously announced would be peace, whilst war broke out almost upon the very day when he reached St. Petersburg after his wanderings, compared by an Opposition newspaper to those of the Wandering Jew. At one time the general belief was that Russia, in spite of the opposition of the Government, would be drawn into a war, and the wildest rumours circulated everywhere in the country. It was said that a secret mobilisation was taking place, and that troops were being sent to the frontier. M. Sazonov, when questioned, declared that he knew nothing about it, and adhered to his protestations that Russia did not want war, and that all that the papers were saying was nothing but nonsense.

He has one great quality: people believe him. Perhaps because it is not possible to imagine that this small, anxious, and fidgety little man can do anything else but speak the truth. There is no guile in him, and he has the frankness of a person who has never sinned, even in intention. It is impossible not to think him honest, and it would be impossible for him to act otherwise than as an honest man.

The fate of Russia is safe in his hands. Under his rule, Europe can sleep quietly and not fear a complication coming from the Russian Cabinet; it may remain convinced that whenever M. Sazonov can find a loophole to escape from a perilous position he will do so. He may not be a clever man; he certainly is not a brilliant one. Sometimes he appears grotesque; he seems insignificant always. But he is earnest, sincere, and will do his best to fight against those who would engage him or his country in a policy of adventures.

Knowing the man, one cannot for one moment believe that those who pretend that Russia is on the point of assuming a bellicose policy have the slightest reason to say so. Russia, whilst M. Sazonov rules at the Foreign Office, will always stick to the position of onlooker on all the complications that shake the rest of Europe; she won't engage in them. Of course, things might change were he to retire and another person to be appointed in his place, or if a new Prime Minister succeeded to M. Kokovtsov. This last eventuality is the one to be dreaded, but even then it is doubtful whether Russia would ever readily engage again in warlike adventures. The severe defeat by the Japanese disgusted the whole country, the Emperor more than anyone else. Russian foreign policy, therefore, for some years at least, will be carried on on the principle of allowing our neighbours to settle their disputes between themselves. The understanding with England is based on this principle, and as for the alliance with France, it will serve peace more than anything else, because it will moderate the thirst for revenge on Germany which exists there. Even the most adventurous of French Cabinets will not dare to move when it knows that it cannot find support in St. Petersburg, and certainly Ministers like M. Sazonov are the best men to prevent useless complications. They talk common sense, and the motive that guides them is love of peace.

It must not be supposed, however, that we have no turbulent elements in our Foreign Office. Our present Ambassador in Paris is of that nature. M. Izvolsky is one of those men whose presence alone seems to be the signal for strife and complications out of which no exit can be found. Wherever this brilliant diplomat has been, something has happened to compromise his country and his chiefs. There are those who say that his tenure as Ambassador at the Court of the Mikado was barren from the point of view of utility, because he never even suspected the military preparations of the Japanese, far less reported upon them.

M. Izvolsky made his career in part through his marriage with a charming lady, the daughter of Count Toll, who for long years represented the Russian Government at the Court of Copenhagen. Whilst there he, as well as his family, had been intimately received by the King and Queen, and had had plenty of opportunities to meet the late Emperor and his Consort during their frequent stays in Denmark. The young Countess Toll had won the favour of the Empress Marie Feodorovna, who continued to protect her after she had married young M. Izvolsky.

As I think I have already related, the post of Copenhagen was always very much sought after among our diplomats, owing to the opportunities which it afforded them of seeing the Sovereigns otherwise than formally, which was the case in St. Petersburg, and it was generally considered to be a stepping-stone to higher dignities. When M. Izvolsky was appointed to the head of the Foreign Office it was an open secret that he owed it to the influence of the Empress Dowager; and it is certain that she never wavered in the kind feelings with which she followed the progress of his career. M. Izvolsky possesses to perfection the art of making himself liked by those who can be useful to him. Brilliant in conversation, gifted also with an easy pen, which allows him to compose dispatches quickly and well, he is shallow and vain by nature. He possesses the belief that he is a genius because he can talk. He is not greatly liked among his colleagues, and especially those in the Foreign Office in St. Petersburg, owing to his arrogant behaviour and his disagreeable manners. The curt way in which he treats his subordinates, and the deferential air with which he handles his superiors have made him innumerable enemies. Considerable gossip has arisen from time to time concerning his actions in regard to promotions in the diplomatic staff during the time when these depended upon him. It was said that rich people always had the preference, and that Madame Izvolsky appeared with new jewels when a certain councillor was made an ambassador. As the lady's reputation had never been attacked, even by the most ill-natured person, it was immediately thought and said that the happy councillor had showed his gratitude to the husband by offering a little present to his wife. Such things, of course, ought not to be discussed in relation to a man in the position which M. Izvolsky occupied, but they were very freely spoken of, as also was his reputation in money matters.

Count Benckendorff, the Russian Ambassador in London, belongs also to the number of happy people who owe the success of their career to a term at Copenhagen. He had, however, more solid reasons than M. Izvolsky to reach one of its most coveted posts. He was the son of a man who had been one of the personal friends of the Emperor Nicholas II.; he had married a Countess Schouvaloff; his brother was head of the Household of the present Emperor; his family had always stood in close relations to the Throne; his sister, the Princess Natzfeld Trachenberg, had been Mistress of the Robes of the late Empress Frederick of Germany. He had therefore every right to expect to become an ambassador, and his appointment to London surprised no one, and was not even criticised by his colleagues. He is a pleasant man, excessively well bred, with irreproachable manners; looks rather like an Englishman. He speaks English remarkably well, with almost no foreign accent. Not accounted a genius, he has tact and the quality not to attempt to assume a part for which he is not fitted. He will never try to pursue a personal line of conduct in matters connected with politics, and will always faithfully execute, without the least attempt to modify them, the orders he receives. He is a *grand seigneur*, and as such is quite in his element in London, where this quality is more appreciated than anywhere else, and, moreover, he likes England and English life and English ways. It would be a pity if private family matters, as gossip in St. Petersburg hints, should oblige him to ask for his recall, and it would be difficult to find a successor, although it is well known that M. Izvolsky believes himself to be qualified for it.

Of our other ambassadors I have but very little to say. Those in Berlin, Rome, and Madrid are what one calls in French, *des diplomates de carrière*, who have risen step by step in the Service and won their appointments by hard work. M. Kroupensky, who has recently succeeded to Prince Dolgorouky in Rome, had been for some years Councillor of Embassy in London, under Baron de Staal, and was extremely liked there, though he did not go much into Society. He is a pleasant man, inoffensive, with excellent manners, and knowing very well how to hold himself in Society, and how to keep his place. He is a well-set-up figure in a drawing-room, and almost as smart as his uniform is well embroidered. His nose is long, his figure thin, his knowledge of French excellent, and of Italian limited. His wife is Eastern by origin, and not perhaps an ideal ambassadress, as experience of the world rather fails her; but she does not attempt, unless absolutely necessary, to impose herself or her manners anywhere, and remains content to be a good housekeeper and a submissive consort to her amiable husband.

I have not seen much of M. Sverbeev, who replaced the late Count Osten Sacken in Berlin, but I believe he is a clever though quiet man, and one who enjoys the sympathies of all who have come in contact with him. His predecessor was so popular at the Court of the Emperor William that he will find it difficult to fight against the remembrance that he had left behind him. I do not think that the Berlin Embassy, under the new regime, will see the brilliance of former days, but very probably it will become the scene of more formal gaieties. M. Sverbeev is a close personal friend of M. Sazonov, whom he slightly resembles physically, and, like his chief, he will always do the best he can to further the cause of peace and to avoid even the semblance of a conflict.

As for Baron Budberg, who occupies the post of Madrid, he is little known in Russia, having spent almost his whole life abroad. I have never met him.

CHAPTER XIX

ST. PETERSBURG SOCIETY AT THE PRESENT DAY

Any habitué of St. Petersburg Society during the two former reigns who, after a long absence, returned to the capital of Russia would scarcely know it again.

The change brought about in the Society of St. Petersburg since the beginning of the present century is so enormous that it is a wonder how it could have taken place in so short a time. The Society leaders of old have either died or gone abroad, or have entirely retired from the social world. Family gatherings, which used regularly to assemble on certain days such as Christmas, New Year, or Easter, at the house of a grandmother, aunt, or uncle, take place no longer. People prefer to go to restaurants to hear a Roumanian orchestra, or some Bohemian singers, rather than cluster round the family hearth. The constraint that formerly characterised the attitude of the younger members of a family to their elders has disappeared so entirely that one wonders how it could ever have existed. St. Petersburg Society, which formerly could boast of some circles entirely shut to outsiders, groups where money was not sufficient to secure an entrance, where those who were admitted within the precincts carefully observed certain rules of politeness, and civility, has now become a kind of cabaret, where everyone thinks he has the right to do what he likes, where good manners are unknown, where even young girls are allowed to go everywhere, not only without chaperons, but even in the company of young men whom they scarcely know, and even go so far as to visit these same young men in their flats, or barracks when they happen to be officers.

The decorum which formerly was carefully observed, and the somewhat stiff but charming way in which women used to welcome even their most intimate friends, has fled. At present politeness is unknown, formality is no longer observed, and gossip has superseded the intellectual conversations which were in past days one of the characteristics of that portion of St. Petersburg Society which belonged to the upper ten thousand.

Salons like those of the Princess Paschkievitch, of the Princess Lise Volkhonsky, or of the Princess Hélène Kotchoubey have disappeared. Those incomparable hostesses, whose judgments made or marred a social reputation, whose smiles were accepted as a favour, and whose invitations were more eagerly sought after than even Imperial ones, have been replaced by women who have pushed themselves to the front, either through their money or through their audacity; who gather round them people to play bridge or to discuss the most trivial and commonplace subjects, who have neither manners, nor charm, nor the prestige of a high personal position independent of an official one.

Of former salons that of the Countess Kleinmichel alone is still existent, and its mistress is as intriguing as ever, and a little less slim, and with a little more "complexion." Otherwise, she has not altered, her dinners are not better; but her evening parties have still kept their attraction for high officials and diplomats of all countries.

Bridge, however, has replaced conversation, and private theatricals the balls of former days. As for flirting, this art, which was carried to perfection in those old times of which I am thinking, is also extinct. Why should one give oneself that trouble when it is so easy to obtain all that one wants without practising it!

Small talk is a thing of the past also; now the only thing that one hears is, "Have you been at the *concours hippique*?" or "Have you been at the skating rink?" An ill-bred familiarity has replaced the courtesy for which Russians of the higher classes were famous. Now no man dreams of calling a lady, or even a young girl, by their family names; one says "Mary" or "Kitty." Young students address maids of eighteen or twenty by their nicknames, and no one seems to wonder at this utter breach of good manners.

Parties are dull and stiff, in spite of their utter want of decorum. They are no longer a reunion of people belonging to the same circle, who meet at the house of one of their number to drink a cup of tea and discuss the events of the day. These intimate little gatherings are no longer considered as being the right thing. They have been replaced by dinners and parties in which hostesses try to outdo each other in the luxury they display. That which indicates more than anything else the emptiness of the minds of the smart set in St. Petersburg is the fact that now no one likes to talk, and that in order to make a party successful, one must have something to occupy those invited to it. No longer are they able to amuse themselves by conversation. One must have either bridge, or music, or some such attraction, else people will not come. Formerly there were dozens of houses where you could go every evening and take a cup of tea quietly, sometimes with two or three people, sometimes with the hostess only, who knew how to entertain you and to keep you talking till long past midnight. Now you will hardly find a place where you can hope to be received without a special invitation. Men and women are no longer sociable, though they are dissipated, and when they meet it is to eat and to drink, though not always to be merry.

One of the reasons for this state of things lies in the number of outsiders who have obtained an entrance into Society. One Grand Duchess, in particular, is largely responsible for this. Her own set is not only fast, but vulgar, and, unfortunately, the admittance is easy. It is sufficient to have money, to be rich enough to entertain her, to talk slang, to go every year to Paris, and to give her money for all the bazaars that she patronises. As her presence at a party makes it at once a smart one, and confers an honour on her hostess, it is not to be wondered that ladies who formerly would never have been admitted into the cream of St. Petersburg Society have seized the opportunity that was offered to them and consistently flattered the Grand Duchess. No one now cares for the family antecedents of guests so long as they have an abundance of money and can give good dinners.

Another reason why the moral and intellectual standard of St. Petersburg Society has sunk so low lies in the fact that now no one controls its decisions. Formerly the Court exercised a strong influence on manners and habits. At a time when invitations to the Winter Palace decided as to the social standing of a person, people had necessarily to be upon their guard. Not to be invited to a ball where one had the right to be admitted constituted a social degradation which was never removed. The Emperor and Empress, going out into Society, and knowing its leading members, were very well informed as to what they did, and knew how to express their disapproval where there were reasons for so doing.

That is now a thing of the past. The Court keeps itself aloof from Society. Balls at the Winter Palace are a thing of the past. Court invitations belong to history; there is no one left to say who ought or ought not to be received at places where admittance constitutes an honour. People are left to their own inclinations, and inclinations always take them where they are well fed, well cared for, where they find luxury, truffles, oysters, and champagne, where there are well-dressed women always willing to be admired, and where cards are always laid out on the table ready for play.

There is one very remarkable thing which cannot help striking anyone who knew St. Petersburg some twenty years ago; it is that the moral and intellectual standard of Society has considerably fallen, while, on the other hand, luxury has increased. Smartness is now general, whereas formerly it was only an exception. Dowagers with caps, and high black silk gowns, which they even wore at the balls and parties where they chaperoned their daughters and granddaughters, have disappeared; grey hair has become an exception; the love of dress has grown tremendously, and the former simplicity which existed, even among very wealthy people, has given place to arrogant display. At one time one was often invited to dinner in a quiet way, when one sat at a table simply laid with some fruit and bonbons, but without flowers, which were considered a great luxury. Now you cannot be asked to eat a cutlet without large baskets of roses being on the table; but, in nine cases out of ten, the food is a great deal worse than when no one dreamed of such accessories. All is for pomp and for show; the intimacy and privacy of life has gone; gone, too, are the friends, who have been replaced by visitors—by no means the same thing.

Another characteristic feature is the indifference which is professed in so-called high spheres to all the moral, intellectual, and political questions of the day. Under Alexander II. social reforms were the one subject of interest and conversation in the salons of St. Petersburg, of which there were many. Under Alexander III. also they were discussed, but more among people who knew each other very well and saw each other very often. Now, after a war and a revolution that should have awakened anew the attention of the public as to these important problems of the life of a nation, it has entirely left off thinking about them. The middle classes, who look ahead towards the future and who discuss what it will bring to them, now talk about these questions. Society, or what goes by that name, gives all its thought to ill-natured gossip. They read nothing except French novels of the worst kind; hardly glance at a newspaper; and their ideas about a journey abroad are summed up in a trip to Paris—where their whole interest centres in the music-halls and other places of the same light character, or worse—or a journey to the Riviera, where they gamble at Monte Carlo.

Where formerly were civilised customs, refinement of taste, chivalrous manners, now exists an ignorance which makes one ashamed of being a Russian. In times of old, families belonging to the aristocracy used to pride themselves on the good education that they gave to their children. Nothing was spared in that direction. Tutors and governesses were chosen with the greatest care, and the familiarity of Russian men and women with foreign languages, foreign literature, and scientific and artistic subjects was always a matter of comment abroad. Now girls and boys are sent to public schools and gymnasia, with the result that when they finish their education they can hardly write without mistakes in spelling in their own language, and they murder all other languages. But of course this easy way of bringing up children saves the parents any amount of trouble, and they are ready enough to find excuse for their negligence.

In fact, Russia as it existed formerly is a thing of the past. New men, new manners, new customs have superseded the traditions that made the country great, and which had raised it above mere savagery. It is now returning to its earlier state. Being an old man I can make comparisons, and regret the passing away of the courtesy of our ancestors, the old ladies in lace caps, sitting in rooms with bowls full of dried rose-leaves dispensing fragrance all around; the thoughtful men who seriously discussed important questions, and who really loved their country, were devoted to its welfare, and lived and died according to the old tradition, so beautifully embodied in those famous French words:—

"Mon âme à Dieu,
  Mon bras au roi,
  Mon cœur aux dames,
  L'honneur à moi."

Russian aristocracy no longer exists; there are men and women bearing great names, but that is all. St. Petersburg Society has turned into a kind of association of people eager only for enjoyment and pleasure, seeking always new subjects of excitement, devoid of serious thought, and hating serious pursuits. It does not see, or perhaps does not want to see, the growing tide of revolution and anarchism that is gaining ground every day and preparing itself for the struggle out of which it knows it will emerge triumphant.

Attachment to the monarchy has been replaced in some by indifference, in many by dislike, in a great number by hatred. Nations as well as women like to see strength in the hands of those who rule, and unfortunately the present monarch is deficient in that respect. His weakness is so well known that apathy has seized hold of all those who by their intelligence, their knowledge of men and things, their honesty, and their devotion to their duty, might have been useful to the Throne as well as to the country. They, as well as the greater mass of the public, have come to the conclusion that there is little that can be done for the welfare of the masses and of the nation. Every effort to raise its moral level has failed, because the Government is unwilling to give its support to those who would have been ready to work in that direction.

When the phantom of Constitution under which Russia is supposed to live to-day was promulgated, some simple souls imagined that a great step was taken towards solving many social problems, but I do not think that there is at present in existence a single person who still fosters that illusion. The last elections have proved that when a Government wants to crush every manifestation of public opinion it can do so. The present, the fourth, Duma is composed exclusively of supporters of the Cabinet; at least, its majority is strong enough to prevent any measure proposed by the Opposition passing through. The Government is forced by its own fault to submit to a state of stagnation, which, perhaps, indeed it desired to bring about, finding it easier to do no work at all. But the Deputies are disgusted and discouraged, and, as one of them said recently to a reporter of one of the daily papers of St. Petersburg, he as well as other members of the Opposition seriously think of resigning their seats, so convinced are they that they can do nothing useful as things stand at present.

The same discouragement prevails everywhere; no one expects or hopes anything; everyone grows indifferent, and gives his thoughts and attention to frivolous subjects, waiting with apathy for the cataclysm which is bound to come. The only thing that absorbs the public mind is how to make money quickly. Financial enterprises spring into existence quicker than mushrooms grow in the rain; for the most part they are attended with success, and at no time has the thirst for money been so great and so general. It is a kind of frenzy that has seized people on every hand, and that frenzy perhaps, unknown even to those that are attacked with it, may be the expression of a feverish haste to get the most they can out of a state of things which they feel cannot last much longer.

And whilst frivolous, stupid, indifferent, smart Society is gathering its roses while it may, under its feet grows another force, earnest, ambitious, cruel, like all those who want to conquer; savage in its instincts and brutal in its actions, a society composed of men who want to brush aside all the old prejudices, all the traditions of greatness and love of country. To them belongs the future, and with them will come confusion, disaster, ruin, the collapse of a nation and of a monarchy.

CHAPTER XX

THE EMPRESS ALEXANDRA FEODOROVNA AND HER CHILDREN

I HAVE already spoken of the Empress Alexandra Feodorovna, and mentioned some of the singularities of her character. These singularities have lately assumed a more decided aspect, and have been the subject of comment by the public. When the Empress was quite young her shyness was attributed to timidity; but as years went on it became evident that her nervous system was seriously impaired. The general report was that she was given to studying the mysteries of occult science, and that these studies proved too much for her nerves. She saw dangers where they did not exist, and was always fearing the catastrophes which were daily predicted to her by spiritualists who sought their own advantage out of her weakness. After a time she was prevailed upon to give up these people, and she turned her mind towards religion. In this connection gossip has had much to say about a monk called Gregor Raspoutine. He was a travelling monk, who went about from one place to another preaching what he called the Kingdom of Heaven. He sprang into notice when he started a campaign with another monk, named Illiodore, who also called himself a prophet, and who wanted to found a religion of his own. He was the abbot of a monastery at Saratoff, where his bishop became one of his adherents. At first Raspoutine was a follower of Illiodore, then they became enemies, and each denounced the other.

THE CHILDREN OF THE TSAR

Grand Duchess Olga   Grand Duchess Tatiana
Grand Duchess Marie Grand Duchess Anastasia

The Tsarevitch Alexis

Photos: Boissonnas & Eggler, St. Petersburg

Illiodore was soon unfrocked after having spent some months as a prisoner in a monastery far from Saratoff; but Raspoutine, in spite of his many vagaries, which far exceeded those of Illiodore, escaped prosecution owing, it is said, to influence in high quarters.

He was introduced to the Empress by the Grand Duchess Elizabeth her sister, who from her convent in Moscow still exercised a great influence over the little Court of Tsarskoye Selo. She suggested to Alexandra Feodorovna to call to her the wandering monk, who was considered by many people in the light of a saint, and to ask him to pray for her and for her children—especially for the Heir to the Throne, who was the object of her particular anxiety.

Not long after he was brought to the notice of the Empress, Raspoutine is credited with having persuaded her that as long as he was allowed to remain she would be safe from any danger, and her children, too, would always remain unharmed, no matter what might occur. He managed to instil in her the idea that it was his protection that kept the Heir to the Throne in good health, and that if he were to be sent away from the Palace something would happen to the child. So intimate became his ministrations that whispers were heard, and the matter became a general subject of conversation among the public, even in far-off provinces. Newspapers began to make allusions to it in veiled words, and it was severely discussed in the Duma.

M. Stolypin, who was still alive, tried to send the monk away from St. Petersburg, but after he had been assassinated Raspoutine came back, and his influence became stronger than ever. Nevertheless, talk became so pointed that when the President of the third Duma, M. Rodzianko, was received in private audience by the Emperor, he ventured to make a remark about Raspoutine and the gossip to which his perpetual presence at Tsarskoye Selo gave rise. Nicholas II. became immediately angry, and told M. Rodzianko in severe terms that no one had the right to repeat idle tales about the private life of his family.

Nevertheless Raspoutine was sent away for some time. He left the capital for his native village in the wilds of Siberia, and for a period nothing was heard about him. Then last autumn the Heir to the Throne fell ill at Spala, and the Empress, who was quite frantic, cried out aloud that this misfortune had happened because they had sent Raspoutine into exile. The monk was recalled, and he was once more admitted into the intimacy of the Imperial Family. He is always at Tsarskoye Selo, but his presence there is kept secret, so that a good many people are not even aware that he has returned. But his influence remains the same, and it is maintained that the Empress is more convinced than ever that it was his prayers that saved her son during his last severe illness.

A lot of rubbish has been written about the illness of the Tsarevitch, and the most stupid tales have been circulated. The reality is sad enough without exaggeration making it worse. The child, who has been very delicate ever since his birth, suffers from an organic disease of the arteries, which are liable to rupture upon the slightest provocation and even without cause. Already, three years ago, he had to undergo an operation, which was performed by Professor Fedoroff, one of the doctors who treated him in the autumn of 1912. The fact was kept secret from the public. Every effort was made to keep secret the state of health of the little boy, and to prevent the world from guessing that it gave rise to uneasiness if not to real anxiety. The child was worshipped by his parents, who for ten years had been waiting for that son upon whose existence so much depended. When at last he was born he became an idol both for his father and for his mother, and indulged to such an extent that it marred his temperament, converting him into a peevish, disagreeable child. Every whim he had was gratified at once, and all his innumerable caprices were obeyed. The result, as can be imagined, has been disastrous.

Generally children born to exalted positions are brought up with the utmost care as regards their moral training and their education. The little Tsarevitch was surrounded with the utmost vigilance, but unfortunately that vigilance was exerted only in the direction of his health and his safety. Training he receives none, and education very little.

The Grand Duke Alexis is now about nine years old, but up to the present no tutor has been appointed to him. He gets a few lessons from his mother, and once or twice a week a master comes to teach him how to read and write; but his only attendant is a sailor, who follows him about everywhere, and who is at the same time his nurse and his tutor and his guardian. The man is of common birth, and though perhaps very devoted to his charge, yet can hardly be considered as the proper trainer for a future Sovereign. But neither the Emperor nor the Empress thinks it necessary to give to their only son a tutor of appropriate rank or birth.

From morning to night the Tsarevitch is told that his existence is so precious to his parents that no caprice of his is to be allowed to pass without being at once gratified. He is constantly impressed with his own importance, and already knows very well his rights, though he entirely ignores his duties. Arrogant by nature, this arrogance is fostered instead of being corrected. No one is allowed to rebuke him, or even to contradict him. The Tsarevitch beats his sisters, tyrannises over his servants, and whenever anyone attempts to correct him he instantly threatens the unfortunate person with all kind of punishments.

His entourage, as well as those of his father and mother, do nothing but flatter him. No one seems to think of the evils such a system of education carries along with it, nor to reflect on the fate that menaces the Russian Empire should it ever come to be ruled by the spoilt little boy who now is Heir to the Throne of the Romanoffs.

A few years ago an anecdote was circulated everywhere in St. Petersburg concerning the small Tsarevitch. It seems that one morning Ministers were waiting to be received by the Emperor at the Palace of Tsarskoye Selo. Among them was M. Izvolsky, at that time head of the Foreign Office. He was talking with another person seated next to him, and did not notice the Tsarevitch, who happened to run through the room. The latter instantly went up to M. Izvolsky, and in an imperious tone told him that "when the Heir to the Throne crosses a room Ministers ought to get up." M. Izvolsky became so confused that he did not know what to do or to say, and his confusion became still worse when, a few moments later, the Emperor, at the end of the audience which he granted to him, asked him what misunderstanding he had had with the Tsarevitch. M. Izvolsky hardly found words to explain, and Nicholas II. told him then, with evident pride, "Yes, later on you will find it harder to deal with my son than with me."

The incident is characteristic, as it shows that the Tsar never realised the importance of the words spoken by his little son. A far-seeing father would have severely rebuked the child for his insolence, and told him that at six years old one ought to learn one's lessons and not make remarks to people whose age and position entitled them to respect; but Nicholas II. was only struck with what appeared to him to be the spirit of independence shown by the Tsarevitch.

Another anecdote was related about the Tsarevitch. It seems that he is always very eager to be saluted by the soldiers whom he meets, and by the regiments assembling at reviews. Now etiquette in Russia exacts that when the Sovereign is present he only is saluted by the troops. The boy did not like this, pride being thus rebuked, so that whenever he was present at a parade, such as takes place at Tsarskoye Selo on the days when a regiment celebrates its religious feast, he used to run in advance of his father so as to be saluted before the soldiers perceived their Sovereign. This was noticed, and upon the representations of the Grand Duke Nicholas, who told the Emperor that the troops got so confused at this that they did not know what they were to do, or who they were to salute, the Tsarevitch was forbidden to leave his father's side.

In spite of a system of education which is only directed towards the care of his person in the physical sense, the little Grand Duke does not grow a healthy child. Perhaps his delicacy is in part responsible for his peevish temper; perhaps it only proceeds from the mistaken way in which he is being brought up. But most certainly the boy is constantly ailing. His mother watches him day and night, and he is her only care; doctors are seldom absent from his bedside, his father forgets everything if his little son has an ache, but all this does not give the Tsarevitch good health. For some years now the Imperial Family have spent months at a time at the Crimea in the hope that the sojourn in a mild climate will do away with the child's weakness, and help him to attain better health. But nothing seems to help; indeed, in the autumn of 1912 it became impossible longer to hide from the public the state of health of the Emperor's only son. Even then, however, the precise cause of his illness was not revealed, and deceptive bulletins were published, and such mystery surrounded the illness of the little boy that it gave rise to all kinds of silly tales which were circulated abroad and in Russia, among people who had no means of coming into contact with the Imperial Family or with Court Society in St. Petersburg.

As I have said already, the truth is sad enough, because it is considered certain that there is very little hope that the Tsarevitch will reach manhood, and this knowledge impels heartfelt sympathy towards his parents, who, after having longed for so many years for the birth of this heir, now have to resign themselves to the probability that his days are numbered.

It is in part that sad knowledge which makes the Empress so extraordinary in her ways, and so inclined to call every possible help, whether mystic or material, which even faintly gives the barest possibility of saving her son. It also explains why she has become so strange, and hates so much to see anyone, or to take part in any festivity, even for the sake of her daughters. Of these the two eldest ones are already grown up and lead sad lives, never being permitted to enjoy themselves as girls of their age generally do. Rumour will have it that the eldest, the Grand Duchess Olga, will soon be married, and one can only hope that for once rumour does not lie.

CHAPTER XXI

THE 300TH ANNIVERSARY OF A DYNASTY

IT was a bleak and wet though not cold winter morning to which St. Petersburg awoke on March 6th, 1913. For weeks people had talked about what the anniversary would mean to Russia, and had been eagerly awaiting it. For it was to commemorate the momentous events that had taken place three centuries before, when the deputation of the Boyars of Moscow, headed by its venerable Patriarch, had set forth for the distant town of Kostroma, to offer the crown of the Ruriks to the young son of the two victims of the cruel Boris Godounov, the monk Philaret Romanoff and his wife Martha the nun, who had been thrown by Boris into cloisters whence he had never expected to emerge. How many important events had taken place in the history of Russia since that memorable day! and how closely the Romanoff Dynasty had identified itself with the nation that had called them to its head in those troubled and dark times, when it had seemed that the country was going to fall for ever under the Polish yoke! How many sad and terrible, how many glorious pages also had been added to the book of its history! Truly it was an anniversary to be rendered for ever memorable.

Had Nicholas I., his son Alexander II., or the late Tsar been alive, it is probable that some stupendous work of charity, as well as a wide political amnesty, would have marked that day. The public expected some such thing to happen. It hoped that some lasting monument would be raised by the initiative of the Sovereign, to render it for ever memorable; that mercies should be shown, miseries relieved, tears dried, an impulse given both to public and to private charities; something attempted to raise the moral standard of the people by the creation of new schools and educational establishments. In short, they expectantly hoped that the monarch would look from the height of his Throne to where so many needs waited to be satisfied, where so much was expected to be done, and had to be done if Russia was to emerge from her present state of semi-barbarism to take her place among the nations. Not only in political and social spheres did dire need exist, but also and especially exigent was the education of the lower classes, which at present constitute in Russia such a dangerous element in her social fabric, and who threaten to overturn the present order of things without being able to replace it by anything rational.

Nevertheless, March 6th was destined to overthrow all these hopes. The manifesto published upon that occasion disappointed everybody, even those who benefited by it. People had expected as a certainty that a wide political amnesty would wipe off old scores, allow old grievances to be forgotten, and permit people to begin their lives over again. One had hoped that on the morning of that spring day some who were living far away in the country of eternal snow and ice would wake up to the realisation that their exile was over, that henceforward they would be free to return to their old homes. Another had believed that the words of the nun Martha, when she blessed her only son on his being called to the Throne, and wished him to reign for the peace and joy of his people, would be remembered by her descendant, and that he, too, would wish to bring peace to those who trusted him and his instincts of mercy. But all these hopes, these tremulous anticipations, these flickering visions of mercy and peace, failed of realisation.

Any Sovereign placed in such exceptional circumstances would surely have had the impulse to do something for the nation in order to improve the general conditions of its existence. Such thoughts may have animated Nicholas II., but if they did they died before they were given expression. A large gift of a few millions coming from his private purse would have made him none the poorer, and would have brought again to him the popularity which he had been steadfastly losing ever since the day of his accession to the Throne of the Romanoffs. That sum, spent in building new schools, or even hospitals in various large towns in Russia, would have made his name and person popular all over the country; would have brought him blessings and thanks from millions of poor people whose needs, physical and moral, such a gift would have met. But apparently no such idea occurred to him or to his Consort. On March 6th their only thought was to admire the decorations and the bunting displayed in the streets of the capital; they accepted the addresses, felicitations, and gifts of their subjects. For all the outward expression evinced they never, even for one single moment, gave their attention to the fact that in return for what was presented to them they also ought to give something to those who offered them all that was in their means to give.

The amnesty so solemnly promulgated proved to be nothing less than a farce. All the thieves and common malefactors who were crowding the prisons of St. Petersburg and the other towns of the Empire were set free, but the political exiles, men of culture and the highest civic and private virtue, were left to their sad fate, with only their sorrow and their despairing memories.

There was one personage who had been the object of the general pity because a feeling of honesty, unknown generally in a man placed in the position he was in at the time of his fall and condemnation, had led him to tell the truth about the conduct and machinations of the political police of which he was the head. M. Lapoukhine had been followed into his exile by the sympathy not only of those who knew him well but also of many persons who had never seen him. It was felt that he was a victim of a corrupt order of things, perhaps also of private revenge coming from such high quarters that one could not even mention them. One had fully believed that the three hundredth year of the reign of the Romanoff Dynasty would bring him a free pardon and the right to take up once more his place in a Society that had never excluded him from its midst. But March 6th came and went, and nothing was heard about this unfortunate man, and this indifference to his fate raised such a storm of indignation everywhere that even the feelings of loyalty of many which until then had never wavered began to be shaken in presence of this arrant injustice.

A few days later, however, the mistake was rectified, and M. Lapoukhine was allowed to leave Siberia; but the first impression could not be corrected. It was felt that this act of mercy, coming as it did after the time it was hoped for, was robbing it of its whole grandeur and generosity. On the Jubilee Day it would have raised a universal acclamation; a week later, it fell flat, because it appeared to have been merely compelled by the general indignation evoked by its neglect on an occasion when peace and pardon ought to have been in the forefront with a strength that no circumstance and no advice from any individual should have been able to restrain.

The only point in which the amnesty satisfied the public was its application to all matters relating to the press and its misdeeds. There, for the first time in the history of modern Russia, the pardons granted were complete and without restrictions, and the satisfaction which they provoked was absolutely sincere and heart-whole.

It is one of the misfortunes of Nicholas II. that he is so badly advised by those who surround him.

The festivities themselves provoked no enthusiasm from the crowds. They were damped externally by the rain, which fell in torrents during the whole time they lasted, and morally by the disappointment provoked by the manifesto. The streets were sumptuously decorated, the illuminations in the town were splendid, the ball offered by the nobility of the province of St. Petersburg to the Sovereigns was like fairyland in its magnificence, but the nation remained indifferent. Its feelings were not in unison with the spirit of the celebrations; it did not share with the Imperial House the joy that House seemed to feel upon so auspicious an occasion.

The jubilee celebrations had, however, one distinguishing feature. The Emperor and his family came from Tsarskoye Selo, and for the first time since the war and the revolution resided for three days in the Winter Palace. On March 6th they drove in state to the Kazan Cathedral for a solemn service of thanksgiving. All the wealth and rank of St. Petersburg were assembled there to greet them. All the high functionaries of the Empire were present. Troops were assembled and lined the streets through which the Imperial procession passed. Their cheers alone, however, broke the stillness of those streets, for the populace was absent. Except a few chosen persons, police, and soldiers, none was present from the nation, which thus tacitly declined to participate in the festival. The Emperor himself looked grave and pale. He drove in an open carriage, with his little son seated beside him, and when he entered the cathedral a Cossack from the escort took the child in his arms and carried him inside the church, where he was placed in a chair beside his mother. The sight was inexpressibly sad, because it proved the truth of what had been whispered ever since the autumn, that the Heir to the Throne was still suffering from disease. The white, pinched, small face of the boy, gazing anxiously round him at all the sea of human beings before him, engrossed with the beauty of the unaccustomed pageant, painfully impressed the spectators in the cathedral, and many a mother among the ladies present sighed as she looked at him, murmuring to herself,

"Poor little fellow, what a pity, and how sad for the parents!"

The members of the Imperial Family who had preceded the Sovereign to the cathedral bowed profoundly as he appeared through the huge doorway. The Patriarch of Antiochus, who had specially travelled to Russia for this important occasion, advanced, surrounded by priests, monks, bishops, and members of the higher clergy, whose flowing hair, long beards, golden robes, and heavily bejewelled mitres added to the picturesqueness of the spectacle. Everywhere one turned the eye rested on embroidered uniforms, glittering cuirasses, ladies attired in white, lighted tapers, and ikons shining forth in the semi-darkness of the vast cathedral, with the glory of the diamonds and precious stones which adorned them. The choristers intoned the anthem for the day in soft harmonies, which gradually grew louder and louder; whilst Nicholas II. and his Consort, bending down before the Patriarch, received from his hands the Holy Water which he presented to them, and kissed the Cross with which he blessed them.

Then they took up their places under the crimson canopy, which had been erected in their honour opposite the altar, and facing the miraculous image of Our Lady of Kazan, patroness of the church and of Russia. They stood there together, the Emperor erect, and with a glance that kept anxiously and furtively scanning the faces of the assembly as if afraid of meeting some secret danger lurking somewhere behind the pillars of the edifice; the Empress robed in white, with the blue ribbon of St. Andrew across her shoulder, sadness upon her classically beautiful features, was immobile as a statue, save when she bent down now and then over the arm-chair in which her little son had been placed. Standing a little before her, on the right side of Nicholas II., was his mother, the sweet Empress Marie, also dressed in white, with tears filling her beautiful soft eyes, the only pathetic figure in the vast assemblage save the child on whom so many hopes were centred, and who, by an irony which perhaps was realised by few among the spectators, appeared to have been brought there for the purpose of showing into what weak and frail hands was entrusted the future of that proud Romanoff Dynasty.

The head of it remained in his place throughout the Divine Service of thanksgiving, which was celebrated by all the bishops. He, too, bent his knee with his subjects during the blessing with which it ended, and then slowly he left the cathedral. As he appeared on its threshold a fleeting ray of sun rested on his head. It reminded me of that other glorious light that on an occasion perhaps even more solemn had hovered above the brow of his father Alexander III. as he emerged from the golden gates of the Church of the Assumption in Moscow, with the huge diamond crown of his ancestors which he had just assumed resting upon it. Nearly thirty years had gone by since that day; the mighty Tsar was lying in his quiet grave, and nearly all those who had accompanied him on that memorable day had also disappeared from this earthly scene. Nearly everything had been changed, but the places and people who knew him no more were weeping for him, even amidst the pomp of the present festival.

As I examined the pale, impassive features of his successor, I wondered whether he gave a thought to another bleak March morning, when, still a boy, he had waited, together with his brothers and sisters, for the return of his parents from the Winter Palace, where they had been summoned to see a monarch die whose Crown they were to inherit. Did he remember, I wondered, the first words uttered by the new Sovereign when receiving the bread and the salt with which his servants greeted him on his entering for the first time his Anitchkov Palace as the Tsar of All the Russias, "I will try to be a father to my people." As the memory of those words rang in the ears of the few among that vast company who had heard them, what a melancholy contrast they afforded to the actual "mercies" with which Nicholas II. had seen fit to celebrate the three hundredth year of the accession of his Dynasty to the Throne of the Ruriks.

As I watched the brilliant procession pass before me, I thought, too, of that other far-away May morning which had witnessed the Coronation of Alexander III.; of the peace and prosperity which his short reign had brought to the vast Empire over the destinies of which he had so wisely presided. Whither had fled that peace he had tried so hard to establish permanently within his realms? The eighteen years that had elapsed since his death had only brought disaster, strife, uneasiness to the nation he had loved so well.

Whatever have been the faults of the Romanoffs, whatever mistakes they may have made, whatever cruelties they have been responsible for, no one can deny that they have been strong men. Fearlessly reckless sometimes, but always sincere in their convictions and their love for their people, never indifferent as to their fate and welfare. The present Tsar is the first representative of their race in whom weakness and indecision find themselves allied; the first whose existence practically counts for nothing in the eyes of his many subjects, whom they neither respect, fear, nor hate.

This indifference as to the importance of his person has never been more apparent than on that wet morning of March 6th, when he left the Kazan Cathedral to return to the Winter Palace, after having rendered his thanks to the Almighty for the protection accorded to his ancestors as well as to himself. The festival celebrated on that day was in no sense a popular one, nor did it leave any definite impression. The nation was simply interested, and perhaps in a certain degree amused, owing to the amount of bunting displayed during the day and the number of lamps lighted at night in honour of the occasion. Cheers of the kind these gauds provoke were heard, it is true; but sincere enthusiasm was totally lacking. And when, two days later, the Emperor, while attending the ball given in his honour by the nobility of St. Petersburg, replied to the address of welcome and loyalty with which they received him, the very tone in which his words were uttered seemed to be utterly wanting in firmness or conviction. True, the National Anthem was sung in reply to the speech of the monarch, and was sung with eagerness perhaps, as one might expect from the cultured imagination of such an assembly. But one felt, just as much, that this eagerness was imposed by circumstances, not that it proceeded from one of these inspirations which happen sometimes in the life of nations and unite it in one thought and one hope.

The words, as they solemnly called upon the Almighty to protect the Tsar, sounded almost defiant, but by one of those strange ironies which happen so often in life, they appeared only too appropriate to the needs of the situation as they remain at present; for never, believe me, in the whole history of Russia did a Sovereign more need the protection of the Almighty than His Majesty Nicholas II., Emperor and Autocrat of All the Russias, does now, in this nineteenth year of his sad and unfortunate reign!

THE END

Printed by CASSELL & COMPANY, LIMITED, LA BELLE SAUVAGE, LONDON, E.C.

back

back

Printed in Great Britain
by Amazon

21435567R00183